ARMY APPRENTICES
Harrogate

HALSGROVE

First published in Great Britain in 2002

Copyright © 2002 Colonel Cliff Walters
Photographs © Royal Signals Museum

Frontispiece portrait: *Her Royal Highness Princess Mary,
Colonel-in-Chief of the Royal Corps of Signals and Patron of the
Association of Harrogate Apprentices.*

British Library Cataloguing-in-Publication Data
A CIP record for this title is available from the British Library

ISBN 1 84114 218 2

HALSGROVE

Halsgrove House
Lower Moor Way
Tiverton, Devon EX16 6SS
Tel: 01884 243242
Fax: 01884 243325
email: sales@halsgrove.com
website: www.halsgrove.com

Printed and bound by
Bookcraft Ltd, Midsomer Norton

CONTENTS

BIBLIOGRAPHY

The Story of the Army Apprentices' College, Chepstow 1923–1983 compiled by Captain John Barnes RAEC and Major David Thomas RAEC.

Sons of the Brave, The Story of Boy Soldiers by AW Cockerill.

Headdress, Badges and Embellishments of The Royal Corps of Signals by Major AG Harfield MBE.

The Royal Corps of Signals: A History of its Antecedents and Development by Major General RFH Nalder CB OBE.

The History of British Army Signals in the Second World War by Major General RFH Nalder CB OBE.

The Vital Link: The Story of the Royal Corps of Signals 1945–1985 by Philip Warner.

Exclusively Harrogate by Malcolm G Neesam.

Princess Marina College, A Brief History 1939–1992 by Captain Bryn Richards RAEC.

'Through to 1970' by Colonel RM Adams of the Royal Signals Institute. *A Pictorial History of the Royal Corps of Signals.*

ABBREVIATIONS

Most, except the obvious, abbreviations have been avoided. Normal abbreviations for ranks and appointments have been used.

AT	Apprentice Tradesman. The normal abbreviation for an apprentice.
ATW	Apprentice Tradeswoman. The normal abbreviation for a female apprentice.
CSM	Company Sergeant Major.
DR or Don R	Despatch Rider.
HQ	Headquarters.
JL	Junior Leader.
PS	Permanent Staff.
RSM	Regimental Sergeant Major.
'Spider'	Name given to wooden accommodation blocks.
STC	Signals Training Centre.
The Wire	The magazine of the Royal Corps of Signals.
The Gate	The magazine of the Army Apprentices' College, Harrogate.

FOREWORD

The wooden buildings of the Army Apprentices' College at Harrogate may have been demolished but if the spaces they left could speak, they would tell the story of the thousands of boys and young men who passed through their doors during the last century. Boys full of hope, boys who were there because life was passing them by, boys from stable backgrounds and those from broken homes. They were different in character but all had one thing in common – they were attending and being trained by one of the foremost apprentice training centres in the country. These were the boys destined to become the leaders and managers in the technical corps of the Army, but since 1961, primarily in the Royal Corps of Signals.

This book recounts that story. Through anecdote and historical record it captures the characters of the boys and those who guided, tutored and trained them. It creates a picture of what it was like to be an Army apprentice, a way of life and a period of character transformation, which only those who experienced it, could ever really understand.

The college did its job well. Its graduates filled the key positions in the Corps' hierarchy, bringing experience, technical ability and zest for life. Some achieved the highest ranks of the Army, but whatever roles they carried out, the Harrogate boys, and later girls, enriched their surroundings.

This book gives the reader a glimpse of why that should be so.

Major General John Stokoe CB CBE
Harrogate, Intake 63A

Major General John Stokoe CB CBE

His Worship, the Mayor of Harrogate, Alderman RJ Riley, takes the salute at the adoption parade on 3 May 1956. The Commandant, Colonel JP Carne VC DSO, is on the right.

INTRODUCTION

The seeds were sown for the writing of this book in 1992 when I was reading myself into my new appointment as Commandant of the Army Apprentices' College, Harrogate. One of the missives on the file entitled 'Royal Signals Corps Matters' referred to a Corps Committee minute that offered, '£300 to encourage an author to record the history of Royal Signals apprentices'. I then realised that none of the official Corps histories made much mention of Harrogate and I decided that the subject deserved my attention.

About ten years later those seeds have germinated although the intervening years have been fragmented with long periods of inactivity on my part. Indeed, there are chapters of this book that have been stored on three generations of computers. Also, I fear that due to my tardiness the £300 is no longer on offer!

Once I had ventured into the bygone years of Penny Pot Camps I soon learned that they were about a much wider range of subjects than just Royal Signals apprentices. The early days were used to prepare soldiers for their various roles in the Second World War and to tend to the wounded. In the immediate post-war period the Apprentices' School was set up but Royal Signals apprentices remained very much in the minority until the 1960s. Even then the college went on to train junior leaders, including infantry, and latterly some single-entry soldiers. Most importantly, throughout the whole period there was a very dedicated and conscientious military and civilian staff. This book chronicles the activities of them all.

I must also take this opportunity to thank a number of people amongst the multitudes who have helped me. Peter Sharp, who was my Senior Instructional Officer at the college, spent hours recalling his many years at Harrogate. Lynne Mee, the Mayor of Harrogate's secretary, guided me through the maze of local politics and put me in contact with many people. Adam Forty, Royal Signals Museum, provided me with the IT support to meet the demands of modern publishers. The Trustees of the Royal Signals Museum have kindly given me permission to use the extensive range of photographs from the archives. In compiling this history I have interviewed and corresponded with many interesting and charming people from as far and wide as Canada and Australia. I am thankful to them all for their contribution even if it did not result in a written entry in this book. I realise that there will be many readers who are justifiably disappointed at the many unaccountable omissions but I had fifty fold information available and condensing it inevitably has left large gaps. For these omissions and gaps I apologise and plead that historical perspective is best achieved at a distance.

It is especially pleasing to know that a period of history that I now realise to be of considerable significance to a lot of people, will be formally recorded for posterity. The writing of this book has brought me hours of pleasure and I hope that it will do likewise for those who read it. For anyone with deeper interests, the totality of my research material will be held in the Royal Signals Museum Archives.

Finally, my happy involvement with Harrogate and its people has fortunately extended far beyond my tour of duty which was happy enough in itself. I continue to meet staff and ex-trainees and my responsibility towards the Association of Harrogate Apprentices will hopefully ensure that this continues. If this book generates further contacts I will be even happier.

Colonel Cliff Walters

Cliff Walters
Royal Signals Museum, Blandford, 2002

From a painting of the three churches by Stephen Maude 1995, to commemorate the closing of the college.

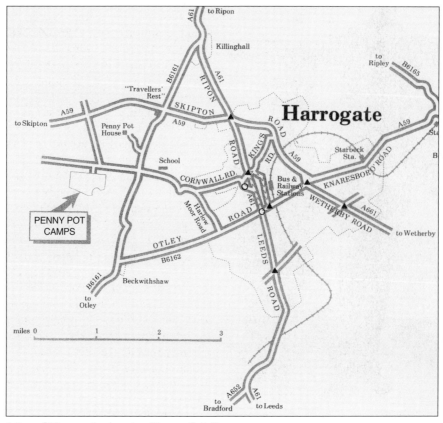

Map of Harrogate showing Penny Pot Camps.

I

TRACING THE HISTORY OF BOY SOLDIERING
AND APPRENTICES IN THE BRITISH ARMY

The history of boy soldiers of the British Army can be traced back to medieval times when it is known that armies, such as those of King Harold at the time of the Norman invasion, comprised under-age soldiers. There are exhibits on display in the armouries of the Tower of London which date back to these battles and show composite half-suits of body armour for boys under ten years of age.

Edward III was himself a boy of only fourteen when he came to the throne and set forth with his army to wage war against the Scots. He commanded his army for over twenty years and there were many young soldiers in its ranks, a good percentage of whom were serving apprenticeships. Undoubtedly the archers and knights employed young boys to assist them. Many of them aspired to knighthoods and commenced their military careers as apprentice harness makers, horsemen, saddlers, minstrels, farriers, wagon drivers or other relevant trades. These boys probably served the original military apprenticeships.

It would be naive to assume that there was any clear distinction between boy or adult soldiers and many of the youngsters served in the front lines. They came from all walks of life, including the multitude of camp followers who used to accompany the armies on their long marches.

The first unit to establish formal training for boys was the Royal Regiment of Artillery. In 1741 the Royal Military Academy (RMA) Woolwich was established. The boy cadets were between the ages of twelve and fourteen, and the aim of the RMA was to teach them the rudiments of military discipline and education. It was at this very early stage that a rank structure amongst the boys was instituted to bring a measure of control and supervision. However, it caused more problems than it solved and was a ready source of bullying, misuse of privileges and unruliness.

The history of Royal Signals boys does not date back as far as these eighteenth-century times but it can be traced back to the days before the formation of the Corps. It is well recorded in an article entitled 'Our Boys', by Major FV Merchant, which appears in the January 1949 edition of *The Wire*.

In the days of the Telegraph Battalion RE, most boys joined at Chatham for training in one of the three main groups of buglers (who became artisans), bricklayers or telegraphists. The latter became known as the 'Tele-boys' and were the envy of the other tradesmen because they qualified for Sapper pay after only six months; this amounted to one shilling and three-half-pence per day (6p). The others, and he at first, received 4s. 8d. (23p) a week less stoppages; 4d. (2p) a day messing, 1d. a day washing, which together with monthly subscriptions for haircutting, library and other miscellaneous items, brought his pocket money down to 1s. (5p) per week.

How did he spend his money? A boy under the age of seventeen was not permitted to smoke; so compared with

RE Signals boys at Crowborough in 1921–22. The three boys were called 'DOT-DASH-DOT' after the Morse code.

the older boys he saved 1d. on a packet of five Woodbines! He could go to the NAAFI and spend 2d. on a 'wad' and tea. This would supplement his evening meal which was at 1715 hours. More likely, however, he would receive his pay on Friday and proceed down town on the binge. He would be smartly dressed in uniform with forage hat, white buckskin gloves and regimental cane. There were no buses or trams so he saved on the fare. The cheapest seat in the local cinema was 4d. and this would be followed by fish and chips for 2d., rice and prunes for 2d., and washing it all down with tea or coffee for a further 1d. It was absolutely essential that the remainder was saved to finance a visit to the NAAFI for at least one ravenous occasion which would be inevitable during the course of the next week.

The 'Tele-boys' were posted to D Company, 1st Training Battalion in Brompton Barracks. The majority were then attached to 2nd Division Telegraph Battalion (later renamed K Company) and would occasionally be employed with the GPO to gain practical experience. It was a great joy to be attached to a major telegraph office, such as Southampton or Plymouth, and work alongside civilians. The occasional night shift would also accrue extra pay.

The preliminary training consisted of sending and receiving Morse code. Pay increases were gained as speeds increased so there was no shortage of incentive. The procedure taught was that set out in 'Rules for Postmasters'. He became proficient at reading Morse from sounders, vibrators and single-needle instruments. He could send on Morse keys and punch up Wheatstone slip. His telephone switchboard operating was carried out at the School of Mechanical Engineering on the 25-line handringing instrument exchange, and at the Electrical School on the 12-line sub-exchange. There was no wireless training but at the time of the Boer War an experimental station was set up in Aldershot, near Mons Barracks, which existed into the 1950s.

On attaining the age of eighteen, a boy would return to Chatham to do recruits drill. He would then be posted to one of the two Telegraph Divisions at Aldershot where he learned his field telegraph work, and after normal working hours he would prepare for his 1st Class school certificate (if he did not already have it).

This procedure continued until the RE Signal Service became the Corps of Signals. The boys changed their badges for their 'Jimmy'and commenced training at Maresfield Camp in Sussex by which time their number had swelled to about 70.

In a manual that was produced by Lieutenant Colonel Boileau in 1945, and is now held in the Royal Signals Museum at Blandford, he records the importance of those early days. The aim of the manual was to provide a permanent record of advice on the policy for the training of boys. Chapter XX provides a 'General Review' of the history of boys in Royal Signals up to that date. It is worthy of repeat in its entirety.

BOILEAU MANUAL FOR BOYS TRAINING
CHAPTER XX – GENERAL REVIEW

1. Origin and early years

Enlisted boys are no new idea. The Royal Engineers – the parent corps from which Royal Signals sprang – had both trumpeters and trade boys for many years. In 1920 the Signals Service RE became the Corps of Signals, and boys, who were then serving with it, transferred to the new corps. There were at that time boys being trained as Signals mechanics and operators, and there were also trumpeters who, besides the musical side of their education, were given instruction in one of the older trades – saddler, wheelwright or smith. At a later date trumpeters were trained as DRs and linemen. During this early period boys lived and worked in whatever men's company dealt with their trades; e.g. operators were in C Company and trumpeters were in E Company. In March 1924 wireless operator boys went to G Company, which then consisted of approximately 75per cent men and 25 per cent boys, under the command of Major Cobb. About fifteen months later all boys, irrespective of trades, were transferred to G Company which was then renamed F Company. In September 1925 the STC (Signals Training Centre) moved from Maresfield Park, Sussex, where it had been since the summer of 1919, to Catterick. Within a few months of its arrival F Company was emptied of all men apart from the cadre required for the training and administration of the boys; and F Company remained as a boy company till the outbreak of war in 1939.

In 1923 the War Office introduced the apprentice tradesman scheme. The arrangement was that:

(i) Army competitive entrance examinations were held for boys between the ages of fourteen and fifteen. Those successful were enlisted to train as apprentices until they were eighteen, and then to serve for eight years' colour and four years' reserve service. Each boy was attested for a definite trade.
(ii) From these examination passes R Signals received intakes of apprentice tradesmen twice yearly, of whom 60 per cent had been enlisted as operators, and 40 per cent as instrument mechanics or fitters signals.
(iii) An establishment of ten trumpeters, who were trained as DRs, was allowed. These did not take the competitive entrance examination, but were nominated by OIC Records from a waiting list and were posted from time to time as vacancies occurred.
(iv) Educational training continued throughout a boy's service with a view to obtaining the 2nd Class Army Certificate of Education and some, if not all, the subjects of the 1st Class.

2. Developments to 1939

These general arrangements remained with little change until 1942. In 1929 ATs of workshop trades joined men's classes for training. Operator boys spent eighteen months attached to the Post Office in the middle of their course. On their return they did a considerable amount of lineman training in their last year, and some boys, who had not proved to be successful operators were mustered as linemen.

In 1933 the school, now known as the Education Centre, was built. Its main function was the education of the boys of F Company. Development continued along two main lines as opportunity arose. These were: (A) The establishment of separate arrangements for boys' training designed to satisfy their special circumstances, as distinct from merely fitting them in with men's training; and (B) Restriction of trades taught to the more highly skilled workshop and operating trades. 1939 found the position as follows:

(i) Strength was 180 boys – 10 trumpeter/DRs, 60 per cent operators signal, 20 per cent instrument mechanics and 20 per cent electricians signal. Intakes were of 25 half-yearly. After a short recruit course, boys were allocated to their trades and spent about seven hours per week in school.

(ii) Operators were trained in the company's own rooms with its own instructors and a reasonable amount of technical equipment. These boys could thus work to definite schedules.

(iii) Workshop boys still had to work mainly with men, as no separate workshops or boys instructors were available, and so had to train by men's programme.

(iv) The trumpeters did not fit in very well. They arrived at irregular times, were usually of low educational standard, and could not start their DR training until they were sixteen years old. They performed duties as orderly trumpeters but it was being urged that their recruitment should stop.

(v) F Company had now been in existence as a boys' company for fourteen years. It was well-known throughout NE England for its achievements in sport, and had regular fixtures with many public schools. Former boys were distributed throughout the Corps, many as senior NCOs. Some had passed into Sandhurst.

3. 1939–1943

On the outbreak of war the Training Battalion became the 1st General Trades Training Battalion with its men companies numbered instead of lettered. A modern barrack block – Sandhurst B Block – which was specially designed for F Company's accommodation was completed and occupied by the company. After a few months it had to be handed over for the accommodation of ATS personnel. Recruitment of boys was suspended and by January 1942 the Company strength was down to 50, practically all of whom were due to pass out during the year.

In April 1942 intakes recommenced – the first two were each of 50 boys, and as the AT establishment was then fixed at 200, future intakes were planned at 35 per half-

year. B Block was still required by ATS but a wing of A Block, with accommodation for 225 boys, was taken over.

In January 1943 a scheme was started in the Army for enlisting general duty (GD) boys in trade corps. Signals had previously tried to get the ceiling for ATs raised to 300, but without success. Now they were asked if they wished to take any of these GD boys, and they replied, 'Yes, 25 every half-year.' Whereas other corps were going to use these boys for general duties and stated they would train them in a suitable trade when they were of age to join the ranks, Signals intended to put them to technical training during their boys' service. At the start the age of enlistment was fifteen years six months to sixteen years, and so they were available for only two years' training. Thus the target of 300 boys – even though not all ATs – was reached. The high age group of the GDs necessitated a special, rather concentrated, programme for them for their first year. Very soon a further serious complication was introduced through the recruiting authorities reporting that it was impossible to carry out the original intention of sending the GD boys in batches twice a year; instead they arrived in trickles throughout the year.

When AT intakes restarted in 1942, the training plan of the Company was redesigned, and after a year's experience this design has been codified in a War Office directive on the training of R Signals boys. This detailed the framework for a complete system of boys' training. Establishments of cadre and equipment to enable its carrying out have been approved. The main points are:

(i) Boys are to be trained in the following trades:
(A) Operator wireless and keyboard Class 3.
(B) Operator wireless and line Class 2 and operator keyboard and line Class 3 (combined).
(C) Lineman mechanic Class 2 and electrician signals Class 2 (combined).
(ii) Boys are not allotted different trades on enlistment. All start as operators, and as the result of observed aptitude during the course of training, combined with DSP results, they are allocated to the target trades. After recruit training, therefore, all boys do the same basic course and specialise on its conclusion.
(iii) The company has its own mechanic training room and instructors, and the use of the well equipped room of the men's main operating school for its operating periods.
(iv) Adequate provision is made for general education. During the first year, time is divided evenly between educational and technical training.

4. 1944–1945

During this period the company steadily increased in strength from 223 boys, 3 officers and 32 cadre in November 1943, to 344 boys, 6 officers and 57 cadre in March 1945. The accommodation question became acute. Owing to demands by the School of Signals who 'owned' Sandhurst Block A and who were themselves extending, the boys had to move into hutments, and have occupied the militia huts and several 1925 huts in Kemmel Lines for living and administrative purposes. Whilst these moves were retrograde from the accommodation point of view, the training side gradually improved and many huts were taken over in Loos Lines as training rooms. By early 1945 all training, with the exception of certain parts of line mechanic and telegraph mechanic, was being carried out in the Company's own huts, and the old headache of borrowing rooms from other Companies and units, with the consequent trouble of trying to fit boys' periods in with dissimilar men's periods, disappeared.

Training objectives were unfortunately constantly being altered during this period owing to changes in War Office policy, and in addition on the workshop side the old instrument mechanic, electrician signals and lineman mechanic trades were cancelled, and those of radio mechanic, telegraph mechanic and line mechanic were introduced. In February 1945 a fresh War Office directive ordered the training of a proportion of boys as lineman PL and lineman field. Thus there are now eight targets viz: OWK A3, OWL B2, OKL B2, radio mech A3, Tg mech A3, line mech A3, lineman PL and lineman field.

These changes in accommodation and training were accompanied by constant alteration of the cadre both on the technical and educational side. Whatever may have been the necessity for these constant postings in war, it must very definitely cease in peace if boys' training is to be of the highest standard. Boys' company is the most important company in the corps and by the standard of its training the whole corps will be influenced. It must have the best instructors – the pick of Royal Signals, who should do a three-year tour of duty with the company – approximately one third being posted each year. Unless the instructors really get to know the boys and their individual capabilities and can settle down and become a real part of the company, an indifferent standard of training will inevitably result.

The present brick system of establishment caters satisfactorily on the technical training side for increases in the size of the company; extra instructors being allocated as each 50 mark is reached. Company Headquarters, however, for Boys' company has a special establishment, which was laid down to deal with a total of six sections. When the seventh section was authorised, a request was put forward for a proportionate increase in Company Headquarters. In view of the restricted manpower then available, this was turned down. The lack of this increase was especially felt as regards (1) the two military training sergeants and the two PT corporals and (2) the orderlies. Reference has been made elsewhere in this book to the necessity of a NCO to act as 'matron'. This job in the past has has been carried out by one of these two sergeants in Company Headquarters: actually Sgt 'Buller' Blades. It has become an impossibility, with the increased size of the company, for one man to deal with the 'matron' side in a competent manner and at the same time to take his proper share of military training and non-technical activities. It has only been by the very loyal help, given by the APTC staff – not catered for in the establishment – in frequently

foregoing the help of the company PT instructors and thus allowing them to be diverted to military training, that this training has been kept going.

The GD boy problem referred to earlier in paragraph 3 of this chapter was solved early in 1944. Permission was obtained by AG 11 for the enlistment of GDs from boys who, although they had passed the AT entrance examination, had been unable to secure vacancies. This new type of GD is in effect exactly the same as the AT. All differences between the two types has ended to all intents, except for their official title and their pay. Incidentally, by enlisting GD boys in this way the total strength of the Company is increased. Previously there were the half-yearly arrivals of 25 GDs, who by their age would stay for only two years in the Company, making a total of 100 GDs plus 200 ATs or 300 in all. Now that they arrive in the same age group as ATs (fourteen–fifteen years), they remain in the company for three years, and consequently swell their GD total to 150, making the company total 350. With the retention of a boy till the end of term in which he has attained his posting age, the company strength may well rise to 400.

Towards the end of 1944 a scheme was started to encourage boys to take City and Guilds examinations in subjects relevant to their trades. This idea was initiated with two main objects. (1) As an inducement to parents to enter their boys for the corps and (2) to enable the boys to get a certificate, which would be of benefit to them when they returned to civilian life. It is a matter of doubt whether object (1) will bring a better type of boy into the corps; and in the case of (2) it is one which requires very careful consideration as to the advisability so early in their career, of turning to the civilian aspect of life the attention of the boys, who are being weaned from civilian life ideas and who it is hoped will become long-service soldiers.

A new feature was introduced in the term ending Christmas 1944, which was named 'The Passing-Out Parade'. A ceremonial parade and inspection with the band in attendance was carried out on the square under the command of the senior boy NCO. Cadre personnel – both officers and ORs – were present only as spectators, except for the OC who accompanies the inspecting officer. The company is drawn up by wings, each wing under its own boy NCO. The parade then march into line and advance to the 'General Salute'. Prizes are presented to the respective recipients (summer and winter terms only). The boys who are leaving, fall out, form up into a squad on the flank and are marched to the inspecting officer, who addresses them. After the address they are played off the square to the tune of 'Auld Lang Syne'. The company then march past in column of threes and off the parade ground. The boys are given a special dinner by themselves and depart immediately afterwards on their last pre-posting leave.

A system of privileges for NCO boys and senior boys was also established in 1944. The details are in Company Standing Orders.

Nearly all the 'old' boys, who had enlisted before the outbreak of war, had departed by the end of 1942, leaving the company with only the young boys of the 1942 intakes. The absence of the senior or top half of the com-

pany had a two-fold effect: (1) Many of the old company traditions and customs became moribund and, (2) The education, which all junior boys at school automatically receive from their elders, was missing. Only by hard and continuous effort were the 1942 boys, who had had no seniors to teach them the way as they grew up, induced to realise that the very fact that they were seniors and had received senior boys' privileges gave them responsibilities to the OC, to themselves and to their juniors. However in mid-1945 the company is nearly through the growing pains consequent in its rebirth, the balance has been restored, a real company spirit is growing and the war-babies of 1942 are now departing, after three years' service, as the tradesmen of 1945.

This detailed record gives an insight into the origins of life and policy for boys. It is further enhanced by an article that appeared in the February 1957 edition of *The Wire* and is entitled, 'The Autobiography of an Ex-Boy; how to do it.' It was written by Captain (QM) 'Bert' Stokoe, Royal Signals. The article is relevant not just because he was a boy but for several other reasons. Firstly, he subsequently became RSM of No.3 Intelligence School, Hildebrand Barracks, Harrogate. Secondly, his son was an apprentice in 1964 who later as Brigadier JD Stokoe CBE, Commander Communications BAOR, was the Reviewing Officer of the graduation parade on 17 December 1992. Thirdly, he became the Quartermaster of 6 (Boys') Training Regiment, Newton Abbot. Fourthly, he had a number of other relatives who joined the Royal Signals, including his grandson who was an apprentice at the college in the period 1991–93. His article recalls:

In the winter of 1927 I arrived at Catterick Camp, aged fourteen. It was, as usual, cold, damp and dismal. The bus conductor showed me where the guardroom was in Baghdad Lines; then the home of the Depot Regiment. From the guardroom I was escorted to the reception hut and handed over to the signalman in charge, who chivvied me around somewhat. (Positions were slightly reversed when I met this character again and I was a lance corporal. A pleasant time was had by all.)

The following day I was taken up to the famous boys' F Company, and within a few hours the comradeship that existed within F Company made itself felt. I had drawn my kit, and having just time to drop it on my bed, was called away, later to come back and find my kit folded up and put neatly in my locker. This had been done by the other boys – a really noble gesture. Life with F Company was a really happy one, under the command of Major FR Cobb, who I am sorry to say passed on. He was a grand Company Commander and I am sure all ex-boys who had the honour to serve under his command will always remember him with affection. Later the command of F Company was taken over by Captain Rance, who as you all no doubt know, is now Major

General Sir Hubert E Rance GCMG CBE CB. Captain Rance used to effect gauntlet fur gloves with uniform – I often wondered how he got away with it.

Technical training was not done actually with the company but in D and E Company Lines. The operator signals' training hut was next to the Royal Signals' band training room – hence the fact that ex boy operator signals could read through interference. The din from the band room was awful. (Major Judd – this was before your time).

Sport and education were a large part of our training. The chief sport being rugby at the time; though we still made our presence felt in all other aspects of the sporting world. I must not forget to mention our CSM – CSM Gibson, known affectionately to all the boys as 'Hoot, the Flying Cowboy'. It was considered a great thing to stand outside the door of his bunk (when he was not in residence) and say, 'Come on Hoot, come out and fight!' When he did come out one day all the boys could say was, 'Is it overcoats on parade, Sir?' (It was August 1928 – really a warm one as well.) Eventually, I reached the age of eighteen and was posted to Aldershot, 2 Divisional Signals, Mons Barracks – a fine unit.

Such was life in the days of F Company. It was by modern standards a comparatively harsh way of life. There was no hot water in the ablutions, and no large steel lockers in which to keep kit. Spring beds were unheard of, and the good old sliding iron was used to press clothes (electric irons were not invented). Climbing into bed was an adventure in itself; the mattress was of the three-biscuit type, the sheets were unbleached linen and the pillow was as hard as a log. Heating was provided by a central fireplace which had to be polished for inspections; as did the coal bucket.

All of this traces the roots of boy soldiers in general, and Royal Signals boys specifically, but it is necessary to return to the time of the First World War to commence a trace of the history of the apprentices' schools. It was not until the introduction of tank warfare and the increased use of mechanised transport in this war that the need for skilled tradesmen in great numbers became apparent. In 1919 the Army Council set up a War Office Committee that was to 'examine the necessity for, and practicability of, establishing a school for training boys as tradesmen for the Army in order to supply the deficiency consequent upon the impossibility of recruiting tradesmen in sufficient quantity from civilian life.' At the time there were already four Army boys' training establishments but they were only small. The recommendation of the committee was to establish a central school for 1000 boys covering 11 trades (in the event only four were selected).

The committee advised that, 'The primary object of the school is to produce tradesmen, and that only such military and physical training should be included as are necessary for the maintenance of the discipline and health of the boys at the school.... a swimming bath or pond should be provided.'

F Company boys at Hut 2, Whinny Hill, Catterick in 1931 after passing off the square.

The site initially selected for the Central Training School for Boys was at Blandford, Dorset, and the planned opening date was 1 September 1923. However, it was soon found that Blandford was not suitable and Chepstow was selected. Unfortunately, this site could not be prepared in time so the first course started in Buller Barracks, Aldershot on 25 September 1923. It was not until 28 February 1924 that the school moved to its permanent location at Bleachley, near Chepstow. On arrival it was also given a new name, 'Boys' Technical School'. This was a name that was to last until 1929 when it was altered to Army Technical School (ATS).

Over the years there have been many official terms to describe junior soldiers: junior soldier, young soldier, cadet, junior leader and apprentice, to name but a few. Those in adult service have used terms of endearment such as jeeps, badgies, rats and brats. The latter two probably derive from the initials of the Boys' and Army Technical Schools. Even today the 'ex-brat' is a well used reference to the Harrogate 'old boy' and there were badgies in Harrogate when the barracks were occupied by the Royal Artillery. apprentices from Chepstow have always been known as robots.

Initially, Chepstow provided tradesmen for the sappers, gunners, RASC and RTR, but from the first to pass out, one soldier joined Royal Signals in Catterick and by 1938, 19 had joined the corps. The course of training developed at Chepstow was

Lieutenant Colonel VTR Ford DSO, The York and Lancaster Regiment. The first Commandant of the Army Apprentices' School at Chepstow.

followed by other corps but not to quite the same scale. The success of 1924 was extended to other schools and by 1937 there were plans for similar organisations at Arborfield, Chatham and Jersey (Channel Islands). Each was to accommodate 1000 boys for RAOC, RE and RASC respectively. The last of these, in the Channel Islands, was over-run by the Germans in 1940 and was never reopened after the war.

Arborfield opened on 1 May 1939 and it was not until October 1939 that all RAOC were rebadged REME. By the commencement of hostilities in 1939 there had been a proliferation of boys' recruiting and it is estimated that over 12,000 were under training within units being operated for infantry, artillery, signals, ordnance, engineers, service, pay and armoured corps.

However, it was not until the end of the war that it was considered necessary to establish a further Apprentices' School at Harrogate. This stemmed from the need to maintain the new-found peace in Europe. It was envisaged that the size and technical expertise required to maintain such a force would only be achieved if boys' units were established to encourage volunteer recruits who would remain in service longer than their conscripted colleagues. So, whilst the history of boy soldiering can be traced back to medieval times, the Army apprentices of Harrogate grew from these comparatively recent seeds of success to meet the demands of peace and modern technology.

REME apprentices working on a Land-Rover at Arborfield in 1965.

Arborfield apprentices work on an armoured turret in 1912.

A 1981 view of the workshops of the Apprentices' School, Arborfield, that were built in 1939.

The Arborfield accommodation in 1950.

It is evident that, in the years following the war, great emphasis was placed on the need to recruit and train boy soldiers, so it soon became necessary to open new institutions to cater for them. There were sufficient schools established to train the apprentices but it was decided to extend the concept of the 'junior leader'. Whereas the apprentices' training included his trade, the junior leader concentrated on drill, weapon training, physical training, leadership, minor tactics, education and basic communication skills. At the end of the term in which he reached the age of seventeen years six months those in Royal Signals moved to Catterick for trade training.

In an article in the October 1957 edition of *The Wire* Major HA Leach, Royal Signals, explains how the Junior Leaders' Regiment became established:

Since the 1939–45 war our own Junior Leaders' Regiment has developed from a squadron which was formed with a nucleus of boys from the Army Apprentices' School at Harrogate. This squadron was attached to No.1 Independent Selection Squadron and stationed in Richmond. By April 1950, both squadrons had outgrown their accommodation and were moved to Beverley, near Hull. The unit continued to grow, and in order to provide more accommodation No.1 Independent Selection Squadron was moved to Catterick where it became No.5 Squadron of 7 Selection Regiment. On 25 August 1950, 6th (Boys') Training Regiment was formed at Beverley near Hull. The first Commanding Officer was Lieutenant Colonel AJ Keddie Royal Signals and Majors G Rowland MBE, and PG Curry were squadron commanders.

After much experiment, and as a result of many complications, a new establishment was written and implemented in 1956. This establishment provided for five boys' troops in each of the two training squadrons, and a recruit troop. A few months later the regiment moved to Denbury Camp, Newton Abbot and settled into Rawlinson Barracks.

The inaugural celebrations were carried out at Beverley in October 1950 when the Royal Signals Corps Band stayed for four days. On 26 October there was a Ceremonial Parade for Lieutenant General Sir Philip M Balfour KBE CB MC, the Army Commander. The parade was commanded solely by boys and the boy RSM was WT Galloway.

Training for junior leaders during the Newton Abbot era was rationalised considerably. Some trade training was achieved in the final term, and greater emphasis was placed on leadership and initiative training; outward bound courses were used

The original shoulder titles of the
Army Apprentices' Schools.

REME cap badge.

The shoulder titles of the Boys' Training School.

Shoulder titles of the RASC.

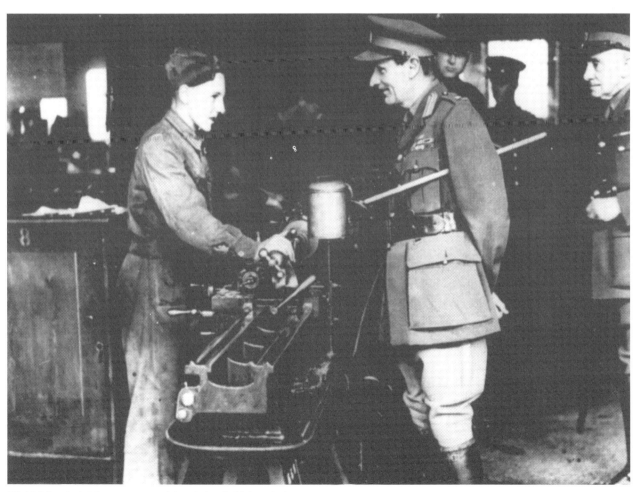

Field Marshal Montgomery visits Arborfield in 1942.

extensively. The Commanding Officer of the day in November 1959, Lieutenant Colonel L Gregory MBE, conceived the '10 Tors Race', and his dream came true when the first race took place from 14 to 17 September 1960; it has since become an annual event in the national calendar.

The concept of the junior leader grew in popularity within the military hierarchy and on 6 May 1959 the first intake of juniors arrived at the All Arms Junior Leaders' Regiment at Tonfanau, near Towyn in North Wales. The staff, which initially comprised mainly Royal Signals, included Major TGH Jackson MBE, Captain DA Barry, Captain EW Hunt, Lieutenant RF Hills, and Sergeants EW Osborne, PF Simmonds and H Chitticks, all Royal Signals. The regiment was responsible for training juniors from the Royal Armoured Corps, Royal Artillery, Royal Signals and Infantry.

The regiment at Newton Abbot continued to train junior soldiers for twelve years until it was closed in 1967. The 39 Royal Signals junior soldiers who had not graduated were sent to the Army Apprentices' College at Harrogate to continue training as junior soldiers and the organisation for the training of juniors had turned full circle. Denbury Camp became one of Her Majesty's Prisons.

From this time onwards there were few major changes to the organisation for the training of apprentices except that in January 1960 a further Apprentices' School was established in Carlisle to train RE and REME trades. This resulted in some rationalisation of trade training within the existing schools and, for example, resulted in all but Royal Signals apprentices leaving Harrogate by 1961. Carlisle became a REME organisation in 1966 but it closed in 1969 as one of the economies of the 1968 Defence Review, and Arborfield took on the whole of the REME apprentice commitment.

Apprentice
"But I don't think I deserve a zero".
Instructor
*"Neither do I, but it's the lowest
mark that I am allowed to give".*

2

THE EARLY DAYS OF PENNY POT CAMPS

Harrogate is a spa town situated in a picturesque part of North Yorkshire equidistant from York and Leeds. It lies on the edge of the Dales and is weathered by the predominantly westerly winds that sweep across the neighbouring moors. The local area makes an ideal apprentices' training base, and the nature of the apprenticeship fits in well with the local lifestyle. From a military standpoint it is near to ranges and training areas such as Otterburn, Strensall, Whitburn and Catterick. For adventurous and external leadership training, the excellent facilities of the Dales and Lake District are near to hand. The families are well served for their everyday needs by Harrogate, York and Leeds.

Harrogate has never been a garrison town and it does not have a great military history. However, during the years before the First World War it was a favoured location for units to hold their annual summer camps. Two sites were used but these have since been developed by builders. Exercising would take place in such areas as Harlow Moor and Blubberhouses Moor. In 1915 there was an increased need to accommodate and train the vast numbers of soldiers required for the First World War. New sites were required urgently and many were considered including one at Ripley. Finally, it was decided to establish a tented camp in the area of Penny Pot Lane on Killinghall Moor (see map on page 8). This commenced in May 1915 and established the current location as a military site. The local paper of the time commented:

The hilly nature of the country round about is especially suitable for troops raised in country districts. It has been found to strengthen the legs and open their lungs in a way that could not have been done in their home roads. No doubt these sentiments have been shared begrudgingly by generations of young soldiers since then.

The camp was given the name of '2nd Reserve Infantry Brigade Group Camp'. Its purpose was to train new recruits in preparation for service in the Great War. The first unit to arrive at the camp was the 13th Battalion, West Yorkshire Regiment.

Mr Bowe, a local farmer whose son was an apprentice at the college in the 1970s, recalls, 'My father used to tell me about military horses being tethered in the fields around "Penny Pot" during the Great War, and to this day we occasionally unearth a horseshoe or two when we are ploughing in the area.'

Conditions were not ideal in those early days. There was a shortage of fresh running water at the top of the hill and in winter it was impossible to tolerate the bitter cold weather conditions living under canvas. Considerable assistance was provided by the local Queen Ethelburga's School for Girls but by December 1915 it was decided to seek more substantial accommodation elsewhere. The troops were moved to permanent camps at Ripon and Masham and for the remainder of the war the spa town became more renowned for its hospitals, convalescent homes and rehabilitation centres.

In the period between the wars the college site remained a moor. Part of it belonged to Sir William Ingilby of Ripley Castle and part to Mr Simpson who

From a sketch by SJ Hughes – May 1995. One of the original huts in Uniacke Barracks that was used as the sergeants' mess, the post office and the woodwork hobby centre and stood until the college was closed.

From a sketch by SJ Hughes – May 1995. One of the original huts in Hildebrand Barracks that was used as the NAAFI, church and Bate Community Centre. It stood until the college was closed.

later became the Mayor of Harrogate. However, as the probability of war drew closer in the late 1930s, the need to have additional permanent camps became apparent. This was particularly so because of the raising of the militiamen by Mr Hore-Belisha.

By May 1939 it had been decided that a militia camp should be established on the Killinghall site to the west of Harrogate where some 200 acres of land on both sides of Penny Pot Lane were taken over. The origin of the name Penny Pot cannot be guaranteed but lore has it that in the days of the First World War there was a publican in the area who would sell ale to the marching troops at the price of 'Penny-a-pot'.

Accommodation was needed for about 1700 militiamen and, for the first time in decades, men in khaki were stationed in Harrogate. The builders of the camp were Sir Lindsay Parkinson Ltd, and the target date for completion was 15 August 1939. The first soldiers arrived in July and the initial contingent of 450 were put under tents in Blue Coat Wood off the Otley Road in the Harlow Hill area. In the event the building programme was delayed and the camp became occupied in September, within a few days of the outbreak of war. It is said that there had been trouble with the workforce during construction. At one time there were 234 carpenters and 646 labourers working on the site. The construction type was of wooden 'spiders' so familiar to servicemen and they were fitted out to a standard of luxury unknown in the early part of the war. Both sides of 'Penny Pot Lane' were used and they later became known as two different camps: Uniacke and Hildebrand Barracks.

Shoulder titles of the RASC.

UNIACKE BARRACKS

The camp to the south of Penny Pot Lane was initially named Killinghall Camp South. The first unit to occupy it was 9th Field Training Regiment, Royal Artillery. The Commanding Officer was Lieutenant Colonel TCD Colman TA (reputedly of the mustard family) who remained in command for about two years. He was superceded by Lieutenant Colonel Blacker who remained until the regiment disbanded in 1943. The first Adjutant was Captain Streather. Shortly after occupation by the regiment the camp was renamed Uniacke Barracks after Lieutenant General Sir Hubert Uniacke KCB KCMG who was a distinguished Gunner Officer. The name of the camp has never been changed.

Gunner Eric Stirk was one of those who received his call-up papers in July 1939 and arrived at the camp just five days after the outbreak of war. He recalls his first winter:

The camp was very exposed and I remember that all the trees leaned in one direction. In the very severe weather 40 braziers were lit and kept alight twenty-four hours a day under the water tower to prevent it from freezing. Trainees were confined to camp for the first twenty-one days while they learned to wear their uniform, bear themselves in a soldierly manner and most important of all, salute! A lot of the permanent staff were ex-Indian Army so we all became familiar with Hindustani terms. Each battery had its boy trumpeters, who were known as badgies, so we had to learn and respond to the various calls. Fairly early after my arrival a company of Auxiliary Territorial Service (ATS) was posted to the camp and accommodated in K Block on the west side of the square. Our roll call was at 10pm and we had to be back by midnight at the latest.

Training was every day except Sunday when we had a church service in the cinema. Compulsory sport was on Wednesday and Saturday afternoons. The Colonel was a hunting man and at first used to hire the Claro Beagles but later he kennelled his own pack of hounds in the camp. Beagling was then accepted as an alternative to any other game. The NAAFI on the east side of the square and the 'Sally Ann' were used extensively.

We were fairly well supplied with rifles, some of them the older Lee Enfields. We had a few Lewis guns with Brens and Stens arriving later. Initially we did not have any guns but eventually some were taken out of preservation. They included 4.5 howitzers from the Great War, 18-pounders and French 75s. They were taken away after Dunkirk but later on they were gradually replaced by 25-pounders. Transport was three-tonners, 15cwts and a few wheeled gun tractors. In addition a number of civilian cars and motor cycles were commandeered. Gun and firing practice took place on Blubberhouses Moor and I recall that a man was killed in that area after the war by an unexploded bomb.

From a sketch by SJ Hughes – May 1995. The original cinema in Uniacke Barracks which stood until the college closed.

The 25-pounder gun used by the Royal Artillery.

We had to dig air-raid trenches on the 'mire dam'. This was the boggy area just to the west of the camp. The regiment did see 'action' twice. On the first occasion, at the time just after Dunkirk, we went to defend Yeadon Airport with pick helves. Then we had to cordon off the Majestic Hotel in Harrogate (20 September 1940) after a German raider jettisoned three bombs. One failed to explode and was lodged in the upper floor of the hotel.

When air raids started in London and the South Coast, the Royal Artillery Mounted Band was posted to the camp and remained there until the regiment was disbanded. The bandmaster was RSM Geary who was later commissioned. I seem to recall that at the end of our time a company of light infantry was in the camp.

Bill Quayle was another raw recruit who arrived at the newly built camp. He was one of the eighteen-year-olds who was recruited into the gunners:

I arrived at Penny Pot Camp on 14 September 1939 together with another new boy, Ron Vickery. We were posted into C Battery where we stayed until December 1940. We were clerks and our offices were in the wooden huts next to the water tower at the top end of camp.

Our barrack block slept about 30 soldiers and we were issued with iron beds, three 'biscuits' matresses laid end to end, two thin blankets, sheets and pillows. There is no doubt that they were completely and utterly inadequate for the bitter winter that followed.

Shortly after arrival we all had to have the dreaded injections. About 30 of us were lined up and the MO came along the line injecting each one of us using the same needle. I got a really sore injection and dared to complain. The MO looked at the needle and turned to his orderly, 'I thought it was getting a bit difficult. The point has broken off the needle. Go back and check their arms to see if you can find anything,' said the MO. Of course, nothing was found!

The officers were mostly TA, some of whom had served in WWI, and the NCOs were Reservists. My BC was Major Plummer and later Major Mytton. There were also Lieutenants Butcher, Pickup and Tate; the latter was a broad Yorkshireman who used to say that no lanyard had been designed that was long enough to fire the 75s with any degree of safety. We also had BSM Houghton, Sergeants Marshall and Skelton and Bombadier Finch. Finch was a spiritualist healer who really could work miracles on injuries. In the office we had Timms and Popham. These people were all excellent types and the officers were real gentlemen.

Shortly after I arrived I was injured in a football match and because I had been a bank clerk before joining I was detailed to fill in the registration forms of new recruits. Each one came forward to my table at which the BSM also sat. One very pale and very thin young chap came forward and nervously gave his details. When asked his religion he said in a very loud voice, 'Centicelestrialist, Sir.' He was, of course, trying to evade church parade. The BSM twitched a little and asked him, 'What did you say?' The recruit repeated, 'Centicelestrialist, Sir.' 'And what do they do?' asked the BSM. 'They worship the sun, Sir,' he replied sheepishly. The BSM was getting agitated by this and picked up his documents. He looked at his home address and said, 'You come from Manchester young man. There is never any … sun there. From now on you are C of E; get over there with that lot.'

A few ATS girls joined the camp for office duties and I remember one of them sang 'Rose of England' at the camp concert; she was magnificent, or so she seemed at the time! For pay I received 2s. per day (10p) from which we had to pay haircuts and barrack damages. So there was not much left for enjoying yourself. To overcome this we did a lot of self-entertainment and Lance Bombadier Baker formed a dance band that used to perform every Friday night at the Odeon in Harrogate. I left Penny Pot after just over a year and joined 125 OCTU in Ilkley. I enjoyed my time in Harrogate and had learned the rudiments of Army life.

941492 Gunner John Dean enlisted in Leeds and arrived by train at Harrogate on 16 October 1939:

Within a few minutes of arriving at the camp I was taken to my barrack block. It was heated by a coal fire and the facilities included hot showers, baths and indoor toilets.

A group of ATS Royal Signals, who were members of the Y Service, outside their accommodation in Queen Ethelburga's School. They were later moved to Penny Pot camps.

There were quite a few of us from Leeds and this was absolute luxury to us all. We were used to back-to-back terraced houses which had no bath or running hot water and the toilet was in the outside shed which we shared with another house.

Many of our NCOs had served in India and I believe the RSM died of black-water fever; the regiment turned out for his funeral. Initially we were very short of equipment and, for instance, there was only an old Albion gate change van for driver training. We had a single Dial Sight but it did not convey anything to us about gunnery. So most of our basic training was PT, drill, small arms weapon training and learning guard duties.

My training at Harrogate set me up for a military life that continued until February 1946; it was a part of my life that I would not have missed for anything. I left Penny Pot and later joined 67th Field Regiment RA.

Towards the end of the war the 116th General Hospital of the U.S. Army occupied Uniacke Barracks following a number of 'temporary' alterations that were to last twenty years. These included providing cover over many of the outdoor pathways so that patients could be moved around the hospital whilst being protected from the harsh local weather. This move was in anticipation of heavy casualties that were expected from the Normandy campaign. Pam Elliott was an ATS Operator at the Forrest Moor Y Service Station. For a time she was billeted at Queen

Ethelburga's School. She recalls that they were asked to visit the wounded soldiers in hospital. A plaque to commemorate the hospital was erected at the entrance to Valley Gardens. It reads:

THIS TABLET WAS ERECTED BY THE
OFFICERS AND NURSES OF THE 116TH
GENERAL HOSPITAL OF THE UNITED
STATES ARMY WHO, SERVING THEIR
COUNTRY DURING WORLD WAR II,
SPENT HAPPY DAYS IN HARROGATE
AND ENJOYED THE HOSPITALITY
OF ALL YORKSHIRE.
JULY 28, 1944   MAY 11, 1945

The plaque was unveiled by Lord Halifax in July 1947 and the ceremony was attended by Colonel William Rich from New York. He had been the Chief Dental Officer of the 116th.

HILDEBRAND BARRACKS

The initial purpose of the northern camp was to accommodate the militiamen of the Royal Corps of Signals. Unfortunately the unit had assembled before the camp had been completed and so a tented site on Harlow Hill, near Beckwithshaw, was occupied. Lieutenant John Sheepshanks (later Lieutenant Colonel) recalled:

Even during the summer of 1939 the Beckwithshaw Camp always seemed to be knee-deep in mud. To combat this there were miles of duck boards. We set about a programme of primary military training for the militiamen but we were delighted, when after about five months, we were able to move over to Penny Pot. We called the camp 'Penny Pot Main'.

The Commanding Officer of the Militia Training Battalion, Royal Signals, was Lieutenant Colonel VJ Westropp (Victor), Royal Signals. He was one of the finest officers that I ever served with and he went on to reach the rank of major general. Apart from myself, the only other regular officer in the battalion was the Adjutant, Captain (later Brigadier) JC Hardy (Jack), Royal Signals. The other officers were supplementary reservists who were seconded to the Army from the Post Office and other technical professional organisations. The battalion built up to a strength of about 800.

It was not long after our arrival at Penny Pot that we received our G1098 stores issue. At the same time we were renamed the First Army Line of Communications Battalion. Due to the outbreak of war the terms of service of the militiamen had been altered and this regular unit was formed.

The only operation that I can recall was in support of Headquarters 15 Infantry Brigade at the port of Andalsnes in Norway. My company was deployed under command of Major Wicks. Other officers included Captain Andrews

and Lieutenant Alan Baker. The Brigade Signals Officer
was Lieutenant JD Yule. The brigade fought hard but was
no match for the German airpower. The local town was
built entirely of wood and was reduced to ashes in a series
of air raids. It was not long before a withdrawal was
ordered. We returned, without any losses, to Penny Pot
via Scotland, courtesy of the Royal Navy.

In mid-1940, battalions became regiments and we
were thereafter known as First Army Signals Regiment.
Shortly after this I was posted, as were the CO and
Adjutant. I think the regiment moved to the Middle East.

Amongst the first people to arrive at the Camp
to the north of Penny Pot Lane was 2363923
Signalman Joseph Cerutti, Royal Signals, and he
recalls:

I was enlisted as a militiaman, in March 1939,
because I was one of those unlucky chaps who was born in
1918. All of us who joined Royal Signals started our
military number with 236. We were to serve six months
with the Colours followed by three years six months on the
Reserves. Unfortunately, the war broke out just after I was
called up so I served a total of six years six months until
12 February 1946.

We were the first troops to move into the barracks in
August 1939. Our pay was 2s. (10p) per day. Our training included drill and Army procedures for lines of
communications. As militia we had three forms of dress.
For fatigues we wore a boiler suit. Best dress was riding
breeches, putties and jacket (Signals was classed as a
mounted regiment). Walking-out dress was a black beret,
black single-breasted jacket, khaki shirt, black tie and grey
trousers; this was made by Burtons, Jacksons & Stewarts.
However, it was not long before we were issued with our
military uniforms.

I recall a few of the members of staff including
Lieutenant Sheepshanks, RSM Strickland (a perfect
gentleman), Drill Instructor Sergeant Lawn (Corporal of
Horse) Dragoon of Guards, and Lance Corporals Gerry
Dawson and 'Horseshoe' Collins. I remained at the camp
until January 1940 when I went to Cavalry Barracks,
Canterbury with 2nd Army Signals. I remained there
until February 1940 when I joined the British
Expeditionary Force as a terminal equipment mechanic.

2593414 Signalman RTH Perkins joined the Army on
10 May 1939 and carried out six weeks' initial
training with the Royal Artillery at Arrow Park,
Birkenhead. He moved to Penny Pot in July 1939 to
commence his line training:

We started our training in Uniacke Barracks because
the huts in the other barracks were not ready until August.
We then moved across into the four brand-new wooden
spiders that had been erected. There were 19, 20 and 21
Line Sections of militiamen and our course lasted about six
months. Each section was about 30 men strong and I was
in 20 Section which was commanded by Captain Dorwood
R Signals. Our sergeant major was WO2 Cousins.

One of my vivid memories is of Bombadier Gunn RA

who was in the Artillery Regiment in Uniacke Barracks.
Later in the war I served in Africa where he appeared as a
Second Lieutenant adorned with the Victoria Cross.

On completion of the course in early 1940 I sailed
with my section from Liverpool to Ceylon and then later to
India where I met Brigadier Rowentree, the father of
Lieutenant Rowentree, who was one of my instructors at
Penny Pot. There is no doubt that the training I received
during these six months set me up for the remainder of my
military career and helped me to cope with nearly three
years as a prisoner of war. I returned to England on
15 April 1945.

NCO TRAINING BATTALION, ROYAL SIGNALS

From late 1939 to 1943 the section of the camp to the
north of Penny Pot Lane was also occupied by the
Royal Signals NCO Training Battalion. The Barracks
was named by the Royal Signals after Brigadier-
General Arthur Blois Ross Hildebrand CB CMG
DSO. Robert Buxton recalled in 1994:

The 23rd Division Signals was embodied whilst in
camp at Scarborough on the outbreak of war. A detachment went with 50th Div to Dunkirk but 23rd were
disbanded with effect from 1 July 1940 and were reformed
as the NCO Training Battalion at Hildebrand. The CO
was Lieutenant Colonel RS White who was followed later
in about June 1941 by Lieutenant Colonel T Sheffield: both
were 50th Div TA Officers. I was the Adjutant.

The battalion was divided into companies. Major
HG Smith was 'Drill and Duties'. Lieutenant Wardman
was 'Line'. I think there was another company dealing
with wireless, maintenance, MT, admin etc.

I also recall Major Robertson, Major Glover, Captain
Renwick and Lieutenants Bell, Maughan, Wills and
Stokes. HRH Princess Mary visited us in spring 1941.
We had joint concerts and sports days with the RA from
Uniacke and our military exercises were carried out on the
local harsh moors.

Eric Markham arrived in June 1940 as part of the
setting-up establishment for the battalion:

I arrived with a party of officers, NCOs and men of
23rd Divisional Signals. This was a TA unit stationed in
Darlington which had been virtually disbanded. Most of
the trained men went to the Middle East. We, the remainder, were to form the core of the NCO Training Battalion.
We were commanded by Lieutenant Colonel Stevenson
Wright who had been CO of the 23rd.

Once a month an input of potential NCOs were sent
to the camp for a three-month course. There were three
companies and HQ Company. No.1 Company for drill
and duties, No.2 Company for technical training, and
No.3 for field training. I was No.1 Company clerk and our
CSM was Sergeant Major 'Taffy' Lloyd.

Having been billeted in rather primitive conditions

in a church hall in Darlington, my first impression of Harrogate was one of untold luxury. We had all 'mod-cons' – spring bedsteads, white sheets and hot baths. The cookhouse was well equipped but it still managed to produce some of the worst food I have ever tasted in the Army.

There are two incidents that stick out in my mind. The first was having to go down to Harewood House, the home of our Colonel-in-Chief, on a cold winter's day in January 1941. We had to clear the snow from the full length of the drive which seemed to go on for ever. The second was having to guard the Majestic Hotel in Harrogate one Friday afternoon after a lone German bomber dropped a stick of bombs and one of them remained unexploded! We provided a cordon until Bomb Disposal arrived.

Following my time at Harrogate I went to Malaya and, after the fall of Singapore, I became a POW of the Japanese in a series of very different camps to that enjoyed at Penny Pot!

Sergeant AP Powell also arrived in June 1940 as one of the founder members of No.1 Company (Drill and Duties):

I arrived to work under Major George Smith who was the officer who instigated the enthusiasm among the staff and students. After my period of teaching new recruits in Catterick it was wonderful to teach these young lads who were so keen to qualify for their stripe. We started with about 200 on the course but this peaked at intakes of about 500 per month. I remained in the battalion until August 1943 and I estimate that we had trained about 15,000 NCOs.

One of the saddest recollections I have concerns one of my fellow members of staff, Sergeant Gordon Winstanley, who was unfortunately killed whilst he was disposing of a cluster of unexploded grenades.

There were many happy times and I recall going to the garrison theatre, ENSA shows and films at the cinema. I was also one of the lucky ones who had to guard the Majestic Hotel when a lone Junkers 88 dropped a bomb which remained unexploded on the fourth floor.

In the spring of 1941, John Phillips was a cadet in 152 OCTU at Catterick. He was detailed to go with a small detachment to Harrogate:

We were to demonstrate the No.21 Set, which was our latest equipment, to our Colonel-in-Chief, The Princess Royal who was visiting Harrogate. When she arrived I gave my well-rehearsed spiel and stressed the robustness of the equipment in being able to withstand a 2ft drop. She liked my demonstration and then, much to my amazement said, 'Will it really withstand being dropped? Is that what you are going to show us? Well, I should like to see it put to the test.'

Of course nothing could have been further from my mind and I obviously looked to my officer for help. Sensing my reluctance she said, 'If I give the order as Colonel-in-Chief nobody can very well complain. So drop it and let us

see what happens.' I duly obeyed by lifting the set from the table and allowing it to fall to the tarmac with a crash. With great trepidation I restored it to the table and switched on. To my intense relief it worked. 'Thank you, most reassuring,' she said with a smile and walked on to the next exhibit.

The AB 64 of Signalman Barry Foreman records on 14 April 1943 that he was graded 'good' as a member of Junior NCO Training Course No.32. Over fifty years later he recollected:

It was a fairly arduous course conducted in (for the wartime Army) excellent conditions. We were told that the barracks had been constructed in 1938 for the conscripted militiamen, though that scheme of course became swallowed up by the outbreak of the Second World War. The standard of accommodation was quite luxurious after the miserable conditions in the 'dark satanic mills' of No.3 TTB in Huddersfield; there were cupboards to keep one's equipment, the toilets were reasonable, I think there were even showers; but the main thing was the food, which was something special. It has remained as a mystery to me, how such a standard of excellence was achieved by the catering staff at Hildebrand – presumably they were only working with the same scale of wartime Army rations issued elsewhere, so if they could do that, why did we have to endure less elsewhere? No doubt the answer lay in the quality of the supervision. The NAAFI also remains in my memory as being of a very high standard, and the same remarks apply to the mess.

The instruction, both technical and military, was of varying standard, but mostly good. The staff were efficient, fair and conscientious; I cannot recall any cause for complaint. My Squad Commander was Corporal Noblett and the section sergeant was called Stebbing. I remember that Sergeant Stebbing was posted away from Harrogate when our course was about half completed, and he had a bicycle which he offered for sale. I gave him £1 for that bike, and I never spent £1 to better advantage in my life. It enabled me to pursue a career of undetected (non-vicious) crime for the remainder of my time in this country, that is to say until I embarked for India in February 1944 to complete officer training at Mhow. Wartime Harrogate hadn't a great deal to offer, but Leeds was within easy cycling distance and a solitary soldier cyclist attracted no attention; I should add that, prior to enlistment in May 1942, I had been working in the Ministry of Works office in Leeds and had friends there.

One item in the training programme which impressed itself on my memory was a demonstration of the art of camouflage. We were marched out to the countryside near Hildebrand. A number of the staff – about 10 or a dozen were concealed solely by camouflage within about 200 yards of us, and at a given signal then revealed their positions, previously not detectable in nearly every case. Although I was born and bred in the country (son of a gamekeeper) I found this demonstration most impressive. No doubt it was a *standard Army stunt (we later did a similar exercise in India) but the Harrogate instruction was especially well done.*

Barry went on to be commissioned and became a Captain in the Royal Signals and a stalwart operator of the Royal Signals Amateur Radio Society.

14316924 Signalman Alec F Morgan (later Staff Sergeant with 305 AGRA, 305 Bedfordshire Yeomanry Troop, Signal Squadron, TA Bedford) remembers well his two months in the NCO Training Battalion:

I was an operator wireless and line (OWL) Class B3. I completed my trade training in 23 Squad, 4 Company, 5 Operator Training Battalion, Slaithwaite, near Huddersfield. I was posted to join No.35 Drill and Duties course at Harrogate on 25 May 1943. Initially my PSI was Sergeant Penman, Royal Signals, of 1 Company. For the first month we carried out military training which included such matters as drill, PT, hygiene, gas training, assault course, weapon training, military law and so on. We covered a wide range of weaponry including LMG, mines, grenades, rifle and the Tommy gun.

After one month we all moved over to 2 Company where Sergeant Ackerman, Royal Signals, concentrated more on our duties as a Signals NCO. Here we covered the No.18, 21 and 38 sets, operators' records, interference and suppression, battery charging, wireless siting, aerials, wavemeter C and Army organisation.

We carried out a number of schemes to practise our skills. 'Foolscap' with the 19 Set took us to Follifoot. We did signal office siting in Bolton Abbey, Guisley and Otley. 'Seventy Six', an RT mobile scheme, took us to Leathley, Ilkley, Otley, Addington and Pateley Bridge. In all we spent most of the second month out and about in the local area on one scheme or another. I completed my training in the Battalion at Hildebrand on 22 July 1943 and went to join 4 Squadron, 8 Corps Signals.

In fact Alec Morgan was one of the last soldiers to undergo training in the Battalion because on 13 August 1943 it was disbanded.

NO.3 INTELLIGENCE SCHOOL

During the Second World War No.3 Intelligence School also moved into Hildebrand Barracks; it was often referred to as the Cypher Regiment. The school had been established at Dulwich and then moved to Knightsbridge in September 1940 before its move to Harrogate. The aim of the school was to train Cypher Operators. Signalman Ron Kelly was a trainee in the school from July to September 1945. He remembers it well:

It was 1945. The war was drawing to a close. VE Day had come and gone. About 30 of us, who were all survivors of a tough 'Special Operations Assault Course' at Scarborough, and nearly all volunteer refugees from the dreaded Catterick, were posted to No.3 Intelligence School; whatever that was! On arrival the shock was complete. From sunny seaside Scarborough to grey, gloomy, wartime Harrogate. From the highly physical course of forced marches, weapon training and assault courses, we had moved to the classroom atmosphere of a cypher course. However there was soon to be some compensation. Living almost opposite us in Queen Ethelburga's School were 1500 ATS who were working at Forrest Moor radio station.

But what were we doing at No.3 Intelligence School? And what the devil were cyphers? All I could think of was invisible ink and secret messages. The course was divided into two parts. The first was Low and Medium Grade Cyphers. The second was High Grade Cyphers.

Low Grade. *This was usually a relatively simple transposition code called Slidex. It was used in artillery instructions and messages of low classification.*

Medium Grade. *Dictionary-type code books (Freddy Books) were used, in which all letters, numbers and words were given four-figure numbers. These numbers were then transposed on a substitution frame and transmitted in five-figure blocks. At the receiving end the reverse of the transposition was carried out and the numbers were read off from a further code book. You had to be able to add up and subtract accurately to carry out the transpositions.*

The low level code SLIDEX Wallet.

The High Level Code machine TYPEX.

High Grade. *These cyphers were similar to the medium grades but the code books were more exclusive. They were only used in selected locations such as the War Office, embassies and important headquarters.*

TYPEX. *This was a letter substitution cypher machine which had a typewriter keyboard in capitals only. Plain language letters would be passed through a number of revolving bakelite discs with a series of brass contacts. The output was a jumble of letters which were then transmitted. The reverse procedure was carried out by the recipient. The important matter on this equipment was to ensure that your discs were set up in accordance with the code for the day.*

One Time Pads. *OTPs was the only unbreakable cypher. It consisted of a pad of sheets of random numbers which were only used once and then destroyed. Only the sender and receiver held the pads so it was impossible for anyone else to unscramble the transposed message. Unfortunately it was very time consuming compared with Typex.*

There were three grades of report from the course. First was fail; posted back to your unit. Second was medium-grade cypher operator in the rank of lance corporal. Third was high-grade cypher operator. I was fortunate in gaining the highest grade and as a lance corporal I eventually made my way to the Signals Headquarters in Palestine and later on to the Transjordan Frontier Force. After further service around the Middle East I was finally demobbed in 1948. There is no doubt that my time at Penny Pot determined my military career.

Signalman John Hardy was called up in March 1946 and, after basic training at Quebec Barracks Northampton, he too arrived for his cypher course:

The course was about two months long and the main elements were paper codes, typing and cypher equipments. I recall learning to set the cogs on the cypher machines which we called 'pianos' because the word cypher was classified. Learning to touch-type was one of the best things that ever happened to me in the Army and was useful to me for the rest of my life.

We sat in classes of about 20 in the wooden huts and we were taught the necessary elements of our trade by sergeants. I recall there being a number of ATS girls around, but I suppose they must have worked in the cookhouse.

WO1 (RSM) Stokoe was a regimental sergeant major at the school and two later generations of his family joined the Royal Signals and served at Penny Pot. Majors Hawkins and Martinson were the last commanders of the school before it was disbanded in May 1949.

115TH GENERAL HOSPITAL, U.S. ARMY

Just as Hildebrand Barracks had been utilised as a hospital so too was Uniacke. 115th General Hospital was set up in 1944 to take casualties from the invasion of Europe. Robert W Rhynsburger was a patient in the hospital:

I was with a Heavy Weapons Company of the 290th Regiment in Belgium. It was January 1945 when I contracted frostbite and was evacuated to Harrogate. There were six wards in the hospital and they were all the same with about 25 patients in each. As far as I recall no critically ill or seriously wounded patients were brought here. Several in my ward had shrapnel and gunshot wounds, several had frostbite, but all were recovering.

We had BBC radio newscasts which were broadcast through a loudspeaker system. Each ward was staffed by a nurse during daytime. At night the whole block had two nurses on duty. The heating system was a coal-fired furnace which was tended by an elderly Englishman.

I was returned to duty on 31 March 1945 and made my way to an Engineer Regiment in Bremen for the final stages of the war before discharge in June 1946.

The war also brought about a measure of mystery to Penny Pot in that it 'gave birth' to the first of the two 'Ghosts of Penny Pot'. The first is the 'Ghost of Stumpy' and AT Corporal S Rogers of Intake 64C (later Major (TOT) Stephen Rogers and the College SO2 Co-ord in 1993) recalled:

Towards the end of the Second World War, a German plane was either shot down or crashed near Harrogate. There was one survivor who was seriously injured. He was taken to Penny Pot Camp, then being used as a military hospital. His injuries necessitated the removal of his left leg. As he recovered , a special cell was built at the end of one of the barrack blocks and he was subsequently moved into it to recuperate; his room is shown on some of the building plans of the time. Each morning and evening he was unlocked from his cell and escorted to the ablutions which were in the middle of the wooden 'spiders'. With the aid of a crude crutch he would hobble to the ablutions, making a loud clump as his crutch came down. He was nicknamed 'Stumpy' by the other patients.

The story is that on VE night there was a big party in the American hospital and when Stumpy's cell was opened the next morning he was found dead. He had committed suicide rather than face the fact that the Fatherland had lost the war. The reported cause of death varies from hanging himself to the rafters, which were great beams across the room, to being 'helped' on his way by some of the patients.

Stumpy's ghost is said to have continued to go to the ablutions each morning and evening from then on.

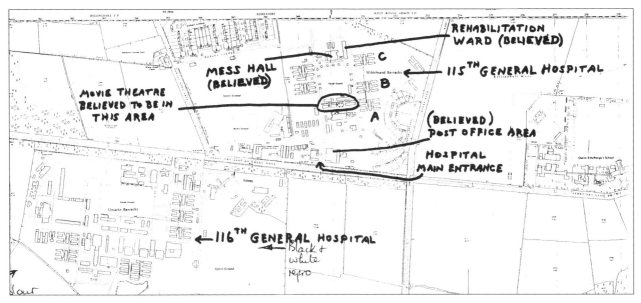

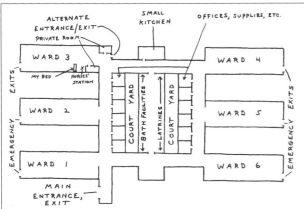

Above: *A 1966 map of Hildebrand Barracks marked by American Bob Rhynsburger, showing the arrangement of 115th General Hospital when he was a patient in Block B in early 1945.*

Left: *The layout of Block B of the 115th General Hospital.*

Members of Scott Troop of 64C were adamant that they heard the clump of his crutch, and I was told several times that his ghost had been seen. His description never varied. Always a tall figure, dressed in a vest and British issued pyjamas, with the left leg folded up and sewn, and a crude crutch, as for Long John Silver, under his left armpit.

AT P Ingarfield of Intake 66B has vivid memories of the ghost:

One evening we returned from a hard day's canoeing on the river at Ripon. The Officer-in-Charge had left us to put the equipment away in the wooden hut but, mistakenly, he had departed with the key. We decided to gain access to the hut through a small window beside the main door. We had just finished tidying up when we all heard the clunk, clunk, clunk coming down the corridor. Within seconds half a dozen 'brave' apprentices were to be seen all trying to make their way through the smallest of windows. I do not know to this day whether someone was messing about or not, but on the day no one was prepared to hang around to find out! It was spooky!

The second ghost is that of 'The Matron'. In the early days many of the military and civilian staff lived in a hut near the main road to Beckwithshaw. One of

these was a matron who allegedly, having got herself into a marital tangle, was murdered by a driver who may have been her lover. Even to the day of disbandment there was talk of 'unusual happenings' in one of the only remaining wooden buildings which was used as a community centre. The playschool teachers reported that items moved and were tidied away, but there was no way that it could have been a member of staff. Others have reported a 'female presence' in the building. Whatever it is, they all refused to return to the building at night unless they were escorted. There were also reports as late as 1993 from the NAAFI members of staff that there were ghosts on the premises.

Hildebrand was also used by A Company of the Infantry Boys' Battalion during the early 1950s. The main elements of the unit were based at Tuxford, near Retford in Nottinghamshire. Boy Lance Corporal John Glazier was Rifle Brigade but later joined the RAOC and served until 1958, reaching the rank of WO1 (Conductor):

In January 1953 I joined 5 Platoon at Hildebrand and I well remember Boy RSM R Arnott, Royal Fusiliers. My OC Company was Captain Lemon of the Wiltshire

Regiment; Lieutenant Hawkins, Dorset Regiment, was my Platoon Commander and WO2 Knocker Walker was my CSM. We did over two days every week on education and I passed my Army 2nd Class Certificate. We went to Hornsea and Strensal for rifle shooting and I recall a three-day exercise on the local Yorkshire moors for map reading and leadership.

To some extent we stole to survive and the NAAFI canteen was raided on a regular basis. I remember being woken up on one of these occasions and being offered 40 Woodbine cigarettes. Next morning Knocker Walker went round and took everyone's fingerprints and eventually a whole pile of fags was found in the rafters. I don't know if they found the culprit. The Red Shield Canteen was a favourite place for us to purchase a wad and a cup of tea to supplement Army rations with our meagre earnings. Soon after my arrival the weather was bitter and the snow was lying very deep, so much so, that it was impossible to carry out any training. Instead, on one occasion, the OC got all the permanent staff on one side of the square and the boys on the other and we spent the rest of the day having a strategic snowball fight!

The turn of the decade also saw the arrival of Headquarters East and West Ridings Area. In 1951 the Commander was Brigadier RJ Springhall and Brigadier Houchin was Commander when it closed in September 1958.

A new recruit!

Fond Parent
"So, service at the School makes you feel confident in decision making".

1st Term Apprentice
"Absolutely. I get up any time I want before 6.30 am and I can finish just when I like after 9.30 pm."

3

THE SCHOOL IS ESTABLISHED
IN UNIACKE BARRACKS

Colonel WH Langran MC – April 1947 to April 1948
Colonel DA Kendrew DSO – August 1948 to October 1950

The permanent staff (PS) for the new apprentices' school began to join in May 1947. The first Commandant was Colonel WH Langran MC who had formerly been in charge of all cadet units in Northern Command. His task was to set up a system of training that included general education, metalwork, signals and military training. Later it was realised that the school also had the special task to train future technical officers and NCOs. This required additional facilities for trades such as fitter, welder, vehicle mechanic, electrician and driver.

The first regimental sergeant major (RSM) was WO1 (RSM) T Rees, Welsh Guards, but he only remained in post for six months before WO1 (RSM) S Lonsborough, Coldstream Guards, took over. He remained in post until September 1955 which gave the school much-needed stability. He was the type of character required to stamp his authority in an appropriate manner. Initially, the school was not prepared for new arrivals and the RSM was one of 12 families who moved into modified wooden huts. There was no running hot water and heat was provided by coal and coke boilers and Calor gas heaters. This situation remained for eighteen months until about 50 new prefabricated buildings were erected. Since then the RSM was always from the Brigade of Guards.

The initial intake of 50 boys was Intake 47B, and they arrived in September 1947. The first Chief Instructor was Lieutenant Colonel LJ Walker MBE REME. He was familiar with the requirements of boys because he had himself enlisted as an apprentice at Chepstow. In his article in the first issue of the school's magazine in 1949 he records:

In May 1947 the camp had a deserted and neglected look and it was difficult to visualise how the large area of dispersed buildings could be adapted for the requirements of an Army Apprentices' School. The existing living

Colonel WH Langran MC, Commandant from August 1947 to April 1948.

WO1 (RSM) T Rees Welsh Guards was the first RSM at the School from September 1947 to March 1948.

Building the school in summer 1949.

accommodation presented little difficulty; but what could be done with old drill sheds and garages? Outwardly the drill sheds remain the same except for a notice which tells one they are now the electricians' workshop, vehicle mechanics' workshop, or one of the closely allied trade workshops. Inside, however, a transformation has taken place, and what were dirty, unsightly interiors, are now bright workshops with benches, vices, machines and sectional models in colours bright to the eye. The garages, not usable at first, are now in the hands of the contractors being converted to workshops and, when completed, will ease slightly the pressing need for work-shop accommodation.

   The first two or three months were hectic in compil-ing syllabuses and preparing the demands for stores required to enable them to be put into operation; also the planning of accommodation and workshops which would be required to cater for the trades we were to teach and would permit the school to function in September 1947. There was much anxious waiting, and wondering whether the stores and equipment would arrive in time, but sufficient stores did materialise.

   At last came the great day when our first boys began to arrive; not so many as had been planned for, but enough to make a start. All our planning and timetables went into operation according to schedule and after three weeks of military training the first Army apprentices of Harrogate started their trade careers.

The newly appointed members of the permanent staff worked hard. In an article reproduced in *The Gate* of spring 1988, one of the first instructors recalls his arrival:

   Getting to the school in 1947 was an adventure. Having talked a 'grizzled' old taxi driver into taking me to the camp we moved smartly out of Harrogate and wound our way along a pleasant country road. The scenery impressed me and when we shortly approached a palatial building, I viewed it with pleasure and guessed it to be my future home. The taxi, however, jolted on doggedly, never faltering, and my expectations were dashed. I have learnt since to recognise Queen Ethelburga's School for Girls.

   Finally, the driver seemed to find his bearings and the car slowed down. Turning off the road we halted in the midst of some matted vegetation. Faintly visible through

the clustering thistles, gorse and tall grass were the roofs of some Army huts. I credit myself with showing no emotion as I surveyed my new station.

The first sub-unit to be formed in the school was Headquarters Company in August 1947, under the command of Major DSL Gregson MBE, the Inniskilling Dragoon Guards. CSM Stevens was in charge of discipline. Intake 47B commenced their training in the company and were soon joined by small detachments from Chepstow and Arborfield. On completion of their initial training they moved into A Company which was formed as an AT Company on 12 February 1948 under the command of Major J Heath, the Gloucester Regiment. They were assigned to become clerks, electricians, vehicle mechanics, fitters and welders. It was normal procedure for initial training to be carried out in HQ Company after which the boys moved on to their respective companies for further training. The system of intake nomenclature that was adopted continued throughout the life of the school. The common short-form used by old boys when they

Colonel DA Kendrew CBE DSO – Commandant August 1948 to October 1950.

wish to determine their origins was, 'What Intake were you in?' The number refers to the year, and the letter to an early (A), mid (B) or late (C) in-the-year intake.

There was considerable movement of permanent staff due to the demobilisation plans. This is well demonstrated by the fact that within a year of being established, the Commandant, OC HQ Company and RSM had all changed. In August 1948 Colonel DA Kendrew CBE DSO, late of the Leicester Regiment, took over as Commandant. He had joined the Army in 1931 and had played rugby for England. He was mentioned in despatches during the North Africa campaign and took command of 6th Battalion the York and Lancaster Regiment in March 1943. During the next two years he won three DSOs before commanding 128 Brigade when he was awarded the CBE. It was his kind of leadership that the school needed to get it under way.

The first Royal Signals boys arrived at the school in September 1948. They came from the Boys' Squadron Royal Signals, of No.1 Training Regiment, Vimmy Lines at Catterick, and altogether there were 400 boys and staff involved in the move. On 9 September 1948 the final parade was held at Catterick and the Reviewing Officer was Major General CHH Vulliamy CB DSO. *The Wire* magazine of November 1948 records the following caption to a photograph of the final parade in Catterick:

It is a great loss to Royal Signals. Ex-boys have always been an ornament to the corps and many have risen to high rank. It is a sorrowful photograph for all of us as General Vulliamy vacates his appointment as Director of Signals in December.

It is evident that the loss of boys from the Catterick Signals Training Centre (STC) caused great disappointment in the corps. In the build-up to the move the Regimental *Wire* notes of August 1948 had stated:

Preparations are now being made for the move of the squadron to join the Army Apprentices' School in Harrogate in September. The future policy for Boys' Squadron is still to be finally decided, but we are hoping that we shall not lose our identity as an individual unit of the corps.

The first *Wire* submission from the Army Apprentices' School was in the May 1951 edition and it was written by Captain GA Horner, Royal Signals. In the article he reflects on the move to Harrogate:

In the Boys' Squadron (in Catterick), apprentice tradesmen and general duty boys arrived biannually in February and September, and were about fifteen years old when they joined. All were given the same training, namely, a full-time education syllabus with Forces preliminary and school certificate as the main object. Boys left the squadron on attaining the age of seventeen years six months to join one of the training

Learning Morse code.

regiments to learn their trades. In April 1948 the recruitment of boys between fifteen and seventeen years six months as general duty boys began, and by the time the Boys' Squadron was transferred to Harrogate, we had received 100 boys under this new system.

On arrival in Harrogate all the boys who had been doing full-time training were put into one company and the newly recruited general duty boys were put into another. The former continued their scholastic training at Harrogate, and the general duty boys' syllabus consisted of general education, some elementary signal training and military training. Both the scholar boys and the general duty boys left the school when they became seventeen years six months and went to Catterick to do their trade training. All of these boys have now (May 1951) wasted out of the college.

Soon after the arrival at Harrogate of the Boys' Squadron, the first two classes of apprentices started training as signal tradesmen. Some of the boys who came down from Catterick, as well as a proportion of the September 1948 intake of apprentice tradesmen, formed the classes. Although there was no equipment with which to train, with the assistance of the Electricians' Department of the school, most of the initial difficulties were overcome. The training was put under the supervision of the Royal Signals Officer, and the Signal Training Wing of the school was born. In those days it was intended to cope with a maximum of 501 apprentice tradesmen and the following trades were to be taught: radio mechanic, operator wireless and line (OWL), operator keyboard (OKB) and lineman.

At the time that the boys arrived from Catterick there were only 110 apprentices in the school. One of those new arrivals was boy soldier Oscar Bell who later became Corporal 'Dinger' Bell, Royal Signals. He recalls that memorable journey vividly:

Reveille was at crack of dawn and following breakfast we were marched from Catterick to the station at Richmond where 400 boys and staff boarded a special train for Harrogate. On arrival at our destination we all detrained and were promptly told by an immaculately dressed RSM to get back on board until he gave the order. We were then ordered to get out, carriage by carriage and line up on the platform. The railway official then counted us through the gate and I can picture now the RSM with the best pair of bulled boots that I have seen to this day. He was standing just beyond the gate and as we turned to the right and past him we all made an effort to stand on his toecaps. He did not flinch or bat an eyelid.

On the way to the school we were all proud that we had taught the RSM a lesson! Little did we know that on arrival at camp we would carry out a long session of drill in double-time and at a rate that, to say the least, we were not used to. I learnt at an early stage in my Harrogate career that you cannot beat the RSM; certainly not Mr Lonsborough.

Another member of the new arrivals at Harrogate from Catterick Camp was AT Dennis Gittins who recalled in 1992:

It was a wet September day in 1948, when our special train pulled into Harrogate Railway Station to herald the arrival of Intake 48. A lone figure stood on the platform, peaked cap but no badges of rank showing, for he was wearing a military raincoat. As soon as the train stopped, 400 khaki-clad boys disgorged onto the platform. The voice said, 'Get back on that train' – or words to that effect. In two seconds the platform was empty, except for the lone figure. We had met WO1 (RSM) S Lonsborough, Coldstream Guards.

Uniacke Barracks was much bigger than the lines we had occupied in Catterick Camp but we were back in 'spiders' again, instead of the old brick barrack rooms. The square was much bigger and we had a cookhouse at each end of it. There were already about 100 boys in residence and the cafeteria catering system had not arrived in the Army of 1948.

I recollect that, as a senior boy, I had to report at regular intervals to the RSM for personal tuition in parade ground duties. Our passing-out parade in the coming February was to be a public relations exercise to promote the new Army Apprentices' School, Harrogate, and I was to command it. That tuition stood me in very good stead for the rest of my military career.

Our Commandant was Colonel DA Kendrew CBE DSO, who had captained the England rugby team in 1934–35. I recollect a rugby practice session over in Hildebrand Barracks for the 1st XV and the Commandant dressed in service dress, crossing the fields to watch our progress. There were several consecutive high tackles and the Commandant shouted, 'Stop! Gittins, run.' I set off at my best wing forward pace, when suddenly I was hit by an express train and grounded immediately, the perfect tackle and in full uniform.

I can recall my first pint of beer in the NAAFI, – legal too! It was a tradition that on the birth of an heir to the throne, each serving soldier received a pint of beer. As I was over seventeen years old and on soldiers' rates of pay, I and the other boys in my age group drank the health of Prince Charles.

I well remember going, with a number of other senior boys, to the Royal Signals OCTU to play for the school permanent staff team in the semi-finals of the Northern Command Rugby Cup. CSM Kelly, Irish Guards, ran the side and insisted I accompany him into the WOs' and Sgts' Mess of the Signals OCTU and that I be accorded the privilege due to a company sergeant major. Royal Signals OCTU had three internationals, Ian Gloag, NIM Hall and Glyn Davies, but we scored first. However, in the end the opposition proved themselves. Within twelve months I was playing for Royal Signals OCTU in the Northern Command Cup but we didn't meet the School Permanent Staff Team.

Much of what happened at the school initially was as a result of experience gained at Chepstow and Arborfield. The establishment at Chepstow had recently been reviewed and the Commandant was raised to the rank of colonel; thus the Commandant at Harrogate was established from the start as a colonel. Chepstow had also, in 1947, changed its name from Army Technical School (Boys), to Army Apprentices' School. A new badge had recently been introduced and this was adopted at Harrogate. The background to this was described in the history of Chepstow as follows:

Colonel Cuddon (Commandant of Chepstow) had felt for some time that the General Service Corps badge then worn by apprentice tradesmen was unsuitable and so, with the Commandant of Arborfield, he approached the War Office. The result was a meeting with the Inspector of Regimental Colours at the College of Arms in the City of London, a building which stood rather isolated among much destruction, having miraculously survived the fire raids carried out by the Germans. Designs were produced, discussed and, finally, the badge was agreed upon. As for the significance of the badge, I can do no better than to quote Col Cuddon's words at the time. 'The cross which forms the spokes of the wheel (the basis of the badge) represents, of course, the Christian virtues and the development of character. The torch of learning, which is superimposed upon the cross, represents that desire to go on learning, which should be the aim of every school to implant in the hearts and minds of all its sons. The crossed swords remind us, as soldiers, of the military qualities of courage and discipline and the importance of a high standard of physical fitness. The wheel, of course, represents the trade and technical training

carried out at the schools, whilst the crown expresses loyalty to our king and country (and therefore to superiors and comrades alike) and devotion to duty.'

Every unit in the British Army has always been proud of its cap badge and the school was no exception. It was retained until the school became a college in 1966 and a poem that appeared in the January 1955 magazine truly reflects this pride:

The crossing blades of steel recall
The martial purpose of us all,
The mould wherein our lives are cast,
That makes us soldiers first and last,
The cogged wheel shows the master's skill,

The cap badges of the Army Apprentices' School.
Left: *1947 to 1953.* Right: *1953 to 1960.*

Field Marshal Montgomery with the Commandant, Colonel Langran (left), on 3 November 1947.

Field Marshal Montgomery inspects the work of an apprentice with Captain CR Rogers MBE RASC.

Derived from hand and brain and will,
That each young soldier will have won
When his apprenticeship is done.
The burning torch denotes the course
Of learning which began at source,
We follow since we know the need
Of learning in those meant to lead,
These emblems three support above
The Royal Emblem of our love,
St Edward's crown in all its sheen,
Proud sign of all who serve the Queen.
Embracing all there is the Cross,
Without which all is surely loss,
That those who wear the badge may feel
Their duty is a great deal!
HEC

Immediately after the war great importance was placed on the recruiting and training of boys. To underline this high priority the school was visited by Field Marshal, The Viscount Montgomery of Alamein, KG GCB DSO, Chief of the Imperial General Staff, on 3 November 1947, only a few months after it had been opened.

An incident that occurred shortly afterwards was recorded by AT Sergeant Webb following a call to muster on the parade square at 1000 hours:

Our hopes rose high knowing that Princess Elizabeth had given birth to a son the previous evening. We expected some outlet for our feelings of loyalty and jubilation... Then the Commandant appeared. He spoke for ten minutes, stressing the greatness of the occasion and all that it stood for in this troubled world. Then, in honour of the event, he informed the civilian and permanent staff that there would be a free half-pint of beer in the NAAFI at 1200 hours and that the officers' and sergeants' messes would drink the royal prince's health at the same time. For the rest of the school, all punishments would be cancelled and at 12 o'clock, a half-day's holiday would be granted.

In December 1948 the first edition of the school magazine was published. It was entitled *The Harrogate Apprentice* and it ran unbroken until September 1966 when it was retitled *The Gate*; initially it was published biannually. The July 1949 edition records a very memorable event in the history of the school which is worthy of repeat in its entirety:

The first passing-out parade in the short history of the school was held on 1 February 1949. The boys passing out were the Boys' Signal Squadron, disbanded in September (1948), and the apprentice tradesmen from the original school intake. The event entailed many weeks of preparation and hard work for the committee. Anxious thought was given to the weather and an alternative plan was evolved which was to be put into effect if the weather proved inclement (comment: was it ever thus!).

The day began with a threat of rain which, fortunately, never materialised. Official guests, visitors, friends and families began to arrive at 10 o'clock and were escorted to their rows of chairs on the edge of the drill square. The press heralded their arrival by taking posed and snap pictures of the preparation and at 10.30am the Band of the Royal Corps of Signals played a selection of marches. At 10.45am the parade, under the command of AT CSM Gittins Royal Signals (who was later commissioned and attained the rank of major), marched on with the company markers and was drawn up and ready for inspection by 11

AT CSM D Gittins commanded the first passing-out parade on 1 February 1949 at the age of seventeen.

o'clock. The General Salute was played and the parade was inspected by Major General CB Callandar CB MC, Director General of Military Training. The inspection over, the boys bore themselves well in the march past, rank after rank passing the saluting base in perfect dressing.

Next came the prize-giving in the Garrison Theatre. The Commandant, in his short speech, reviewed the events of the past year and gave a forecast of future policy. He then introduced Major General Callandar. The General, who presented the prizes, emphasised the value of training the youth and read a passage written by Mr Winston Churchill:

When I look back, I cannot but return my sincere thanks to the high gods for the gift of existence. All the days are good and each day better than the other. Ups and downs, risks and journeys, but always the sense of motion and the illusion of hope. Come on now, all you young men all over the world. You are needed more than ever now to fill the gap of a generation shorn by war. You have not an hour to lose. You must take your place in life's fighting line. Don't be content with things as they are. The earth is yours and the fullness thereof. Enter upon your inheritance, accept your responsibilities. Don't take 'no' for an answer. Never submit to failure. You will make all kinds of mistakes but as long as you are generous and true, you cannot hurt the world or even seriously distress her. She was made to be won and loved by youth.

The Commandant's prize for conduct, discipline and example was won by AT CSM Gittins and the school prize for all-round excellence by AT Sgt Fieldhouse. Lunch was served to the visitors and in

The senior squad march past on the first passing-out parade on 1 February 1949.

the afternoon the school was 'at home'. There were then tours of the workshops where samples of the apprentices' work and handicraft were on show. Several working models in the various 'shops' were of particular interest to the visitors and the technical staff never tired of explaining them. A demonstration of another sort took place in the east gymnasium where a neat and brisk PT display was given. Afterwards the Band of the Royal Signals gave a concert in the theatre, playing popular music much appreciated by the audience.

After tea the evening was rounded off by a cinema show and a dance for the boys of the leaving squad and their partners. The visitors proclaimed the day a success and the school can be proud of the fact.

A Morrill

The above passage is worthy of repeat not just because it is a record of the first passing-out parade at the school but also because it represents a format that has changed little in over forty years. Anyone who has been involved in these occasions through the decades will instantly recall it. It is also interesting to see that the words of wisdom written by Mr Churchill and spoken by the Reviewing Officer have been the subject of many subsequent speeches, albeit not specifically from that text.

Religion plays an important part in the life of the services and specifically in any junior training organisation. Arrangements had been made for prayer and worship at the school from the start with a part of C Spider set aside. However, it was quite basic and drab so it was not long before improvements were sought. By November 1948 a new church hut had been decorated, furnished and made ready for use. The first great occasion in the new hut was on 28 November when the Garrison Church of St George was dedicated by the Lord Bishop of Ripon in the presence of as many of the school as could be accommodated. Amongst the congregation were the District Commander, Major General JY Whitfield, and the Rural Dean of Knaresborough. Other religions were also well catered for and, for instance, the spiritual welfare of Catholics in both camps had been looked after by Father Bickerdike OCF, since 1939. Their own church was the Church of Christ the King; a name that was to continue throughout the life of the college.

The Commandant had placed great emphasis on the importance of religious life in general and on padres' hours and parade services in particular. Considerable effort was put into obtaining further improvements in the church facilities and by February 1950 the school was able to boast its own

Apprentices learning about vehicle mechanics.

Mr Muggridge teaching carpentry to RE apprentices.

chapel. It had been built in one of the wooden spiders and was opened by the School Chaplain, Captain (Reverend) ROR Wood RAChD, in the presence of members of the school. The apprentices had put much effort into the conversion and the c haplain reported in the school magazine of July 1950:

> As I write, some new items of furniture for the chapel are nearing completion or in the process of installation. They are a beautiful set of altar rails worked in heavy oak – the proud joint achievement of AT Sergeant P Crellin and AT Corporal TB Hawton – and a delightful little font for which the staff in the carpentry section, together with AT J Lucas, who chiselled out the top in stone, are responsible. AT CSM Young turned his hand to making hymn boards and produced a lovely set in light oak.

In June 1949 the establishment of the school was extended to accommodate 1000 boys. These were to be made up of 700 apprentices and 300 GD boys. It was expected that the increased total would be achieved by early 1950.

At the time the school was established there were already three other apprentices' schools in existence at Chepstow, Taunton and Arborfield. The oldest of these was Chepstow, which came into being in 1923 in response to the greater technical needs of the Army. The Army Apprentices' School, Taunton, which had only opened in 1947, was closed in September 1949, and 400 of the apprentices were posted to Harrogate; it had been a close decision whether to close Harrogate or not but the northern outpost survived. This put greater emphasis on the need for Harrogate, which absorbed the extra sappers, including the building trades, and in doing so became the largest of the apprentices' schools with 1070 apprentices under training. It also resulted in some of the tradesmen moving to either Chepstow (welders and sheet metal workers) or Arborfield (vehicle mechanics and fitters). Thus, by September 1949 the school was predominantly Royal Engineers. It was decided at this early stage to cease lineman training and operator keyboard lasted a further year.

AT Peter Radnidge was one of the boys who joined the Army Apprentices' School, Taunton, on 15 February 1949 and five months later moved to Harrogate:

> ... and so I moved to dear Harrogate. In those days I would not have described the AAS as dear. The three years I spent as a boy soldier there, and previously at Taunton, were the hardest of my career in the Army, which came to an end in December 1973. At the time one was not considered a lad, a human being or a person. One was just there to be shouted at, bullied, vilified and the object for all sergeant majors to vent their frustrations upon ... but it did assist in making a man of me.

The first Commandant was Colonel Kendrew. He already had three DSOs. He was posted to Korea and got a fourth DSO there, so I heard. His place was taken by Colonel Thicknesse of the Rifle Brigade. I remember having an informal chat with him towards the end of my fifth term. For my sins I was in the school's athletics team, having come second in the long jump (I still have the medal somewhere in the attic). I was all alone on the sports field at the long-jump pit, having finished training. I was sitting down, shaking the sand out of my track shoes, when Col T. came along and sat next to me. I wasn't sure who he was at first. Then I realised it was the CO. In those days anyone with rank, even a corporal, was God, but the CO! He soon made me feel at ease, asking the usual general questions about life before and during boys' service and had I decided on what course my career would run.

I mentioned Taunton and named an aunt there who used to supplement my food rations a little during my initial six months provided I could get out of camp at the weekend. He replied that he had been brought up in Taunton and went to King's College there. He asked if my aunt's husband was called 'Duke' Dyte and when I said 'yes', he expressed surprise at how small the world was. His father used to play rugby or cricket for Taunton and Somerset and had frequently mentioned 'Duke' Dyte, who had played for Taunton, Somerset and England at both sports. My uncle never ever spoke about this to me and years later, when I was a sergeant and was visiting my aunt and uncle in Taunton, I was at last allowed to step into the front room, which had always previously been banned to me. The walls had shelves on them, each shelf displaying the caps he had won. This verified what Colonel Thicknesse had said to me!

Now we come to C Company. My platoon was 3 Platoon, whose sergeant was a Glaswegian called Sergeant Chisholm HLI. He did not like me one little bit! In fact, I never knew of anyone he did like and, if the truth be known, I don't think he even liked 'hisself'. The platoon corporal's name I cannot recall, nor his corps, but he was understanding and did have some intelligence! As far as I can remember, we had no platoon officers at Harrogate. We lived in spiders, similar to those at Taunton. Even so, they were warm and comfortable enough. In the initial stages of the course one's time was taken up with polishing one's bedspace, cleaning windows and kit. Seemingly unnecessary, but all part of the discipline process. Some of this is still with me today; I spit and polish certain pairs of my footwear and I always press my clothing – not with brown paper, I hasten to add.

It would be rather hard for a young person to imagine it today, but our initial pay was 10s. 6d. per week (52p). We were allowed to draw 5s. over the table, the rest was retained by Imprest for such small things as paying for worn-out and lost kit, barrack-room damages and, if there was any left, saved for leave. On reaching seventeen years of age, one went onto men's rates of pay (28s); (56s when one reached eighteen years of age). Food was another bone of contention with everyone. We just did not get enough to eat. How I remember the number of times I went to bed

feeling so hungry! The food was strictly rationed and rarely did the junior groups manage to get any supper, which was the left-overs, if there were any. As the pay increased, so one could make up in the NAAFI. How amazed I was to see the catering arrangements at Harrogate in the mid-seventies, when I went to see my son at his initial passing-out parade. What a difference. You will notice that I referred above to the 'junior groups'. At each meal queue the senior groups moved up ahead of us. The odd toughie tried to argue against this, but was swiftly 'dealt with'. Then, as one became senior, one did the same thing. It might seem only a small point now, but it was a most aggravating custom at the time!

The leave entitlement was adequate and was issued on a par with schools outside: two weeks at Christmas and Easter and four weeks in summer. If one was in the choir, one got two days extra each time one went on block leave. Naturally, I sang like an angel.

On the subject of education, I found very little time to study. The atmosphere, in any case, was just not conducive to academic pursuits, certainly not as far as I was concerned. The certificates I achieved were ACEs 2 and 1 and one GCE 0 level (in handicrafts) – purely because it was faintly connected with carpentry and joinery! The only slight claim to fame I might have had in this area was my knowledge of the Russian alphabet and about 10 words of vocabulary which caused a certain Sergeant Jefferies (no relative of the Hanging Judge Jeffreys of Gloucester I might hasten to add) of the Education Corps to advise me to see the Education Officer, Major Henderson, with a view to studying the language further. This took place in the last couple of months of my stay at Harrogate. The advice I was given was to apply for a correspondence course in Russian and then to submit a further application to attend a six-month full-time course. Naturally I had not heard of anything like this and since I had not shone in the field of education at Harrogate, I felt somewhat reticent to heed this advice. However, I did apply for the correspondence course, the beginning of which coincided with my arrival for man-service training at No.1 Training Regiment Royal Engineers, Malvern.

AT Peter Mitchell (later Major, Royal Engineers), arrived at the school, as a fifteen-year-old recruit, on 16 February 1949. He subsequently served at Harrogate and Chepstow and recalls the following about his first few months:

My first few hours in the Army were disastrous. I arrived early because I travelled from Hull. On arrival, in my wooden billet, I met the only other AT who had arrived equally early. I looked out of the window and saw a bald-headed man digging the garden. There were two soldiers, with white belts, watching him. 'Everything all right, mate?' I shouted. Before you could say 'Jack Flash' the two with white belts had dragged my fifteen-year-old frame through the open window and carted me off to the guardroom. About half an hour later, after not having a clue about what was going on, a military gentleman (I knew later that he was the RSM) arrived to

The Corps of Drums on parade in Uniacke Barracks, 1949.

advise me that I should never again speak to prisoners who were doing fatigues. Fortunately, he also released me from gaol.

Our initial training, as general service corps apprentices, was a mixture of military training and aptitude testing for trade. I wanted to be a vehicle mechanic in REME and, although I thought I had done well in the mechanics module, I was allocated the trade of clerk. Following complaints from my father it was eventually changed to welder. After my first six months, there was a shake-up in the establishment and welder apprentices were transferred to Chepstow (still not knowing which corps we were going to join). On arrival I was told that I was going to be a sheet-metal worker/welder and, in 1952, along with a lot of others who also wanted to join REME, I graduated into the Royal Engineers! Chepstow was a much harder regime, mainly because there was a rank structure amongst the juniors that I had not been subjected to at Harrogate. This lead to a lot of bullying amongst ourselves.

At Harrogate I remember people doing stupid things, like drinking Brasso as a half-hearted way to commit suicide. We were also up to all the pranks to evade exercises, like wrapping your knee in wet towels and banging it until you had water on the knee. All our pay went on cleaning kit and we supplemented the cookhouse food with sweets stolen from the NAAFI or Sally Ann. We always

seemed to be ravenous and raiding the kitchens after lights-out was another favourite pastime.

We occasionally walked into town, in uniform of course, for fish and chips; we were not allowed to drink or smoke. If we met a girl and she accepted an invitation to the pictures, she then had to pay for both of us because half-a-crown a week just didn't stretch that far!

By mid-1950 the school was becoming well established and much of what was being arranged would last the test of time. Sport was already a major part of the training programme and there were regular fixtures for cricket, basketball, athletics, tennis, rugby, boxing, soccer, cross-country and shooting. It is recorded that the boxing went down from flyweight to mosquito, midge and gnat-weights; this was to cater for the junior boys! The rugby team had great incentive as the Commandant, Colonel Kendrew, was international standard and was often to be seen refereeing school matches. The RSM was the spearhead of the staff cricket team's bowling and took twice as many wickets as anyone else. Major Cragg represented the Army and colours were awarded to ATs Thompson (Capt), Chalk, Williams, Dunn, Corrigan, Spurgin, Wilsher and GD Gribble. On 27 June 1948 the school held its first cricket match against Arborfield but unfortunately a loss was recorded.

Where facilities did not exist on camp they were often found elsewhere, as in the case of swimming which was carried out in the town pool.

C Company won the Boys' Army Football Challenge Cup in 1948/49 with a 1-0 victory over Arborfield. On 23 June 1949 Captain Sturge held the first sports day. A Company were winners, AT Pearce (36) was the senior champion (winning all the sprints) and AT Irvine was the junior champion. On 2 June 1950 the school participated in the first athletics quadrangular with Arborfield, Chepstow and RAF Halton and won by one point from Arborfield. The RAF presented a new trophy and it was proudly received by AT Sergeant McDonagh who was a sprinter.

Providing entertainment for up to 1000 young men was no easy task. To cater for their requirements a dance was held in the NAAFI every fortnight and was arranged by Miss Roberts and her staff. A Company reported that, 'each Company takes turns to organise the dance. Our first one was on 30 September 1949 and it suffered badly from lack of partners!' It was not long before the local girls were being transported to Penny Pot by the busload. The dances became very popular all round! The Globe cinema was used extensively and was cheap, and boys used to sell ice cream at the interval. Trips were arranged to local amenities and whilst Bolton Abbey on a Sunday may have been appealing it is difficult to see how many would have enjoyed *Twelfth Night*.

Educational visits were a prominent element of the programme. Most of them were related to the trades of the ATs. Plumbers went to the Lead Works in Huddersfield; electricians went to the Exide Battery factory; painters went to Williamsons Ltd of Ripon; others went to the Pool Paper Mill, Doncaster Railway, Phoenix Electric or Low Moor Iron Works.

Hobbies also got off to an early start. One of the first was bee-keeping and was due to the enthusiasm of the Padre, Rev. EF Jessup, who was the self-appointed Bee-keeper-in-Chief. As early as December 1949 he had reported a profit of £14.12s.0d., a lot of money in those days. Others included photography, philately, amateur dramatics, woodwork, plastics, amateur radio, cycling and the choir. The library benefited greatly from the closure of Taunton and boasted over 16,000 books and attendance of 50 per cent of the boys every week.

The School Corps of Drums was quickly set up under Sergeant Stone, R Fusiliers, and Mr Gardner. Their first performance was at church on 16 October 1949 and three days later, Drum Major AT CSM Howson went public with 46 musicians at a rugby match in Harrogate. Later that term they acquired 25 bugles.

In August 1950 Colonel Kendrew, who was responsible for such great progress and had handled the multitude of changes with such calmness, departed on promotion to command 29th British Brigade in Korea. Whilst in command he won a further DSO. He was later posted to Headquarters, Northern Ireland District, where he became Brigadier AQ. His appointment at the school was taken by Colonel RN Thicknesse.

From an Instructor's Report
"If ignorance is bliss, this boy is assured of a very happy future".

4

THE SCHOOL SETTLES DOWN
IN THE EARLY 1950s

Colonel RN Thicknesse – September 1950 to March 1954

Colonel Thicknesse arrived at what he called 'the mid-point of the century'. He was keen to impose a period of stability and settling in. This was not easily achieved in post-war Britain when there were still shortages of many items especially training materials, and many of the permanent staff moved on having reached the end of their military service. He wrote:

Young plants do best when they are not dug up by the roots and replanted, and we venture here to express our earnest hope that we shall now remain undisturbed. Flexibility is an admirable military virtue, but so are continuity and the growth of valued tradition and honest precedent; we congratulate ourselves on our ability to say with truth that those qualities exist here. It is for us to see to it that their seed-bed never lacks cultivation.

Colonel RN Thicknesse with his orderlies ATs Hancock and Lance Corporal Gardiner.

During his time in the school he made considerable effort to ensure that PS and ATs alike enjoyed their military training. He took the trouble to get to know them and what made them 'tick'. He also recognised that life at the school was extremely busy and leave periods were for relaxing:

If we had twenty-five hours in a day and thirteen months in the year we should have no difficulty in filling them with some activity that no one had so far thought out. All very stimulating and rather exhausting... I would urge all ranks to relax during their well-deserved leave, being perfectly aware that none of them is likely to do anything of the kind!

The passing-out parade of 30 January 1951 was one of the Commandant's earliest formal occasions. The Adjutant General was the Reviewing Officer which reflected the importance of the apprenticeship to the Army. General Crocker spoke of:

...the momentous and important times in which we live, of the growing threat to peace and the spread of unrest throughout the world. It was necessary to build up reserves and this demanded more and better regular soldiers. He presented the newly established Champion Company Cup to B Company and the Army Commander's Prize for conduct, discipline and example to AT CSM McDonagh. He finished by reminding the boys, 'Above all your technical skill, you are, first and foremost, soldiers!' Words that would be echoed many times down the years.

By 1951, the school was organised into four companies (later five) and 14 departments (all accommodated in Uniacke Barracks by February 1953) which are described in a later chapter. The changes in the various apprentices' schools resulted in the following trades being taught within these departments:

RE. Bricklayers, carpenters and joiners, painters and decorators, plumbers and pipe fitters, electricians, architectural draughtsmen, survey trades, quantity surveyors assistants.

REME. Clerks (Class B), electricians (vehicle and plant).

R SIGNALS. Operators (wireless and line), line mechanics, radio mechanics, telegraph mechanics.

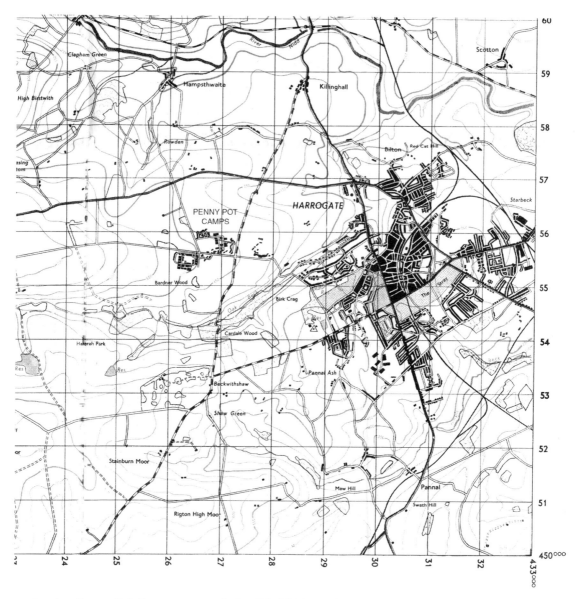

The map, showing Penny Pot Camps, was made by ATs CSM Newberry, Sergeant Isherwood, Corporal Cook, Lance Corporal White, Lance Corporal Beale and Mayhew. They were all RE apprentices of Intake 52A.

The staff of the RE Survey and Printing Department with graduating apprentices in 1954. Captain Geoff Seaton and CSM John Bickmore are in the middle of the front row.

AT CSM G McGilvray joined Intake 50B on 5 September 1950 at the age of sixteen years and six months. He was to be a telegraph mechanic (later telegraph technician) in Royal Signals and, within three years of graduating from the school, was promoted to acting sergeant. He completed a full career and was commissioned in 1974 before leaving, as Major Mac McGilvray MBE, to become a non-regular permanent staff, permanent staff administrative officer with the TA. He recalls his time at the school:

AT NCOs had considerable privileges. They were allowed to wear approved civilian clothing on appointment; the other ATs had to be in the second year before they were authorised. AT sergeants and WOs were allocated a bunk each at the entrance to the barrack rooms. This was much appreciated as privacy was at a premium – there were no doors in the toilets or baths in HQ Company during recruit training!

AT CSMs were appointed for each Company. The Commandant presented them with their Warrants at prayers on the first day of the new term (this was a custom that was reintroduced in 1993 based on this information). The AT RSM was selected from the four CSMs for the last month of his apprentice service.

I enjoyed my time as an apprentice. I was able to look after myself so I was not bullied but a fair amount of bullying did take place. Some of this was due to boys not repaying loans from money-lenders (either cash or cigarettes).

Enduring memories are of excessive 'bull', kit and room inspections – the bucket was polished like a mirror and the broom and dry scrubber were scraped with razor blades. The table was scrubbed endlessly. All of these items were reserved for inspection purposes only and 'working utensils' were obtained for everyday use. The daily layout for inspection was bedpack, white belt, best boots, web equipment and greatcoat 'dolly' fashion. Webbing and belts had to be blancoed and all brasses gleaming – this was before staybright buttons!

We worked seven days a week – Saturday was the RSM's parade followed by cross-country running or fatigues. There was sport in the afternoon. Every Sunday morning was the big parade of the week. There was a series of inspections by AT NCOs, permanent staff and then the Commandant. We then marched to Hildebrand Barracks behind the Corps of Drums for the church service. Sunday afternoon was free.

On the social side, highlights of the week were the films shown in the camp cinema on Wednesday and Sunday evenings. I think a ticket cost 4d. (2p). The projector often broke down with the normal catcalls and comments from a very critical audience. During off-duty periods, before the advent of TV, we organised our own fun which included lots of sport. All ATs could play football, cricket, hockey or rugby and boxing was compulsory.

Social life was restricted by the roll call by the company orderly sergeants at 2230 hours and everyone had to stand by their bed to be counted. However, as the orderly sergeant invariably started his room checks at the room nearest the sergeants' mess, a member of that room could be checked and take your place in your bed when the sergeant called the roll in your room. This enabled us to go down town without booking out and come back late at night. Many of the other antics we got up to cannot be repeated here, but suffice it to say that we left Harrogate well prepared for a military career.

Whilst a chapel was being set up in 1945 to meet the religious needs of the school, further work was being done towards building a more grandiose chapel by converting the old NAAFI building in Hildebrand Barracks. This took over a further year to complete and the Dedication of the Chapel to Saint Alban The Martyr took place on Sunday, 29 April 1951 in the presence of Her Royal Highness, The Princess Royal. It was one of the major events in the early history of the school. The dedication service was

Her Royal Highness, Princess Mary, arrives for the Dedication of the New Church in Hildebrand Barracks on 29 April 1951.

conducted by the Chaplain General, the Reverend Canon FL Hughes CB CBE MC TD MA. He was assisted by the School Chaplain, Captain HW Summers RAChD, and senior chaplains from Catterick and York.

Unfortunately, the day started in true Yorkshire fashion with weather that necessitated cancellation of the opening review. The Princess Royal, wearing full military uniform, was met by Colonel Thicknesse, and in church the congregation included as many of the 700 young soldiers and permanent staff of the school as could be squeezed into the available seats. The school choir sang and the Band of the Royal Corps of Signals played under the baton of Captain JL Judd MBE, their Director of Music.

A reception was held at the officers' mess and this was followed by a visit to the school's exhibition hall and library. The party then had tea in the sergeants' mess after which the Princess Royal was presented with a bouquet of flowers by Miss Anita Lonsborough, the RSM's daughter, who in the 1960 Rome Olympics was to win the nation's only gold medal in swimming. Immediately prior to her departure, the smallest apprentice in the school, Boy K Logan, presented to the Princess a fine gold replica of the beautiful wrought-golden key used for the opening ceremony and bearing the school crest. The key had been made by AT Carenco who was a plumber and it is now displayed in the Royal Signals Museum.

In conclusion, no more fitting words could best sum up the feeling of those privileged to witness the day's events, than the Apprentice's Prayer, spoken by the Chaplain General and recorded in the school magazine of the day:

Almighty God, who didst suffer Thine only Son to live on earth, and there be apprenticed to a carpenter's shop in Nazareth, in the hills of Galilee, favour with Thy loving care these Thy other dear and faithful apprentice sons on these Yorkshire moors.

Grant them, we beseech Thee, all the golden qualities of soldiers; loyalty, courage, endurance, patience, faith. In the day of the battle and in the night that follows it, be Thou their constant General to lead them against the forces of anti-Christ, to protect them against the assaults of the Prince of Darkness. In ordeal by fire, by hunger, by thirst, by fear, by loneliness, be by their side; their sword and armour in the hour of Victory.

Grant to them, and to all who now serve with them in this School, the proper fortitude of brave soldiers and servants of our Sovereign Lord, King George, and the Faith to sustain their apprenticeship to the service of Thy dear Son, so that when their long battle is done, they may be received into Thy glory, and there, in peace, remain, through Jesus Christ our Lord. AMEN.

The activities of the church have always been an integral part of school and college life. Many of the young soldiers have had little opportunity to learn the benefits of religion prior to their joining the Army. padres' hour has always been a regular feature of the curriculum and a strong choir has provided joy to many of the apprentice choristers and permanent staff alike. There have also been many baptisms and confirmations through the years. Most important of all, the padre, being outside the chain of command, has always been a person who can be trusted to give the right guidance to a young soldier in need of assistance at a time of personal concern.

Field Marshal Slim talks to AT Sergeant Innes during the inspection on 19 July 1951.

Her Royal Highness, Princess Mary, is escorted by Major T Leahy, King's Own, to inspect the Guard of Honour on 10 April 1951 when she was presented with the Freedom of Harrogate.

By this time the Princess Royal was becoming familiar with the Harrogate environs because a little earlier in the month, on 10 April 1951, she was presented with the Freedom of Harrogate. This may not be too surprising as she was married to Lord Harewood and resided only a few miles away at Harewood House. The school provided a guard of honour in front of the Municipal Offices which was commanded by Major T Leahy, King's Own, and

Her Royal Highness, Princess Mary, arrives for the passing-out parade escorted by the Commandant and General Balfour on 23 July 1952.

Apprentice Sergeant Majors Dunn and Murray of B Company raise the Champion Company Cup which was presented by Princess Mary on 23 July 1952.

comprised three officers and 100 ATs. The presentation was made by the Mayor of Harrogate, Alderman CE Whitely, in the presence of Lord Halifax and the council members.

The Princess Royal further increased her association with the school on 23 July 1952 when she was the Reviewing Officer at the graduation parade. In her speech she said:

I have been immensely impressed with your parade. To produce a parade such as I have inspected today means the perfect co-operation of all ranks, and illustrates the value of your training. I am glad to see so many of you wearing the badge of my corps. I know how pleased the Royal Corps of Signals is to receive you.

The progress made since I was last here in April 1951 is symbolic of the constant progression of young soldiers through this school and afterwards in their Corps. Those soldiers who are old boys of this school are of equal importance to it as those still apprenticed to the service.

I congratulate those soldiers who are now leaving. I know they realise the immense advantage of the start given to them by this school; both to the individual and to the Service. Wherever you are you will always belong to the school and carry that responsibility with you. You have the power to do it harm, as well as credit.

The happiest tale that a lifetime can tell is to work among those who co-operate well; those who listen with interest to an idea and lend every project a good atmosphere; those who do not add stumbling blocks just to be mean, nor bring a discordant note to the scene; those who join for the good of the cause every time to make the path smooth and the purpose sublime. All are not leaders, but life would be hollow if those who can lead had not those who follow.

In conclusion, a word of thanks to the parents. To them is the credit of the right background in your lives, and I know with what pride they have watched this fine ceremony today. Do thy duty that is best – leave unto God the rest.

A copy of this speech, signed 'Mary', was always subsequently displayed in the Commandant's office.

The Adjutant during the period November 1950 to December 1952 was Captain WT Macfarlane (later Major General). He remembers vividly some of the battles to maintain discipline:

RSM Lonsborough was as fine a soldier as you could hope to meet. He was loyal, maintained highest standards and was a very intelligent man. On one occasion he entered my office in his usual manner with the smartest of guard's salutes. He wished to brief me on the minutes of the mess meeting because he would have to speak about one matter to the Commandant, Colonel Thicknesse. It concerned two of the warrant officers who wanted to change mess rules so that it was permissible for mess members to remove jackets whilst playing snooker or darts. The RSM was against such a change because he thought it was a lowering of standards. The Commandant was duly briefed and the RSM was summoned to discuss the matter and put

WO1 (RSM) Stan Lonsborough, Coldstream Guards.

Lieutenant General Callandar meets apprentices newly arrived from Nairobi. Left to right: ATs McPherson, Lori and White.

his case. 'Fine,' said the Commandant 'but, RSM, my uncle is the Dean of St Albans and was recently at that fine London institution, The Athenaeum, where he played snooker with another eminent member of the cloth. What is more they removed jackets to play their game.' The Commandant realised that the sergeants' mess was no place for democracy but thought that his explanation would convince the RSM to relax the rules a little. However, without the bat of an eyelid the RSM remained bolt upright and replied, 'Sir, such rules may be fine for that great London institution but they have no place whatsoever in the sergeants' mess at Harrogate.' The mess rules remained unchanged.

We also had a disciplinary problem with the YMCA staff on one occasion. The YMCA was situated in Hildebrand Barracks and was run by a husband-and-wife team. Unfortunately, the wife took a liking to some of the boys and she became over involved with one of them. Colonel Thicknesse, who always wrote so stylishly and with a tinge of humour whenever appropriate, decided that he could not tolerate such behaviour and she would have to be removed from her post. He wrote to the Regional Director of the Young Men's Christian Association (YMCA) and explained the reasoning for wanting to remove her. He finalised his letter by saying, 'It is a great pity that she appears to have more concern for the YM than she has for the CA!'

AT Mike Abraham was a member of Intake 50B and passed out as an operator wireless and line (OWL) in 1953. He served for a further eight years and during this time he was in Northern Army Group, Korea, Cyprus and Suez before returning to 30th Signal Regiment in Blandford. On retirement he continued to teach Morse to aspiring amateur radio enthusiasts. In 1994 he recalled his training:

The Operator Wireless and Line Syllabus included:
    Wireless telegraphy and procedure. Q and Z codes. Taught by 'Bluey' Dutton.
    Radio telephony and procedure.
    Telephone switchboard and procedure.
    Teleprinter operation and procedure.
    Aerial propagation theory, types and erection. Taught by Mr (Professor) Heald.
    Fullerfone and field telephone operation.
    Minor fault finding and repair of radio apparatus.
    Battery charging and maintenance. Taught by Mr Tyrie.
    Slidex code and one-time pad.
The equipment that I can recall in use included:
    Wireless Set No.88. VHF for local use only. Pouched on Belt.
    Wireless Set No.32. HF W/T or R/T, 10–15 miles depending on aerial. Back-packed.
    Wireless Set No.19. HF W/T or R/T, could be worldwide with only 20 watts.
    Wireless Set No 53. H.F. 150 or 250 watt, long-distance communications.
    Switchboard field & fortress. 40 line.

Amateur Radio Station G3HKR opened in 1951 using a No.19 set, W/T only. The licence was held by Bluey Dutton. I am on the first page of the original log book. Our aerial was a half-wave multi-band Dipole. We could only work on 40 or 80 metres with this set.

Members of the band received two days extra leave as did the boxing team. On road runs we ran out of the gates and down to Queen Ethelburga's School for Girls. On the verge opposite we did our exercises while the girls watched from the windows. This was stopped after a complaint was made. Shame really!

The cookhouse was raided at nights on a regular basis and the bones from joints of meat or whatever were consigned to the static water tank behind the spider block. This was mostly done by the tearaway types (myself included), lads who in the main came from a harsher background during the war years. It has to be remembered that children from London and the suburbs had been through five years of the Blitz followed by another five of very austere and difficult conditions prior to joining the Army. Many of us had been bombed out or lost family and friends and were therefore not very nice lads at all. There was no counselling or social workers at that time. A lot of us were only in the Army to ease the strain at home.

Discipline was harsh. Six strokes of the cane was a common punishment handed out by the OC B Company, Major Thomas Leahy. CSM Laurence gave the punishment and the offending AT, after thanking the OC for the punishment, ran and howled in private. In retrospect, I can see no real justification for the current 'anti-corporal punishment' lobby. If we got it, by the Lord Harry we deserved it, and it never did us any harm at all!

Money lending was rife and each company had its permanent staff member who turned up with a book once a week. Money was loaned on 50 per cent per week compounded and no excuse was accepted. The system was run by a permanent staff member and local administration was under the control of the barrack-room NCO.

Boys who were found dirty or were bath-shy were taken to the ablutions, dumped in a cold bath and scrubbed with a bass broom. It rarely needed to be repeated. It should be said at this time that it was very, very common to have fire buckets full of cold water heaved over the wall and into the bath. A lot of the lads were put off using the facility for that reason.

The wooden floorboards in the spider-hut accommodation were polished with black 'Kiwi' shoe polish. This was paid for by each boy for his own bed space out to the centre of the floor. There was also a room job rota for the corridors, ablutions, etc.

We used lengths of 2 x 1 timber to box our blankets and sheets and if it was not of the standard required it was very swiftly spread across the room. Field packs were blancoed and stacked on the locker top with a 'best' boot each side.

Trousers were pressed by using a mouthful of water run down the creases and then placing the said item between a blanket and the mattress. Body heat did the rest. For added sharpness, soap could be run along the inside crease line. The uniform was 'gently' shaved with a razor to smooth it off a bit. This was frowned on and could cost you a new uniform.

On parades a boy was placed on the roof of the NAAFI. He would obey all the orders and do the old, 'one-two-three-one' business. The parade would follow him so that timing was good.

Hildebrand Barracks was used for some of our instruction. An AT would be put in charge of a squad and would march them out of Uniacke and down into Hildebrand hoping that no officer would appear to demand an eyes-right or left from the squad. I believe the REME LAD was at that time in Hildebrand.

When leave came around groups of boys would stay up all the previous night playing cards or whatever. All kit was put away into the locker, including the mattress. In the early morn we would then walk down the lane all the way to the station singing and chatting. Some of the lads who were in the band would take their dress cords with them to pose in their uniform. Impressed the girls no end.

In 1950 we still had sheets of ration coupons as well as a railway pass and leave pass. Our credits had been paid out and it was really something to have one or two of the old black and white, single-sided £5 notes… My God I feel old!

When I was a member of the band we used to march sometimes through Harrogate, Richmond or Ripon to the strains of 'Sweet Lass of Richmond Hill' and 'Begone Dull Care', breaking into the 'British Grenadier' at the busiest part of the route. The cleaning of the instruments was a real chore and I believe we were short-changed rotten with only two extra days on our leave.

Weapon training was done with what I still consider to be superior arms. The Royal Enfield 303 and the Bren gun were, and still are, weapons with real knockdown stopping power with a range of 1000 yards plus. They were fairly heavy for a young lad to carry and did the shoulder no good at all having a brass butt plate that opened to store a pull through and oil bottle.

Half past one in the morning and all is well. Eight of us had decided to raid the cookhouse and have a 'pig out'. The spider block was silent as we made our way out and across to the square. At this time of the night we could have cut straight through but desisted; the square was sacrosanct and, even in our clandestine adventure, we would not walk upon it! Along the west side of the square was an asbestos corrugated roofed tunnel that led all the way through to the HQ area. It ended at the cookhouse, our target for tonight. The metal Crittall windows were always left on the security latch; a jackknife eased in and lifted would unlatch the window and allow us to climb in. It was dark, silent and a little menacing, we were after all mere sixteen-year-old lads.

Padding across the kitchen towards the ovens, we passed the large cauldrons that were used to make soup and crept very quietly on towards our goal, the ovens. A roast was provided once a week and, as with all mass military catering, was always cooked the day before. After cooking in the afternoon it was removed from the oven and placed on racks above. We could smell the enticing aroma of roast lamb and, having reached the ovens, were about to reach up for the spoils. Suddenly all hell broke loose. There was the sound of running, then the voice of Geoff Gates, 'For Christ's sake run, there's someone here.' Oh yes, you bet your life there was. It was A Company; another small group of lads also bent on pillage!

We had a sort of heart-to-heart discussion on the merits of what we were about. Two leg joints would be a bit over the top so, using the butcher's tools, we cut a leg in half and all departed very swiftly for our respective lines. Back in the barrack room we shared out the spoils among the now wide-awake members of our room. Sitting in the dark and chatting amongst ourselves, we savoured the delights of an illicit, delicious and well planned take-away meal. In retrospect, it was nothing short of theft. At the time, however, it was an adventure and, like scrumping apples from an orchard, it added a little bit of spice to what was in those days an extremely hard life!

One of Colonel Thicknesse's major innovations was in June 1952 when he formed the Association of Harrogate Apprentices (AOHA). This was primarily for the benefit of past and present apprentices but civilian and military staff could join as Associate Members. Within a few months the Association was set up on formal lines.

It is clear that ex-ATs' recollections in later years revolve round a small number of situations that occurred time and time again. Two such incidents, the weather and the graduation parade, were recollected in 1992 by AT Doug Bell (Intake 52B):

The one event of my three years as an Army apprentice at Uniacke Barracks, which still remains fresh in my mind, is the occasion of my final parade, the passing-out ceremony, which transformed me, and the 140 other members of my intake (52B), into a fully-fledged, adult member of the British Army. For the parade, which lasted about 75 minutes, the senior passing-out squad, held pride of place, forward of, and central to, the 600 or so apprentice tradesmen then at the school. We were, for the first time, wearing battle dress and blue beret adorned with the cap-badge of our new corps, not the high collared, brass-buttoned service-dress and peaked hat of the apprentice tradesman.

The climax of the parade was a manoeuvre which led to a 'gate' opening in the centre of the main body, while the senior squad about-turned and, to the strains of 'Auld Lang Syne', slow-marched through the gate, which slowly closed behind us. As the gate closed, the band ceased playing and we left our apprenticeship days, and boyhood, behind us to the sound of slow-marching foot-steps. I still remember the pride and elation of those final few moments of my three years at 'Maniac Barracks'. I can recall too that those feelings were tempered by more than a little trepidation at the thought of what lay ahead in the real man's Army. I needn't have worried though. Those years at the Army Apprentices' School were more than enough to prepare me for life as a regular soldier, and later, as a civilian. Now, forty years on, I am still proud to say, 'I was a Harrogate apprentice.'

A further vivid memory is that winter was never a pleasant experience at Uniacke Barracks. In the early 1950s, accommodation for the inmates was wooden 'spiders', theoretically heated by radiators fed by a small coke-burning boiler housed in a small room of the building.

One year, I think it was 1954, winter came early and with a vengeance. Heavy snow showers over several days at the beginning of December were followed by temperatures which plummeted well below zero. One effect of the conditions was the inability of vehicles to get out of or into the camp – and that included the trucks delivering coke for the boilers. It didn't take long for a rumour to circulate to the effect that if conditions failed to improve, the school would close early for Christmas and we would all get some extra leave. Some of us in A Company decided to give

The Director of Education, Brigadier Beddall, discusses carpentry with ATs Sergeant Eades and McLaughlin on 29 January 1953.

Eamon Andrews of the BBC interviews ATs Maung Maung Aye and Hla Thwin of Burma, in the 'Welcome to Britain' programme of 8 March 1953.

nature a hand and, after much thought, hatched a plot to turn off all the radiators in our spider and at the same time keep the boiler fully stoked. That we reckoned would cause the boiler to explode and us to get some 'buckshee' time at home. Then an apprentice plumber pointed out that an exploding boiler would probably flatten the spider and us with it.

Before we could formulate plan B, the school hierarchy solved the problem. Half of the boys took their beds and chattels and 'double-bunked' in other spiders, thus halving the demand for fuel. But nature still had the last word. Hardly had the move been completed when the temperature soared, the ice and snow departed and we had to move everything back whence we had just left. And Christmas leave was no longer than usual!

Some of the medals won at sport by AT ID Loney in the 1954–55 seasons.

AT ID Loney (Intake 54A) later joined the Engineers as an electrician. His eighteen years' service included a tour at Christmas Island on the nuclear testing programme before he finally retired in 1978 as WO2. He remembers those early days:

There is no doubt that my early Army days were a dreadful shock and I was very homesick. My first severe haircut revealed the scars of an early misspent youth. But more than anything I remember some of the characters I met. One of them was Mr Heald who taught us electricity. He was very clever and had been a university lecturer. In his spare time he was a hypnotist, magician and escapologist and would appear in local shows as 'The Great Heldino'. In class he was very easy to distract and we would bring in handcuffs and tie him up. Usually, he managed to escape but not always. I recall that he used a set of AT twins to demonstrate telepathy. Unfortunately for them they took it too far and at a later time were caught 'using telepathy' in an examination! On another occasion he used a plumb-line hanging over a number of envelopes containing the names of horses, to select all the winners of a race meeting at Catterick. He never gave us the secrets of his success and he never made us rich.

Our sporting fixtures at Chepstow and Arborfield were always a highpoint of the term. On one occasion two

ATs Corporal Mackenzie, Clarke, Than Aye, Clifton, Gould and Semple take to the water.

A Company, winners of the Army Boys' Soccer Cup 1952–53 proudly displayed by their Captain AT Lance Corporal Armstrong. Major Chubb and Bombadier Johnstone are on the left with WO2 CSM Cross and Sergeant Chisholm on the right.

of the ATs at Chepstow died of polio and, on return, we were told to watch out for symptoms. Of course a couple of idiots found out what the symptoms were and feigned the disease just to get a few days in sick bay.

Another incident that sticks in my mind concerned the barrack block inspections which counted towards the Champion Company Trophy. In our endeavour to be impressive a number of us went down town into Valley Gardens after lights-out. We returned with a load of plants out of the flower beds and planted them in the border immediately around the wooden barrack block. What we did not realise was that the 18 inches around the building was a fire-break. You can imagine the trouble that we got into!

The needs of up to 1000 young men at any given time required the attention of a dedicated staff. Sport was a major resource for keeping fit, team building and developing leadership. For most ATs it was based at company level with ATs being divided into half-companies alphabetically for major sports such as football. A Company were Boys' Army Cup football champions when they beat Chepstow 4-2. Boxing produced many champions. In 1951 there were three Army champions in ATs Trehearne, Conway and Neiles. Trehearne and Cooper went on to be Inter-

Services winners. AT Corrigan gave an outstanding performance when he took 7 wickets for only 10 runs against Harrogate Cricket Club. AT Sergeant Devanney captained the rugby XV.

Not all spare time was taken up on sport however. Hobbies flourished and broadened in scope as new expertise arrived with new staff. The school Corps of Drums improved in playing ability and performed widely at public engagements under Drum Major AT CSM Dixon and Commandant's Bugler AT Lance Corporal Talbot. The Amateur Radio Society was also established under Captain DH Baynham (G3DHB) which was very popular with future Royal Signals operators.

On 27 February 1954 Colonel Thicknesse relinquished his command of the school and retired from the Army. He had been Commandant for three and a half years and in that time over 1400 boys had been trained. Throughout this time one of his trademarks was that, 'He knew "his boys" personally, not only by name but also their background, interests and peculiarities.' Unfortunately, his last few weeks were marred by illness but he was able to attend a farewell function to complete thirty-two years' service in the Army.

From an Essay
"The teeth arms are the regiments which engage in hand to mouth fighting".

5

CLOSE LINKS ARE FORGED WITH THE LOCAL COMMUNITY

Colonel JP Carne VC DSO – April 1954 to April 1957

The most highly decorated soldier ever to serve in the school was Colonel JP Carne VC DSO. He arrived in April 1954 following his experiences with the Gloucester Regiment at the Battle of Imjin in Korea. The school magazine recorded, 'We can have no finer inspiration than a Commandant who has shown powers of leadership which can seldom have been surpassed in the history of our Army.'

It was therefore a significant connection with the school when, in 1990, the Royal Corps of Signals commissioned an oil painting by Peter Archer entitled 'Last Transmission at Imjin'. It depicts Lieutenant Colonel JP Carne DSO with two soldiers of the Royal Signals. In April 1951, 1st Battalion the Gloucester Regiment of the 29th Infantry Brigade Group, was holding part of the UN line on the Imjin river in Korea. On 22 April their position came under heavy attack from a force made up of three divisions of the Chinese Communist Army. The 'Glosters' held on for three days denying the Communist army a quick breakthrough and effectively saving the 29th Brigade. It proved impossible to relieve the battalion and on the morning of the 25th the Commanding Officer, Lieutenant Colonel Carne DSO, was ordered to attempt to break out. Communications with the brigade were maintained by the Royal Signals' Rear Link Detachment consisting of Lance Corporal S Ward, Lance Corporal H Jennings, Signalman Cairns and Driver AE Mills. The painting depicts the moment when Colonel

Lieutenant Colonel Carne on the Imjin River.

Carne sent his last message to Brigade Headquarters. Lance Corporal Jennings is shown preparing to destroy the No.62 radio set while Signalman Cairns burns the codebook. They were all taken prisoner. Colonel Carne subsequently walked with a slight limp and for this reason all commandants were thereafter often referred to as the 'Gammy'.

By the time Colonel Carne arrived at the school it was reasonably well established and much progress had been made; a lot of it being self-help. It is worthwhile looking at how the school was organised.

ORGANISATION OF THE SCHOOL IN 1954

School Headquarters (SHQ)

SHQ comprised the Commandant's staff and those personnel who had responsibilities throughout the school. This included the chief instructor (CI), senior education officer (SEO), administration officer, adjutant, QM, MO, chaplain, dentist, RSM, chief clerk, etc. The role of SHQ was to deal with external matters and to carry out the policy set by the Commandant.

THE COMPANIES

Headquarters Company

HQ Company was established in August 1947 as the Intake Company under the command of Major DSL Gregson MBE, the Inniskilling Dragoon Guards. All boys were initially posted into the company, into platoons of about 30, to carry out their basic recruit training which could take up to six months. This initial six months was a very important part of a boy's training as it set his attitude for the remainder of his time at the school. On completion, boys were posted to companies according to their intended trade.

A Company

A Company was formed on 12 February 1948 under command of Major J Heath, the Gloucester Regiment. The trades were electrician, vehicle mechanic, fitter and welder, and clerk. When the apprentices' schools were reviewed in 1950 following the closure of Taunton, the REME trades were lost to Arborfield and the welders went to Chepstow. A Company was also reviewed and resulted in seven trades being retained; surveyor, draughtsman, quantity surveyors 'assistant (QSA), electrician, painter and decorator, and plumber and pipefitter.

B Company

B Company commenced life as a general duty boys' company in mid-September 1948 under the command of Major WVR Cragg, the Royal Lincolnshire Regiment. It took some of the initial intake from the Boys' Signal Squadron in Catterick. Training then centred on general education, metalwork, military training and some signals training. In 1955, line- and tele-mechanic moved to D Company and clerks moved in. Later it became all Signals trades.

C Company

Most of the original members of the company were from the Boys' Squadron in Catterick in September 1948. Shortly after this, on reorganisation, bricklayer and carpenter, painter, clerk, and mason were added.

D Company

The company was formed, under command of Captain RT Hone, Royal Signals, on 11 February 1949 when B Company was renamed. There were 78 mechanic and operator tradesmen of Royal Signals. Major BN Bleakley, the Royal Sussex Regiment, assumed command on 25 April 1949. On 31 October 1949, 30 of the boys left for Richmond to form the Boys' Signal Squadron. Early in 1950, the Commandant approved the wearing of Royal Signals' badges and flashes. The squadron closed in early 1951 but was resurrected on 17 February 1954 under the command of Major WH Wade, Yorks and Lancs. At this time the trades were line, telegraph and radio mechanic, operator wireless and line (OWL) and operator keyboard and line.

THE EDUCATION WING

The Education Wing was set up under the first Senior Education Officer, Lieutenant Colonel AS Cronshaw RAEC, with a staff of eight. As well as teaching the boys they had to draw up syllabuses, find classroom equipment, establish a library and assess the needs of the trade wings. The wing grew quickly in both size and responsibility. The early aim of the wing was to qualify each boy to the best of his ability. Examinations were taken in Forces Preliminary, the Royal Society of Arts, the Army Certificate of Education or GCEs.

It was not long before the SEO was reporting that the rate of growth was prolific as staff increased to 28, the classes rose from seven to 30 and boys increased to 600. The wing moved into 19 and 20 Spiders of Hildebrand in 1955.

THE TRADE DEPARTMENTS

In its initial stages the school taught 13 different trades. This was greater than any of the other schools, including Chepstow, which had been established longest but only taught nine.

There was a serious shortage of both equipment and appropriate teaching facilities. There was considerable movement of departments between Hildebrand and Uniacke as buildings were adapted and commissioned for use. Much of the work was done by the apprentice tradesmen.

Departments were assigned to specific trades and each department had its own staff, equipment, dedicated classrooms and accommodation as far as was possible. In most cases trade training commenced almost as soon as the department was formed so it was necessary to compile the syllabus and stores list, and arrange classrooms and workshops at the same time as carrying out instruction. Most of the departments took City and Guilds examinations in their appropriate subject and did very well.

ELECTRICAL DEPARTMENT

AT Lance Corporal David Kipling – Electrician.

The Electrical Department was formed in 1947 under Captain SJ Male RE and taught 79 apprentice electricians (RE, RAC and RASC) and electrical fitters. This changed in 1950 to electrician vehicle and plant (REME) (formerly the responsibility of AAS Chepstow) and electrician RE. The syllabus encompassed such subjects as magnetism, secondary batteries, cable jointing, vehicle electrical equipments, DC and AC theory, overhead lines, instruments and electronics.

As time progressed the apprentices proceeded in accordance with the syllabus. First term was an introduction to the use of hand-tools which required frequent visits to the first-aid box! Second term was basic electricity and magnetism. Third and fourth terms involved workshop practice on DC machinery

and internal wiring. Fifth term was for specialised courses when the apprentices had completed the common course and decided which trade they were to become. The final term was preparation for the Class III trade tests. Selected apprentices sat the Motor Vehicle Electrician papers and the Preliminary DC and AC papers in the City and Guilds examination.

Many visits to relevant branches of local industry were arranged; for example most apprentices visited the British Electrical Power Convention in Harrogate in June 1950. Some also visited the Harrogate Power Station but visits had to be restricted in distance due to the rationing of fuel.

CARPENTERS' & JOINERS' DEPARTMENT

The department was formed on 5 September 1949 in time to take the trade, together with some of the staff, from Taunton following its closure. One of the first tasks of the department was to prepare a stand at the Ideal Homes Exhibition of 1950. The second major task was the conversion of the NAAFI building in Hildebrand Barracks into a church. This work included the construction of choir stalls and other furniture, as well as the bulk of the main structural carpentry work.

The apprentice tradesmen became adept at construction of various types of display stands which included the local Careers Exhibition in Valley Garden in 1954, and the Ideal Home Exhibition later in the year in the Royal Hall. The department also carried out significant work around the camp as part of the general improvements that were being made.

PLUMBERS' & PIPEFITTERS' DEPARTMENT

The department was built by the apprentices of various trades but everyone benefited greatly because the plumbers could install central heating! There were instructional visits to local industry, and in 1950 these included the Leeds Building Exhibition and a lead-piping firm Heaps, Arnold & Heaps of Leeds. Most of the department were also on free haircuts in the early stages as a favour for installing wash-basins in the barber's shop.

BRICKLAYERS' DEPARTMENT

The department was a product of the move from Taunton and, having formed in 1949, was faced with a mass of building projects to improve the barracks. They built the carpenters' timber store, converted the NAAFI into a church and generally assisted around the school. Initially the department included masons but these were lost to Chepstow in 1950.

AT Jim Rogers – bricklayer.

ATs Anthony Metcalfe and Corporal Drummond – surveyors.

PAINTERS' & DECORATORS' DEPARTMENT

The department was formed in the summer of 1949 and found a mass of improvement work to carry out around the school. The apprentices also represented the school at the Ideal Homes Exhibition at Olympia and went to exhibitions to recruit for the school.

SURVEY DEPARTMENT

The department was formed when the school began and the aim was for the apprentices to obtain all three survey qualifications – surveyor trigonometrical, surveyor topographical and draughtsman topographical. To achieve this the course was divided into modules through which the apprentices progressed. These included cartographic drawing, cadastral survey, air survey, trigonometrical survey and topographical survey. Considerable amounts of the syllabus were completed in the field, such as Ripley Park, the Nidd Valley and Darley.

In 1952 a new system of training was adopted which also included printing. For twelve months all tradesmen carried out a common course of printing and surveying after which they went to print or field to cover the basic trade of surveyor topographical or storeman survey. The trades then could go on to specialise in the various elements of these basic trades.

ARCHITECTURAL DRAUGHTSMEN DEPARTMENT

The draughtsman trade was started in Taunton and transferred to Harrogate. Initially the department was joint with the quantity surveying assistants (QSA). The first tradesmen passed out in summer 1950. Visits were an important part of the course and included local builders' merchants, Harrogate Council Architects' Department and the Building Trades' Exhibition.

QUANTITY SURVEYING ASSISTANTS DEPARTMENT

The QSA course was new to the apprenticeship and teaching commenced in mid-1948. The initial syllabus was prepared by Major CF Berry RE. The trade of QSA was seen as the stepping-stone to quantity surveyor and the aim was for apprentices to leave as Class III tradesmen. The apprentices followed a set syllabus. In the first term basic draughtsmanship was taught. The second and third terms were building construction. Fourth and fifth terms concentrated on abstracting and billing, mensuration, taking-off and contract procedure. The final term was surveying and levelling, and the law relating to quantity surveying.

The department made visits to industry which included the Leeds Building Exhibition of 1950, seeing the new married quarters being built in Ripon and seeing a new school being erected in York. A film, *Easiform Houses*, gave a good insight into the speed at which houses could be built, but it is understood that *Pluto* held the attention of the apprentices for longer. In 1954 ATs took the City and Guilds exam for the first time. ATs Nurrish, Hancock and Broadbent were the first to pass.

SIGNAL TRAINING WING

The training of Signal trades commenced in February 1949 in Uniacke but this was transferred to Hildebrand in August 1949 so that the former could be updated. By this time equipment was beginning to arrive and a battery shop and a large number of radios were already on the inventory. One of the officers to set up the wing was Captain HAJ Sturge, Royal Signals, (later Major General).

The apprentices were taken on many visits which included the BBC Transmitter Site at Moorside Edge, GPO Repeater Station in Leeds, Oldhams Batteries and English Electric in Bradford.

As well as teaching the Signals trades there was

AT Lance Corporal David Sugden – electronics.

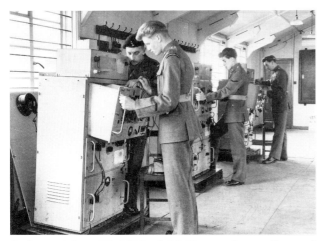

Left to right: *ATs Michael McGowan, Lance Corporal David Graham and CSM David Sharp – radio technology.*

also a General Practical Signals training course for other trades; mainly those in D Company. As is normal in Royal Signals it was also the responsibility of the wing to provide the power amplification (PA) equipment for a multitude of internal and external events. The AAS display van (the Red Van) also included a display of tele 'F', 10-line exchange, a No.62 wireless set, two 88 sets, and a number of typical Signals layouts. These were very popular displays amongst the viewing public.

In July 1951 the first Royal Signals fully trained apprentices left the school. It was a proud and historic moment for all concerned. It was a year later that the wing moved into its new accommodation under Captain WW Webb R Signals.

CLERKS TRAINING WING

Intake 47B was the first intake in the school and it included clerks of A Company. The aim was to qualify the apprentices as Class III tradesmen and to obtain the Royal Society of Arts certificates in shorthand and typing at various levels of competence. In 1950 all clerks were posted to REME owing to the reorganisation of that corps but later they were also posted to RASC.

ROYAL ARTILLERY SURVEY WING

The first class of six RA surveyors for locating regiments commenced training in March 1952. All six were eventually posted to units in BAOR in February 1955: ATs Alexander, Clarkson, Edwards, McCauley, Barel and Wilde. Initially, there was a severe lack of stores and equipment. Director RA, Major General KF Mackay Lewis CB DSO MC visited soon after BSM C Woods BEM RA was in post. The wing borrowed an SP gun and crew from 270 (WR) Field Regiment to complete the display.

PHYSICAL TRAINING DEPARTMENT

Inevitably the PT department (or muscle factory as it was known) was one of the first to be set up. Special fitness tables were set out which incorporated the standards to be achieved in mobility, strength and agility. For success in this field a 1st Class PT certificate was awarded prior to graduation. Training schedules were also made to improve the standard of the various major team games including the famous novices' boxing competition.

There was also a course in gymnastics, and the school was called upon on several occasions to provide a display at local events such as that given by 6 and 7 Platoons on the County Ground for the May Day celebrations in 1949.

Learning pottery in December 1955. Hobbies have always played an important part in the life of apprentices.

HOBBIES

Much effort had been put into establishing hobbies from the very early days of the school. Progress made depended on three main factors: money available, facilities available and permanent staff with the knowledge to run the hobby. The chief instructor was OIC Hobbies. The authorities recognised the importance of hobbies in developing the interests and character of the apprentices but they were unwilling to provide adequate funding. In 1954 there were 40 recognised hobbies.

Model Club	Badminton
Cycle Club	Philately
Canoe Club	.22 Rifle Club
Amateur Radio	Wood Carving
Marquetry	Archery
Sub Aqua	Fishing
Fencing	Hiking
Gardening	Table Tennis
Chess	Mountaineering
Sailing Club	Golf
Art Class	German 'A'
German 'E'	Drama
Scouts	Dance Band
Ballroom Dancing	Photographic Club
Carpentry	Stage Management
Senior Wranglers	Scottish Country Dancing
Bee-keeping	Plastics Club
French	Field Study
Play Reading	Popular Science
Debating	Music

It is inappropriate to delve into the background of all these hobbies but a few of the early archives are worth a mention.

Bee-keeping
The first hobby to be mentioned in the school magazine of July 1949 was bee-keeping. It was set up by the Rev. EF Jessup …'in a club house converted from the old gas chamber on the SW corner of the camp… almost every department of the school has contributed… in the next issue we hope to report that the two school hives have increased to four and that a surplus of honey has been taken. Signed Beekeeper-in-Chief: The Padre.' Sure enough the next issue reported; …'the sales of honey have been sufficient to repay half the sum loaned by the investors (PRI)! Actually the sum of £14. 12s. 0d. has been repaid – a dividend rarely obtained today.'

Dramatic Society
The society was founded in March 1949 and the first show was a revue with the cast coming from A Company. This was soon followed by plays such as *The Housemaster*, *Rookery Nook* and *Blithe Spirit*. On many occasions the society performed at external venues in Catterick, York and Wetherby.

Photographic Club
The club was formed in March 1949 in J Spider and by the end of the year there were over 24 members, with Mr Middlemiss taking charge of stores, accounts and projects. Obtaining cameras and other equipment was difficult but the club was soon providing the school magazine with most of its photographic material.

Radio Club
The club was formed in 1950 by Captain DH Baynham who was a keen 'ham'. He was the only licence holder and so his call-sign G3DHB was used for the first transmissions which brought in an amateur in Finland. The first transmitter was a derelict No.53 Set which was rebuilt by the radio mechanics of Sergeant Taylor of Signals Wing.

Gardening Club
The club commenced in autumn 1948 and was one of the earliest hobbies. Mr Milward was the head gardener. The object was to beautify the camp and its surroundings. During the early years the club seeded grass lawns and planted hundreds of trees, flowers and plants.

Golf Club
The most recordable event that had occurred in the short history of the golfers was a hole-in-one by Major J Wheel REME in November 1952 at Oakdale GC where special rates had been negotiated for school players.

Corps of Drums
A limited stock of ordnance issue pipes and drums lay in the QM's Department from an early stage. Unfortunately, it was not possible to encourage boys to play and there was also the absence of a bandmaster. This was put right in January 1949 with

the arrival of Drummer NCO Sergeant Stone, Royal Fusiliers. Within a year he was also teaching buglers. On a self-help basis, and with some extra funding, the necessary trimmings were produced. This included painting the drums with the school crest, and purchasing dress cords, card pouches, buff leg aprons, buff gauntlets, white gloves, badges and mace. Almost immediately the Drums were providing music for the Sunday church parades and it was not long before they were playing at local events in the town such as the Civic Parade and Remembrance Parade in November. The first apprentice drum major was AT Corporal Lawrence.

By 1954 the Drums were well established and under Sergeant Slattery and Drum Major AT Dent they totalled 27 musicians. Recruiting new members was always a high priority so in 1950 the Commandant allowed all Drummers to wear dress cords when walking out. This seemed to have a 'fatal attraction' for the local girls and thereby swelled the ranks with volunteers, thus 'killing two birds with one stone!'

SPORT

Sport has always been regarded by the military as an essential part of training and from the first days of the school it is clear that this unit was to be no exception. One complicating factor then, and has ever remained so, was the need to cater for apprentices and permanent staff at the same time. The staff are needed to coach the apprentices and there is a need to share the facilities.

The availability of sports fields and other equipment was problematical in the early post-war years. By late 1954 new sports fields were ready for

use in Uniacke which reduced the pressure on the Hildebrand and Cross Roads grounds. They included two hockey pitches, three football pitches, a grass athletics track and a cricket pitch. By 1954 there were 10 main sports being played.

Athletics	Cross country	Cricket
Hockey	Rugby	Football
Boxing	Basketball	Tennis
Swimming		

Matches against other apprentices' schools were arranged at an early date but the quadrangular

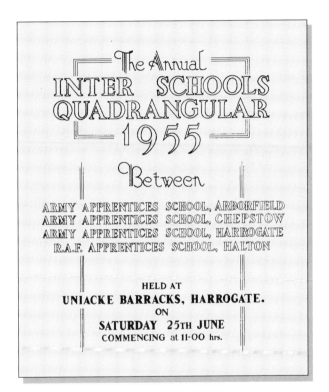

The athletics team for the 1955 quadrangular competition. Front row: *AT Gloyne, Gooch, Truesdell, Purcell, Jepson, Birtwistle, Captain Williams, Colonel Goldsmith, WO1 Cooper, ATs Russell, Newman, Wilkinson, Height, Aung Cheng, Khin Aung, and WOII Jenkins.* Second row: *Sgt Rowland, ATs Yelland, Smith, Firman, Devanney, Hobbs, Loney, Lowe, Thayer, Edwards, Lister, Findlay, Godden, Saunders, Walker, Sgt Paul.* Third row: *Sgt Coxon, ATs Pepperel, Colvin, Smith, Turner, Brooks, Parsloe, Thompson, Walton, Price, Simons, Nichol, Gibb, Missen, Sgt Porter.* Fourth row: *Bdr Johnson, ATs Hoare, Davies, Wilmott, Shaw, Tracey, Graves, Dobson, Downie, De Burgh Percival, Hare, Collins, Snowden, Bdr Bakewell.*

competition was soon established as the cornerstone of school sport. Until 2 June 1950 the Army apprentices of Arborfield, Chepstow and RAF Halton had held a triangular contest but Harrogate then joined the athletics for the first time. The result was a win for Harrogate by a single point from Arborfield. The new trophy, which was presented by RAF Halton, was lifted by apprentice Sergeant McDonagh who was a sprinter. Whilst not every sport can be included here it may be appropriate to look at a few comments from the archives.

Boxing

Most weights up to light-heavy weight were usually contested by the boys but, because of their size and age, the range was extended below flyweight to include mosquito, midge and gnat! In 1954 the school had Army champions in AT R Paton at bantam, and AT R Ayres at mosquito. There were also three beaten finalists from the school in AT J Graham, AT J Richie and AT Lance Corporal A Harris.

Cricket

Cricket became instantly very popular despite the likelihood of bad Penny Pot weather. In 1948, an astounding 47 matches were played, of which 28 were won. Matches against Arborfield and Taunton were both lost! It was not until 1955 that the school had the honour of winning the quadrangular, and as a result colours were presented to Perry, Payne, Russell, Stevens, Goodinson and Birtwhistle.

THE MILLER REPORT

In April 1955 a War Office report was completed by a Committee headed by Lieutenant General Sir Euan A Miller KCB KBE DSO MC and it became widely known as 'The Miller Report'. The Committee investigated the organisation and administration of all boys' units in the Army and it had a profound and lasting effect on the way that boy soldiers were treated and trained throughout the remainder of the century. For instance,

A display board in 1955 to show the badges of the corps to which apprentices were posted.

note was taken of the report when the Army opted for a single-entry system of recruiting in 1993 and thereby ended junior leader training. So important is the report that it is worth outlining its contents here. The terms of reference given to the Committee were:

To investigate the organisation (including staffing) and administration of those units of the Army which have been set up to train enlisted boys and to report whether such units best meet, under present-day conditions, the Army's requirements for enlisted boys, bearing in mind that the object is to provide long-service regular NCOs for the Army.

In 1955 there were 11 units for training boys which included the four apprentices' schools. As well as visiting all these units, the Committee also visited the military schools and they were very impressed with the high standard of facilities provided at such establishments as the Duke of York's School in Dover. This impressed them and resulted in them recommending that the units should conduct training more along the lines of a school than as a military unit.

The report was in great depth and included recommendations on discipline, security, games, quality of staff, accommodation, amenities, curriculum, levels of care, buildings and many other important matters. It recommended many changes to practices current at the time and it was not long before they were being implemented. For instance, within a year, adventurous training had been introduced. There was also concern over discipline and the need for the permanent staff to show a more humane approach to the boys; to this end the standard and continuity of the staff were improved. The need to control the activities of the boy NCOs was also highlighted; this was a major source of bullying at the time. By the end of the year the school had the unique addition of the first Women's Royal Voluntary Service lady, Miss Pat Ward, and one of her first duties was to claim the Scottish dancing hobby. This excellent service continued throughout the life of the college and the WRVS lady always held a key welfare appointment.

Within a year of the report the charter of the school had been significantly altered and, as a result of these recommendations, a rebuild of the barracks took place in the 1960s.

AT Terry 'Korky' Cawthorne was a member of 54A and was present at the final parade at the college in 1996. During this parade he recorded his recollections of his own time at the school which included:

Seeing the sergeant major I drifted back to the day I took command of the Roman Catholic squad of B Company. It was early morning muster parade. My squad were at the front of the company and our CSM, GT Harris (known in the Guards as 'Bomber' but known to us as 'Harry Boy'), was watching me with interest. I bawled out in my best voice, 'RC SQUAD ...SHUN'. Turning smartly to Harry

Boy I said, 'RCs all present and correct, Sir.' Harry Boy took his pace stick and pointed it at my midsection. Emphasising each word with a jab into my middle he said, 'You report them present Korky – I'll decide whether they are correct.'

As AT RSM Gray marched his troops off parade to the strains of 'Auld Lang Syne' I recalled my parade commanded by AT RSM Brian Lay. The standards of today were certainly as high as in my day, and I was delighted to see it. As a leaf blew across the parade ground it reminded me of stronger winds when the roof was lifted off B Company rooms one winter's night. I thought of the times when we raided the coke stocks and stoked up the boilers in our spider. A blind eye was turned by PS when pyjamas could be seen peeping from under our denims. The drying room was the most popular place in the spider. I thought of the AT who died after a training run. I remembered the AT who underwent corporal punishment for his crimes. He never came back for a second helping!

It was time to go home. My wife and I walked down the exit road and stopped to look at the commemorative stone. The date of the adoption was recorded; an event in which I was involved. As I walked down Penny Pot Lane I tried to recall other faces. The face I recalled most clearly was that of Harry Boy as we waved him goodbye by the main

gates. Even as we drove down the road away from the camp, he didn't seem to get any smaller.

Intake 54B included five Burmese ATs. The passing-out parade on 20 July 1955, at which Major General Wheatley was the Reviewing Officer, was the final parade for WO1 (RSM) Lonsborough. He retired from the Army to Huddersfield where he worked in security.

In November 1955 No.214 Army Dental Centre opened in the camp. Much of the preparation for the centre was done by the building trade apprentices. It was noted in the school magazine that, 'Living in a closed community as we do, it is our duty to our neighbours as well as ourselves, to maintain every part of our bodies, including our mouths, clean and healthy.'

A red-letter day in the history of the school was 3 May 1956 when the Council of Harrogate formally adopted the school. The Commandant accepted the honour from the Mayor.

On 9 June 1956 the sergeants' mess bade farewell to one of the longest-serving, most well-known and best-liked NCOs in the corps. Sergeant Tommy Blades BEM, Royal Signals, retired after over forty years' Army service, much of it with boy

Burmese apprentices meet their Military Attaché. Left to right: ATs Lance Corporal San Hlaing, Hla Thwin, Lance Corporal Mg Mg Aye, Maung Maung and Lieutenant Colonel Tin Maung.

WO1 (RSM) King was the School RSM from September 1955 for three years.

Sergeant Tommy Blades BEM encourages canoeing at the school exhibition.

The school march past Major General AH Hornby CB CBE MC, the Representative Colonel Commandant RA, on 18 July 1956.

soldiers. He joined at sixteen and served his first ten years in the Royal Sussex Regiment before joining Royal Signals. He saw service in the First World War, France, Bermuda, Jamaica, Trinidad and Gibraltar. In 1936, 1937 and 1939 he won the Army cross-country championships and had many other running titles to his name. He had been a member of the staff of the Boys' Squadron in Catterick and had spent nearly eight years at the school, arriving with the squadron at Harrogate in 1948. His activities as a runner and a coach, and his continuity, were valuable assets in the early days of the school and latterly he took on canoeing. At his farewell 'Tommy' was presented with a gold watch and, following his departure through the school gates with the Corps of Drums leading, he retired to New Zealand. The school magazine quoted Kipling's famous lines, 'Think where he's been, think what he's seen, think...' After he died, his medals were presented to the Royal Signals Museum and displayed ever since.

Ex-WO 1 PJ Smith was a member of Intake 55B and recalls being on duty:

I was on fire picquet. The only turn out we had was nearly a disaster. Sod's law – we were in the top gym on a PE period when the alarm went. No one in the gym heard it. Our first indication of being wanted was when a body came screaming into the gym.

Out we flew to see the whole school already formed up on the square. We made our way as fast as we could

with every WO and SNCO in the camp shouting at us as loud as he could. The fire was in a small 'Sally Bash' where the stove had been over-stoked and scorched the wooden wall behind it. When we arrived the Provost had already put out the fire and little damage had been done. But you can guess who got a lot of extra fire drills for the remainder of our stint.

Summer 1957 saw the last term in which REME electricians were trained at the school. Considerable effort was also made in bringing closer the education and trade training so that one was supportive of the other. In the same term Colonel Carne was appointed Honorary Colonel of the 5th Battalion, the Gloucester Regiment.

A unique event took place in July 1957 when, at the request of the Mayor of Harrogate, a party of 17 apprentices from the building trades went to assist refugees in Austria. The scheme was sponsored by the UN Association and lasted for fourteen days. During this time the aim was to assist in building as many houses as possible.

April 1957 was the end of an era for the school as Colonel Carne left Harrogate after three years in which he had consolidated the apprenticeship. His successor commented that, 'He has those qualities which we should always strive to attain – courage, wisdom and sincerity and an understanding of the essentials of life.' He retired from the Army on 30 November 1957 and returned to Cranham in Gloucestershire.

> ### End of Term Report
> *"The improvement in his handwriting has revealed his complete inability to spell".*

6

THE ENGINEERS MOVE OUT

Colonel NAC Croft DSO – March 1957 to May 1960

The new Commandant was Colonel NAC Croft DSO MA (late Essex Regiment) who arrived in March 1957 and embarked on a tour that lasted just over three years. He was a renowned Arctic explorer and a fine soldier. His opening statement to the apprentices was one of great vision in which he advised, 'Go flat out in all you do. Yours is the opportunity of a lifetime and yours is the age to learn. Do not consider that your learning should end with trade and education, but ensure that you become proficient in at least one sport and one hobby, that you form the habit of reading, and above all, that you become a man of initiative and self-reliance – one who, by example, shows a true sense of service to his fellow-men.' How many times would similar words be repeated in the years to come?

Colonel Croft's first formal occasion was on 6 May 1957 when the first anniversary of the adoption by the town was celebrated. The period also saw great emphasis being placed on the importance of the apprenticeship. This arose because of the imminent phasing out of National Service and the recognition that, in future, the schools would be a major source of the high-calibre tradesmen that the Army needed. This importance was underlined by the number of high-ranking and important visitors who came to the school.

The Signal Officer-in-Chief, Major General RJ Moberley CB OBE, inspecting the parade on 17 December 1958. Colonel Croft and AT RSM D Blake are in attendance.

On 27 August 1957 the Secretary of State for War, the Honourable H Hare OBE MP, visited with the C-in-C Northern Command, Lieutenant General RW Goodbody KBE CB DSO. He was followed, on 5 September, by the Director of Army Education, Major General S Moore-Coulson ERD. In November there were visits by Major General RJ Moberley, SOinC(A), Sir Stanley Rous, the Secretary of the Football Association, and Sir John Hunt, the explorer. Finally, in December, the Quartermaster General, General Sir Nevil CD Brownjohn CBE KCB CMG MC ADC, visited just prior to the SOinC(A) taking the passing-out parade. Indeed, these were times when the apprenticeship was seen as all important and it was announced that the school population would rise from 850 to its maximum of 1000. By 1960 the Grigg Report had stated that between a quarter and a half of the future Regular Army should be recruited through boy service.

The effects of the Miller Report were also taking greater effect. Adventurous training was now held at the Army Outward Bound School, Trawsfynydd, for all apprentices in their senior term. Other intakes exercised in more local locations and carried out 'self-reliance' training on the North Yorkshire Moors. At this time the school was still directly under the first Director of Army Boys' Training, Major General K Bayley CB CBE, who retired in 1957. The Commandant commented that, 'The General has never spared himself and has the ability to know what is best in any boys' unit and what to introduce or improve; he has, in my view, been largely responsible for ensuring that the vital importance of boys' units to the Regular Army is appreciated. Baulked by finance, he has not yet been able to realise the greatest single improvement that could be made to this school – the building of additional married quarters, which would enable company commanders and myself to live within a reasonable distance of the apprentices for those whose welfare they and I are responsible.' The General retired and in fact the Commandant did not acquire a married quarter in Hildebrand Barracks until 1970.

Building projects in other areas did gather momentum and planning for the central cookhouse, the three-storey barrack block (later to be named the

The new barrack block which eventually was named the Forge Block.

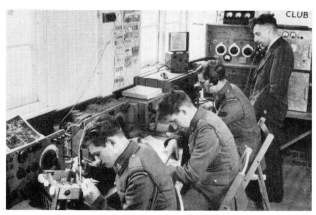

The Radio Club was always a popular hobby with the apprentices.

The new dining hall.

The new boiler house.

The area of the new playing fields.

Forge Block), the boiler house, two company offices and the cinder running track enabled these to be built by the end of the decade. The school commenced its long conversion from wood to brick, a process that took ten years to complete.

In January 1959 the school moved from a two to three-term year. There was also a bonus for staff and apprentices alike in the form of an extra week's leave at both Christmas and Easter. This resulted from a decision by the War Office that apprentices' schools should have ten weeks' leave each year in line with junior leader units.

In 1959 volunteers were entered for the Duke of Edinburgh's Award Scheme for the first time. A year later the school made the first gold award in the Army to AT Robert Baldwin. He was an apprentice carpenter and joiner and joined the Engineers.

Raising the profile of the apprenticeship to the general public was also a vital part of the public relations strategy. The school had its own 'Red Van' which toured the major public events of the North of England with an impressive display. Open days were also held for parents of apprentices who were then encouraged to 'recruit internally'. Regular visits by headmasters and youth employment officers were also introduced and this policy continued throughout the life of the college.

The end of the decade saw a shift in War Office policy, and recognition that more apprentices were required for the modern Army. A new school was opened at Carlisle in 1960. This resulted in a rationalisation of trades taught at each of the schools. Finally, it was intended that Harrogate would train only 'X' and operator trades of Royal Signals. Planning towards this goal commenced immediately.

September 1959 saw mainly a Royal Signals intake and the engineer trades started to move down to Chepstow, commencing with electricians and plumbers and fitters. It was not until late 1962 that the last of the engineer trades ended at Harrogate; the gunner survey trades transferred to Bramcote in 1959.

The East and West Ridings Area Headquarters, located in Hildebrand Barracks, closed in September 1958. This, together with building improvements, gave the school the opportunity to carry out some much needed reorganisation. Many of the company lines and trade wings were relocated. Anyone visiting in the early 1960s would not have recognised the school of a few years earlier; even the skyline had been altered by the boiler-house chimney which could be seen from miles around.

As mentioned earlier, considerable effort was made to integrate trade and education and this meant that rescheduling of many courses was required. Maths and science studies for the Army senior certificate were devoted to passing papers based on trade requirements. In the Signals Wing, for example, the technician first-year syllabus was based on the City and Guilds standards.

Immediately prior to the major move towards becoming a Royal Signals trade-orientated school there were 247 military and civilian members of staff excluding clerical and industrial personnel. The outline organisation in 1960 was:

College HQ – HQ, A, B, C and D Company
RE Survey Wing – Field and Lithographic
RE Wing – Carpenters and Joiners
Draughtsmen Architectural
Bricklayers
Painters and Decorators
Electricians
Signals Wing – A and B
Education Wing
PT Department
Technical Stores

As the school numbers grew so the standard of sport improved. In 1957 there were three Army boxing champions in ATs Chadwick, Brown and Howells. AT Stewart also received his inter-services colours and went on to reach the finals of the ABA championship. In the 1958/59 season 26 school boxers entered the Army junior championships and seven reached the finals. AT LCpl Carslake, ATs Pendleton and Chadwick were all victorious, the latter for the third time. ATs Hodgson, Lecky-Thompson, Spinks and Ulokwe were runners-up.

Cross-country runners were plentiful and in 1957 the school were Leeds and District youth champions. Colours were awarded to ATs Binar, Latham, Dawson, Dove and Short. In 1957 the school had six Army athletics champions: ATs Manley (both sprints), Hobson (440 and 880), Binar, Missen, Flower and Stokes. In 1959 the highlight of the season for the team was winning the quadrangular at Harrogate with 113 points and the trophy was raised by AT Sergeant Lee Manley. The nearest rival was Arborfield with 84. In the Army Boys' Athletics Championships at Aldershot on 17–18 July 1959 the school won 35 medals. Medals were won by ATs Martin, McInnes (2), Mathie, Powell, Hughes, Meadows, Perry (2), Fountain, Payne, Irvine and Gledhill.

On 16 December 1957 the first final of the Army Youth Football Cup was held at Aldershot. This was a competition suggested by the FA President, Sir Stanley Rous, in order to raise standards. The winners by 3-2 were D Company against a team from Chepstow. The goal scorers were ATs Pratt (2) and Balfour. Two years later C Company won the trophy by beating the junior leaders from Pirbright but this time by the larger margin of 7-2. The tournament continued to flourish to the end of the millennium. AT LCpl Bob Lee of Intake 57A remembers it well:

In 1958 C Company lost in the final by 3-2 and we were choked. I recall that our coach and my platoon sergeant, Sergeant Reg Thompson RE, took us all down to the NAAFI in Aldershot to get pie-eyed on a couple of beers. There were Jock Fraser, Steve Stokes, Satch Lancaster, Jock McCallum, Jock Barrie, Ray Harrop, Lou Griffiths, myself and a few others. He said something like 'cheer up, we'll be back next year.' By the time the following season came round we had three additions in the side: Paddy Wylie in goal, Bob Millings at full back, Taggy Arnold at centre half, Jock Arnold moved to right half and we had a defence as tight as Fort Knox.

*When 9 December 1959 arrived we had again reached the final. With half of C Company behind us in at least three coachloads, we ran out 7-2 winners. This time I will never forget the euphoria. One sad point was that Reg Thompson had been replaced after the previous year's defeat and posted to D Company. His successor was WOII George Footner, a very different character but a good coach. Despite Reg's accurate prediction of a year earlier it seems that the penalty for failure in football management has not changed from the 1950s through to the 1990s. Nevertheless, I am sure that we were the finest team **ever** to come out of Pennypot. Oh happy days, well most of them anyway!*

AT Alan Harwood training for the pole vault in the gymnasium.

The youth team also went on to win the Harrogate and District League in 1957 and followed this by winning the higher division in the next year. The PS were league champions in the York Half Holiday League in 1959 with WO II Footner RE and Sergeant Blake RE playing important roles.

Not to be outdone by the boys, the permanent staff were area champions at hockey in 1958 and went on to beat 10 Wireless Training Squadron in the final of the Northern Command competition by 3-2. Sergeant Nourrish, Captain Holmes and Captain Rogers were the goal scorers with the last two goals coming within the final three minutes of the game. All players were SNCOs or above. In 1959 the team did even better by winning its way to the Army Cup semi-final and winning the District Cup final.

The cricket season of 1958 was noticed mainly because well over half of the matches were called off due to bad weather. At least the team won two out of the three quadrangular fixtures with ATs Layton, Turner and Smith performing well in all matches.

In July 1958, the school swimming team won the enlisted boys' championship and returned, for the first time, with the Mackillop Trophy. The winning team was ATs Vutirakis, MacPherson, Thorpe, Carney, Cooke, Paton, Ashford, Pettifer, Parkin and Foote. This performance was all the more remarkable as the school did not have a swimming pool.

THE FIRST WEEKS OF A HARROGATE APPRENTICE OF INTAKE 57A

AT Lance Corporal Truman (Fred) Carslake was a member of Intake 57A who trained as a painter and decorator before joining the Engineers. Whilst at the school he showed outstanding talent as a boxer and became well known for it. He was an individual title winner in the Army junior championships of 1957, and in December 1959 he was school captain and awarded full colours. He served until 1967 having attained the rank of corporal. Since leaving the Army he has formed a 'Reunion Group' of the Engineer members of his Intake. This is as Fred remembers the school:

It was early February 1957 that a crowd of waifs and strays from all over the country arrived at the Army Apprentices' School, Harrogate, and what a mixed bunch they were. There were Jocks, Geordies, Brummies, Taffs Scouses, Cockneys and a whole tribe of West Africans from the Gold Coast.

In those days there was no personal selection like there is today. You went to your local recruiting office and told them what you wanted to be and then you sat an entrance exam which consisted of maths and English papers. Although these two exams were compulsory you were also given the option of sitting a general paper which could pull you through if you were weak in the other two subjects; if you passed these tests and a medical you were on your way.

On 8 February 1957, at the age of fifteen, I reported to the recruiting office where I signed on and picked up my train ticket. I was very excited at leaving home for the first time and embarking on a new career. It was not long before I was on the train to Harrogate. The journey seemed to take ages, but the further north I got the friendlier the people seemed to be and I had tea and sandwiches bought for me by people on the train.

It was about 5 o'clock in the afternoon when I reached my destination and, on coming out of Harrogate railway station, I was greeted by a large blackboard telling all the apprentices to wait in Lindy's Cafe across the road (this was to become a popular meeting place when we came to town). About an hour later we were picked up by a 3-ton truck and taken up to the camp where we were booked in and given a bed for the night. It was too late for an evening meal but we were taken to the bottom cookhouse and given a pint of cocoa and a huge doorstep cornbeef sandwich. There were about 100 of us in the first draft and we were split up into the different wings of two spiders at the bottom end of camp, HQ Company. A further 60 were due a couple of months later, after the Easter holidays.

We were split up into groups of about 17 to a room, in alphabetical order, and each room had an apprentice NCO from one of the senior terms attached to it. That first night away from home felt strange but it was good fun getting to know all the other inmates. One of the first things to happen that night was that nearly everyone picked up a nickname. No one seemed to be called by their Christian name; little did we know what problems this would present us with thirty odd years later when we wanted to hold a reunion. What were they called? We found Taff Simpson, Geordie Pattinson and Ginge Reed, but where have Bootlace Barton, Doggy Bone and Taggy Arnold gone to ground?

I mentioned earlier that we had some Africans in the Intake who were possibly from Ghana. There were seven of them altogether with names like Affram, Chukwu, Ilube, Kumah, Papafio, Ugwu and Ulokwe. Being a little older than we were and better educated, they took up technical trades and then went on to become officers in their own army; it is possible that they went on to Sandhurst first. We got on well with them over the years and one or two of them stood out very well on the sports field.

Each of our barrack rooms had its own loud-speaker system and we were blasted out of bed the next morning at six o'clock by Lonnie Donegan singing 'My Old Man's a Dustman' and 'Cumberland Gap'. Our two resident DJs were Sergeants Jock Bowley and Nobby Clarkeson and they had some lovely (unrepeatable) phrases!

The first day was all about 'admin' and we had to fill in endless forms, have various medical checks and injections, and be issued with our uniforms and various items of kit. Then we went to the cinema and had a welcome-to-Harrogate talk by the Commandant, Colonel Carne VC. In the evening we started to learn all about 'Bull...t' when our room NCOs introduced us to bedpacks, and showed us how to present our kit for morning inspection. It was gone midnight when we got to bed that night as it was a hard job to please them. In the morning, when we thought we had got it all right, all our work was pulled to bits by the troop sergeants; nothing seemed to be good enough for them.

We then had Bull, Bull and more Bull. I make no apology for wanting to use the stronger terminology because it was something we had to live with the whole of our service life, and perhaps it is of interest to explain some of the things we were made to do.

• We had to run a bar of soap down the inside of creases in our uniform before we ironed them to keep the creases in, and shave the outside of the creases to make them sharper.
• We had to put black polish on the bottoms of our best boots and put white blanco on the studs, heels and toe plates.
• Our bedpacks had to be made up with plywood boxes to make them square.
• All our clothes had to be boxed up with board when laid out for kit inspection.
• Big packs, small packs and ammo pouches all had to be boxed up.
• Spare bootlaces had to be tied up like a Catherine wheel and bulled up with black polish.
• Army numbers had to be stamped on everything.
• We had to burn the bumps off our boots and bull them up so you could see your face in them.
• Everything had to be laid out in your locker for inspection at all times with your packs on top.
• We had to polish our mess tins so you could see your face in them.
• Boot and utility brushes had to be painted white.
• Greatcoats had to be done up 'dolly fashion' and hung on the side of your lockers.
• The centre floor of the barrack room – a 4ft wide strip right down the length of the room – had to be polished so you could see your face in it. I remember pushing the bumper up and down the floor to polish it with someone sitting on the end to add extra weight. White lines were painted either side of the centre to make it stand out.
• Everything in the room had to be lined up, the beds, the lockers, bed packs and kit on top of the lockers.
• The room's galvanised bucket had to be bulled so you could see your face in it.
• On a regular basis we had room and kit inspections when everything had to be laid out the same as in a photograph on the room noticeboard. I still have a treasured copy of that photo, having pinched one off the board before I left.

AT Sgt Dave Winship (57A) was an electrician who went on to serve a full career with the sappers and reach the rank of major. He recalls:

AT Taggy Arnold, who never seemed to have any money, was given a forty-eight hour pass for being the best at something or other. He was desperately trying to borrow money for the train fare home but as we all knew what he was like he had no luck. Anyway, off he went and dutifully returned before midnight on the Sunday and on our inquiring how he got home he replied, 'I hitched a lift to Leeds, bought a 2d. platform ticket at Leeds Central and

boarded the express to King's Cross. On the train I stood in the corridor until an oldish lady went to the toilet. I waited a few seconds until I thought she was incapacitated, knocked on the door and demanded to see her ticket which at my request was slipped under the door. Fortunately for me it was a return ticket so I pocketed it and went and sat down as far from the scene of the crime as I could get. A good weekend followed and having given my mother a sob story about spending all my money on getting home she also gave me a few bob to spend!'

Asian flu had descended on Harrogate and as a result there were one or two empty bed spaces in the barrack room. Sergeant 'Bow Wow' Bowsley decided that this looked too untidy for the forthcoming OC's inspection and he ordered us to rearrange the room. This was the last thing we wanted as we had cut holes in the floor boards under our lockers for storage of illegal (sometimes stolen) articles. Our protestation that the lockers were too heavy to move only succeeded in making Bow Wow so impatient that he gave one locker a big shove and promptly disappeared through a hole in the floor. It was almost worth seven days' Jankers to see the look on his face.

Towards the end of the passing-out parade senior term's dance I had managed to convince the girl that I had been plying with drink to come back to my bunk with me. In the dark, and in my alcohol-induced state, we managed to find our way back to the window of the barrack block. I heaved her up through the open window only to find that it was the wrong spider and I had succeeded in delivering a very attractive girl to a room full of third-term boys. A tug-of-war ensued but I lost and retired hurt to the dance licking my wounds. I never did find out what happened to the young lady.

At the end of term we were issued with our Post Office savings book (POSB), travel warrants and credits. We then had to make it to the 3-tonner without being filched by the senior term moneylenders who loaned money at exorbitant rates of interest. Very few escaped unscathed and those in junior term (Sprogs) who had succeeded and felt safe in their railway carriage were in for a shock:
Sprog 1. Hello Sergeant what are you doing on this train? I thought you lived in Hull!
Sergeant. I do but I have to go to London and I thought I would keep you company.
Sprog 2. That's good of you Serge.
Sergeant. Well now how many of you play poker? It's an easy game and helps to pass the time!

AT John (Ginge) Reed was a carpenter and joiner who went on to complete twenty-two years' service with the sappers and RAPC before retiring as a WO2. Most of his recollections have a financial bias so it is evident that he was always going to end up in the Royal Army Pay Corps:

My overriding memory of life as an apprentice at Harrogate was always being broke. When I joined up my gross pay was £1. 11s. 6d., of which we were only allowed to draw 10s. (50p) per week. This was deemed sufficient to buy copious quantities of boot polish, Brasso, blanco (khaki

Colonel Croft departs, in a Champ, along the route lined by apprentices on 21 May 1960.

and white), and Zebo for mixing with the floor polish to enhance the shine of the barrack room floor. This left just enough for five Woodbines! The total lack of liquid assets gave rise to many moneymaking enterprises.

The Fish and Chip Run. So called because each evening a mobile van (nicknamed Greasy Jane's) would ply its trade outside the camp gate. I would go through all the company, take orders and then go to the van with my issued suitcase to return with the orders. This service cost 2d. and from it I could afford my own fish and chips which were essential to make up for the poor quality and quantity of the Army food.

Stick-Man. Every night a number of apprentices had to do guard and they were inspected by the orderly officer who picked out the smartest as Stick-Man and he was let off the duty. AT Ray Pattinson had the best kit in the Company and was the first man to get Stick-Man three times. For a small fee he would hire his kit out to anyone who would pay so that they could avoid patrolling the camp at three o'clock in the morning. This hire charge was extremely expensive at anything up to 2s. (10p).

Money Lending. Money was lent out at extortionate rates and boys would get into serious debt from borrowing small sums initially. These 'Shylocks' were usually big senior term boys and repayment was usually enforced by

bullying. I recall a syndicate being spearheaded by a boy in B Company who was known to us only as 'Planet'. Planet was always around on pay day and end of term!

TV Room Search. After the TV room emptied on a Saturday evening one or two enterprising souls (me and Dusty Miller included) would search the lounge chairs for those coins that had slipped out of people's pockets as they reclined. This would sometimes raise a few bob and was most profitable immediately after a pay day.

Such were the recollections of some of the apprentices who saw out the 1950s. It is also noteworthy that Intake 59C would later provide the first ex-apprentice Yeoman Warder when WO1 TE Trent moved to the Tower of London on retirement.

Colonel Croft also saw out the 1950s but on 21 May 1960 the school bade him farewell on parade and he departed in a Land Rover with the route lined by the ATS and PS. He retired and became the first Commandant of a brand-new apprentice scheme for cadets in the Metropolitan Police. His parting words were, 'If any of you have Scotland Yard trouble you have a friend in court! To serve youth is a challenge and an adventure. To serve you all is a privilege. I hope you all love this place, and what it gives, as much as I do. Good luck.'

> From an essay
> *"The police farce was started by Sir John Peel".*

7

ROYAL SIGNALS ONLY

Colonel JP North – May 1960 to January 1964

Colonel JP North CBE (late Royal Signals) was firmly in command to see that the new decade got away to a smooth start and from this time onwards all commandants were late Royal Signals. His tenure was to last nearly four years until January 1964 and was dominated by two main issues. The first was the setting up of the school as a Royal Signals apprentices' training establishment. The second was the planning of a complete rebuild of the school. In his second submission to the school magazine in June 1961 Colonel North remarked:

This edition of our magazine closes another chapter in the history of the school as it is the last to be issued whilst there are Royal Engineer apprentices with us. We are indeed sorry to see them go, and the school will be the poorer for their absence. Sapper apprentices have left many permanent reminders of their stay here, which will remain even when the school is rebuilt, and the good they have done will not easily be forgotten. We wish all those who are leaving us the best of luck and good soldiering in the future.

Colonel JP North CBE

At last there are visible signs of the rebuilding of the school even if they are only scars left by the engineers who have completed the ground survey for the foundations of the future buildings. However, planning is now nearing completion and the architects' drawings are in an advanced stage. There is every hope that the construction will begin in the spring of 1962.

Like most military men Colonel North was an optimist but his hopes were to be dashed and in his final entry in the magazine before he left he recorded:

It is my greatest regret that the biggest change in the school that we had hoped for has not happened during my time here, namely its rebuilding. I am assured that it will start during mid-1964 and I pray there will be no further hold ups.

A high percentage of the detailed planning for the rebuild was completed early and by June 1961 the architectural drawings were made public and were never substantially altered. Despite all this, the

An aerial view of Uniacke Barracks looking west in 1961. The cinema, which remained until the closure of the college, is the large building, centre right.

In 1960 all catering, in the new dining hall, was undertaken by Industrial Catering Ltd on contract.

January 1963, using a Stenzil Apparatus to demonstrate Electricity and Magnetism.

rebuild did not get underway until 1965, and was not completed until early 1968. It was originally envisaged that the cost of the rebuild would be about £1¹/₄ million but as early as 1962 the estimate had risen to £3 million. The only building to be completed early was the new cookhouse. AT Brian Houldershaw (59A) recalled in 1994:

The existing cookhouse in Uniacke Barracks was completed and commissioned some time during 1960. It was a remarkable improvement on the two old cookhouses which had stood at either end of the parade ground. Furthermore it was civilian staffed and initially the food was infinitely superior to that which had been 'murdered' by the ACC in the old establishments.

As Christmas approached, the four main companies were all seated together to receive their Christmas dinner served by the officers and senior NCOs of the permanent staff. The Commandant, Colonel North, duly arrived to wish everyone the usual Yuletide platitudes and a prosperous and industrious New Year. He referred to the new cookhouse in glowing terms and asked of us what more we could want. 'A pint of beer, Sir' came the reply from one audacious AT. Although somewhat taken aback, Colonel North ordered 'A pint of beer for that man and one for me.' The AT received his pint of beer from an attendant sergeant, much to everyone's surprise and delight. The Commandant then stood on a table, toasted each and everyone of us, downed his pint in one go and despatched his empty glass to the far corner of the empty mess area used by the junior ranks of the permanent staff. He departed to a rousing round of applause from the ATs.

The rearrangement of the apprentices' schools, including the opening of AAS Carlisle, took place over a period of about two years. However, they remained under the control of the Director of Military Training and were not 'Arms Schools'. The move of the RE Wing from Harrogate included the transfer of architectural draughtsmen, carpenters and joiners, bricklayers and painters and decorators

ATs Stephenson, Watkins, Brooker, French and Gledhill practising keyboard skills in December 1960.

in September 1961 immediately after the summer leave. This meant that 58B passed out as planned, but it was decided that 59A should continue in trade until December 1961 and pass out from Harrogate, thus negating the need for a short-term move. By the time these trades arrived at Chepstow the building of their new accommodation was well underway. By 1962, trades were taught as follows:

AAS Arborfield. Only REME trades.

AAS Carlisle. RE and REME trades.

AAS Chepstow. RE trades, ammunition examiner RAOC and marine engineer RASC.

AAS Harrogate. Royal Signals trades only: telegraph operator; electronic technician; line technician; radio technician, light; radio technician, radio relay technician; telegraph technician.

AT Brian Houldershaw was one of the ATs who moved to Chepstow:

December 1960, first-year technicians learning battery charging.

January 1963 an apprentice radio technician checks a teleprinter.

Lieutenant General Sir William Pike presenting prizes on 26 July 1961 with Lieutenant Colonel AR Glanvill assisting. The coveted Champions' Cup is on the table.

At the beginning of the summer term of 1961, my group of Intakes 59A and 59B, together with 59C and 60A of the Field Survey Wing departed from Harrogate for Chepstow to join the print section apprentices of RE Survey. The latter had been transferred twelve months previously and only Intakes 58A and 58B groups of Field Survey were left at Penny Pot to complete their training.

On arrival at Chepstow we were divided amongst the three main companies. Harrogate employed a trade company system which did perhaps create a form of elitism. Chepstow's method of completely mixing its companies with representatives of all trades was probably more far-sighted. It also promoted incentives, indicated by stars worn on the right sleeve, whereby privileges such as the right to wear civilian clothes, extra pass-outs and small pay supplements, could be gained by attaining high marks for educational, trade and military attainments. This system particularly helped those ATs who were not NCOs.

However in many respects Chepstow lagged behind Harrogate as far as encouraging initiative and responsibility amongst its ATs. This was particularly noticeable amongst its boy NCOs. Some resentment crept in amongst the Beachley boys and the permanent staff, as time and again they saw the ex-Harrogate NCOs run away with the most senior appointments. All ex-Harrogate ATs had to take a lot of stick as a result of this situation, but it was bravely borne as we all considered ourselves to be superior and felt extremely proud of our ex-Harrogate status.

The cap badge of the Royal Corps of Signals.

The progression at Harrogate towards an all Royal Signals teaching environment was quickly under way, and the standards had to withstand scrutiny by Her Majesty's Inspectors of Education. The Signals training organisation was divided into A and B Wings. A Wing comprised Basics Group and Operator Group. Teaching the basics of the trades was difficult enough but the root of the problem was, and has ever remained so, 'that many apprentices are shocked when they realise that it's even worse than school – sitting at desks and studying; wielding a pen rather than a screwdriver!' One suggestion for the Wing motto was 'Libri damnosi' – which loosely translated was 'Don't forget your books or the instructor will blow his top!' In the spring of 1963 there were 316 first-year technician apprentices under training.

The operator course was based on typing in term 1, Morse in term 2, and teleprinter operating and Morse transcription in term 5. The syllabus included over 30 exercises and schemes between the fourth and ninth terms. The Class III trade test was taken in term 7 and in term 8 the better tradesmen visited 24 Signal Regiment in Catterick to take their AII trade test (by 1963 this could be achieved in the school). The Tape Relay Centre at Boddington was visited in term 8 and a complete 'Commcan' exercise was undertaken at 14th Signal Regiment. Facilities were also being improved step by step. A new Morse trainer was installed which allowed an operator to plug into any one of five selected speeds. New radio vehicles arrived and were used for training exercises.

B Wing undertook technician training once the apprentices had completed their first year in Basics Group. Improvements in the availability of equipment were made gradually. Radio-relay vehicles were added to such equipment as the D11/R210 (who could forget Lissajou's figures!) and the T100 teleprinter (with its J bell to provide entertainment), which improved considerably the standard of exercises and hands-on training. Voice frequency (VF), carrier and telephony laboratories were also established.

In addition to the normal syllabus there was also the option to train for the Ordinary National Certificate (electrical) and a few achieved Higher National Certificate. By 1964 many of the apprentices had classified as TII tradesmen by the time they left.

The emphasis being placed on Royal Signals training also resulted in the renaming of the companies. They were redesignated Rawson, Phillips, Scott and Penney after distinguished officers of the corps. Initially they were referred to as 'houses'; presumably a throwback to the Miller Report. However, by 1964 they were firmly established as squadrons.

In the mid-1990s AT (RSM) David Gardner recalled some of his memories of AT life. David

December 1960, Holy Communion.

retired from the corps as a colonel and took up employment with the Cabinet Office in London:

After leaving the Duke of York's Royal Military School in the summer of 1960 I joined the Army Apprentices' School, Harrogate, on a three-year apprenticeship. Fortunately, as I was already accustomed to living away from home and was used to a military environment, I had little difficulty in settling into this new way of life. I could already march proficiently, wear a uniform and clean my kit, compete at a reasonable standard in most sports and play a number of musical instruments. The youngest recruit at that time was only fourteen years old and some of them were extremely homesick.

On arrival at the school new recruits were not allowed out of uniform for the first term and could not leave the barracks until they had passed off the square. I discovered, however, that if you were selected to represent the school at sport or were in the band these rules were quietly ignored. Needless to say I immediately joined the band, which was probably the best Army boys' band in the country. I also took up cross-country running as this was the one that managed to get the most trips around the country! Whilst at the school I ran in every Army championship, every English national championship and all the inter-school meetings and was subsequently awarded my Army colours for athletics and school colours for cross-country and athletics.

Within four weeks of joining the school I was selected to be a senior apprentice tradesman which involved being in charge of the barrack room and marching the recruit squads around the school. This entailed wearing a half stripe, which was unfortunately removed on joining one of the four senior companies at the end of the first term.

Once we had passed off the square we were put into basic trade groups. A number of us already had 'O' levels and for the first time the top-grade class was formed entirely from students with these qualifications. We went on to study for ONC which included attending Bradford Technical College on day release; yet another way of defeating the system! Some of our trade classrooms had the old pot-bellied stoves which had to be stoked up at frequent intervals; always a good excuse for having a smoke break. During our first term we were also required to take our Army First Class and Second Class Certificates of Education. Despite protests that some of us were exempt with our 'O' levels we were still made to sit the exams as we were told it would look good on the school records. Surprisingly, I achieved higher marks in some of the subjects at first class than at second class!

At the end of the first term I left Recruit Company and joined C Company where, I discovered later, the Guards sergeant major had still to pass his first-class education. I was part of the first Royal Signals intake into that company which previously had been the bastion of the Royal Engineers. The sappers were mainly brickies and chippies and had a reputation of being extremely hard; hence the company was called 'The Zoo'. They had little time for Royal Signals, especially those who needed to swot

for their trade tests and, as a consequence, many a trade book got ripped up in 'friendly rivalry'. Fortunately, I found the trade training well within my capability and, with my experience gained at the Duke of York's, knew how to look after myself. At the end of the first year I was the first outsider in the company to become a lance corporal and a couple of terms later was promoted sergeant.

I thoroughly enjoyed my time at the school. The pay was £2. 2s., which was not very much; however this increased to about £6. 15s. on reaching the age of seventeen, plus 1s. 9d. for every promotion. Trade training was never a problem and day release once a week to Bradford was a pleasant break. Most weekends I was either running somewhere or playing in the band, including the Royal Tournament in my second year. It seemed that everything I did was marked by a degree of success.

I have few specific memories of my time at Harrogate. I do however recall the time we had an enormous storm, probably some time in 1962; it blew down the ration store at the top of the square and the following morning the bottom of the square was covered in oranges. During the storm a few of the wooden barrack room roofs started to lift off, assisted where necessary by the boys, with the odd radiator managing to fall off the wall!

At the end of my apprenticeship I had risen to the rank of apprentice regimental sergeant major. This was not a foregone conclusion, the appointment was keenly competed for and there were one or two other apprentices in the running. On the final Graduation Day Parade everything went to plan. We had practised so often that, apart from the crowd at the front, it was just like another rehearsal. I suppose my training over those past three years enabled me to take the event in my stride and, I must say, I have never looked back.

Five eventful years later, during which I became a member of the first Joint Service Satellite Communications Project Team, competed for the Royal Signals' representative ski team and was awarded two international athletic vests for Singapore, I was commissioned into the Corps from Mons Officer Cadet School and, in effect, started my career all over again.

There were a few 'administrative' milestones at the school in this period. On 7 February 1960 the catering for the apprentices was contracted to Industrial Catering Ltd. This was a step that was to be regretted subsequently, and it was not until a decade later that the Army Catering Corps resumed responsibility. The apprentices were also relieved of the duty of guarding the school because War Department Police were assigned to the task.

On 22 June 1960 the school was readopted by the Borough of Harrogate in a formal ceremony and parade in the town. It was also during this event that the school rebuilding programme was made public. Following the ceremony, five companies of apprentices marched through the town past the Victoria Memorial where the Mayor, Councillor L Roberts, took the salute.

In 1962, AT Corporal Nyameke, Sergeant Tontoh and Corporal Frimpong were the last Ghanaians to train at the school.

On 30 March 1961 a thanksgiving service was held in St Alban's Church to commemorate the tenth anniversary of its dedication. The last of the Ghanaian apprentices left in 1962 when three of them passed out together; they were AT Sergeant Isaac Tontoh, AT Corporal Martin Frimpong and AT Corporal Samuel Nyameke. Sergeant Garland RAEC, who was an instructor in Education Wing, departed at Easter 1962 and was the last of the National Service instructors to leave the school and in April 1963 the RAEC became an all-officer corps. Thus ended 114 years of 'schoolies' in the sergeants' mess.

In the early hours of 12 February 1962 Penny Pot had one of the fiercest storms ever witnessed. The gale destroyed all in its path including barrack blocks, cookhouse and office accommodation. The School Orderly Officer was WO2 (CSM) Furner Kings. His prompt action in evacuating the apprentices from their accommodation ensured that nobody was injured and earned a public commendation from the Commandant. In all, £12,000 of damage occurred which included many buildings and the loss of many old trees. This also heralded one of the worst summer seasons recorded.

The Pipe Band and Corps of Drums continued to flourish, and the musical capability within the school was enhanced considerably when, in September 1961, the School Brass Band was formed. Cornets, horns, baritones, euphoniums, trombones and basses were obtained. This brought the total number of instruments in the massed bands to 95. Recruiting was intense and the musicians made steady musical progress. The years 1961 and 1962 brought heavy schedules for the apprentices, which included the Royal Tournament on 10 June 1961 and a display in front of a crowd of 65,000 at Roundhay Park in Leeds in the same year. The Pipes and Drums undertook their first public engagement at the Remembrance Day Parade in Harrogate on 12

November 1961. ATs Scaife and Walter performed Last Post and Reveille respectively. On 15 June 1962 the massed bands beat retreat on the square for the first time. In front of the whole school and guests they provided one of the most impressive displays of any kind seen at the school. The event owed its success to the endeavours of Drum Major Hall, Pipe Major Yule, Colour Sergeant Evison, AT Drum Major Lawson and AT Drum Major Cooke. Major DW Sutherland, Royal Signals, had also spent many patient hours teaching the Pipers. The parade was followed by 29 instrumentalist of the brass band playing in fine style at the September Great Yorkshire Show.

Sport continued to play a major part in the programme of the school but the 1960 season saw a lot of washed out matches owing to bad weather. Maurice Leyland, the England and Yorkshire cricketer, held nets and ATs Harrison, Worsley, Lawrence, Lindehringhs, Palmer and Nunley were all awarded colours.

The athletics team of 1960 was extremely strong and won the quadrangular from Chepstow by five points with RAF Halton and Arborfield following on. In the Army boys' individual championships the school won 24 medals; more than any other unit. School athletes set up four Army records:

Youths 100yds	AT Cpl Perry, 10.5 secs
Youths 880yds	AT Cpl Gilbert, 2m, 4.6 secs
Jnr Triple Jump	AT CSM McInnes, 42ft 11in
Jnr Hammer	AT Cpl Cartwright, 56ft 10in

The school also had Yorkshire County champions in AT Truluck for youth pole vault and AT Lance Corporal Payne for the junior triple jump. In 1961 the school produced six Army champions: ATs Minns, Newman, Fountain, Greenall, Randall and Pilbeam. AT Fountain was successful in both the hurdles and the high jump. Perhaps the outstanding achievement of the season was the success of ATs Tontoh, Lawson, Perry and Edwards when they broke the Army record for the 4 x 110yds in 45.2 seconds. The Athletics Officer, Major SE Miller MBE, continued to provide success in 1962 albeit to a lesser extent than before. ATs Baynes, Randall and Newman were Army champions and were selected to represent the Service. Baynes was awarded the Victor Ludorum for his efforts in the 880yds and thus took over the honour from AT CSM Fountain. The Quadrangular Trophy was regained in 1963 by a clear five points from Carlisle. AT Fenge broke the Army record in the pole vault and ATs Baynes, Randall, Escott and White were Army individual champions. Once again the relay team of ATs Randall, Harris, Smurthwaite and White ran to victory in the 4 x 110yds relay.

The main claim of the basketball team was that for four seasons they remained undefeated in all quadrangular matches. In 1961 AT Sergeant Thompson was selected for the All England Under 23 squad and Penney Squadron were Army champions. ATs Simpson, Newman and Meredith were also selected for the Army team. In 1962 the permanent staff were Northern Command champions and in 1963 Penney Squadron repeated their Army Cup success of two years earlier; Sergeant H Jennings was their coach.

In 1961 C Company, under the captaincy of AT Harrop, repeated their success of the previous season by beating A Company of Chepstow in the Army Youth Football Cup. Sergeant Hall guided them to a resounding 9-3 victory. A year later, as Scott Squadron, they were narrowly defeated in their fourth consecutive final by a Chepstow team that was predominantly ex-C Company transferees! In the 1963 season the PS team became League and Cup double winners when they produced an emphatic 6-0 win over Corinthians, in which AT Frost played in goal, and kept a clean sheet, and Sergeant Graham scored a hat-trick.

In the 1960 rugby season D Company were narrowly defeated in the Army final by a strong C Company, Chepstow. But revenge was to be sweet a year later when Penney Squadron defeated the same team by 6-3 with ATs Davies and Lowry (the captain) scoring the tries.

Canoeing was a popular sport in the early 1960s. Good canoes, in the form of K2s, were purchased from Nuffield and school grants. A lot of effort was put into preparation for the Westminster/Devizes race which was held annually at Easter. In 1961 moderate success was gained when ATs Brett and Harrison completed the course in twenty-six hours twenty minutes. A year later ATs Rayment and Tucker finished in twenty hours twenty-seven minutes with six of the school's teams in the first 13. Then, in 1963 ATs Harrison and Irving won the event in the time of nineteen hours eleven minutes.

Sailing too had its strong support and six new National Enterprise dinghies and two RNSA 14ft dinghies were provided from Nuffield grants and launched at Semerwater. In 1963 the Captain of Boats was AT PH MacCulloch; he returned some thirty years later as OIC of the sport!

Hockey remained ever popular but without great success under the guidance of Captain JR Garratt and the coaching of Staff Sergeant Loates. The outstanding achievement at the school was that of AT Sergeant Coldwell who played for the Army team on six occasions. The team suffered to some extent until 1961 because the opposition were senior sides. It was then decided to play schools only, thus providing similar calibre opposition.

Whilst many hobbies went from strength to strength, other new ones were being formed. Within a period of three years, six new hobbies were formed: karting, model railway, judo, archery, riding and angling.

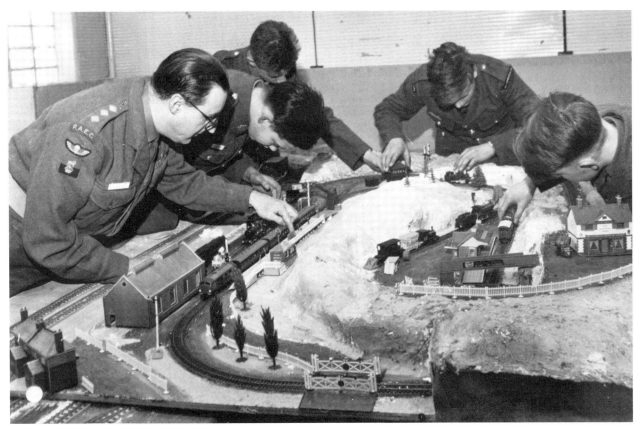

Captain JH Robinson with members of the Model Railway Club in 1962.

In 1962, with the assistance of Captain (TOT) AC Earl G3FGN and assistants P3DPS, G3DBU and G3FMW, the Amateur Radio Club successfully updated its equipment with a grant of £300. AT Percival was the Club Secretary and G3HKR became one of the best stations in the north with both DY-100-U Heathkit and KW Viceroy model transmitters and a Hammerlund HQ-170 receiver.

Separate to this was the CCF/ACF wireless station for which Captain Garratt was OIC and AT Galliard was the secretary. It broke away from the Radio Club and set up on 5 November 1960.

Sports and hobbies were important in the development of the apprentices, but the arts were also not without their place at the school. In 1961 the chief instructor announced a new competition:

A new development has been the inauguration of the 'Arts Pentathlon'. I appreciate that the pedant may find fault with choice of the title, but surely in an establishment of this sort, the combination of the artistic with athletic is a highly satisfactory aim in the development of the complete young man! But seriously, this new competition, which involves the participation of the competitor in the five subjects of designing, drawing, craftsmanship, poetry and essay writing in drama and music, is to be highly commended to all apprentices, and I would like to congratulate Captain PE Creedy (who was himself an accomplished artist) on his initial thoughts which led to this competition. A cup will be awarded termly to the successful competitor and we look forward to the first results of this interesting innovation in the extra-curricular life of the apprentice.

The first winner of the competition was AT J Porter who was an RE tradesman and transferred to Chepstow. In all, 13 complete entries were received and external judges selected the winner.

The following year AT J Porter was deemed to be the best actor in the school for his part in the Army junior music and drama festival. Also in 1962, AT J Collins entered the NATO poster competition with the theme of 'Freedom before Bondage'. Having shown little previous artistic talent he took the second prize of £3.

The school always had strong entries in the Army art and crafts competition. In 1962 it was held in the Pillared Hall, near Horse Guards and there were over a thousand entries. The school provided 36 entries and won 13 prizes; the strongest being in boat building. First prizes were won by AT Beers (drawing), AT Harrison (boat building), AT Etchells (miscellaneous, for which he made a fishing rod), Captain Creedy (drawing), Lieutenant Colonel White (boat building) and Lieutenant Kay (miscellaneous for artificial baits).

The main visitors to the school included the Secretary of State for War, The Right Honourable John Profumo MP, who visited on 17 March 1962, St Patrick's Day. His successor, Mr James Ramsden, was the graduation parade Reviewing Officer in December 1963. There was also a visit by Sir John Hunt, the Everest explorer, on 6 June 1962.

Over a period of three years most military people come and go and, of course, in so doing they leave their mark. Most definitely in that category was Lieutenant Colonel AR Glanvill TD R Signals, the Chief Instructor and initially the senior R Signals officer, who on departure retired from the Army and handed over to Lieutenant Colonel PH Brown. In his departing notes he thanked his staff for supervising the many changes that had occurred during his tour. They included Major Worrin, WO1 Neale, Mr Storer, Mr Tindall, Mr Moxam, Mrs Mount and Mr McGrail.

Major Frank Parker R Signals left after four years of taking new recruits and moulding them into proficient soldiers. Major SE Miller MBE came from the TA and moved on to the Junior Leaders' Regiment, Royal Signals, but not before taking D Company and school athletics to new heights. Major LL Scott RA retired to Guildford after three years with B Company. He was then the near neighbour of Colonel CEC Burton (late RA), who had, as PRI, held the school purse-strings before his second retirement to Farnham.

The change-of-command parade from Colonel North to Colonel Piddington was held in January 1964 when, in true Penny Pot style, there was snow on the ground. The ceremony ended with Colonel North being towed away in an apprentice-drawn Champ as the remainder of the school lined the route.

From an Instructor's Report
"There has been a good improvement this term especially in his maths, but I feel I could do even better".

REBUILD OF THE BARRACKS

Colonel JR Piddington OBE MC – January 1964 to September 1966

Colonel JR Piddington OBE MC became the Commandant in January 1964 and remained in post until 1 September 1966. He had enlisted in Royal Signals, as an electrician fitter boy soldier, in F Company at Catterick on 4 May 1932 and had seen service in many parts of the world including Palestine, India, Burma and Egypt. During his time in Burma he was awarded the Military Cross for his skilful and determined defence of 7 Indian Division Signal Regiment Headquarters against Japanese invasion. In August 1959 he assumed command of 30 Signal Regiment and was later appointed an Officer of the Most Excellent Order of the British Empire, for what he called 'services rendered'. His move to the apprentices' school was not his first time in the training organisation as he had commanded the Technical Trades Squadron of 1st Training Regiment at Catterick during 1945.

His period of tenure was eight terms and it was a time of consolidation and preparation for the rebuild, rather than one of many startling changes, and in his farewell notes he reflected on his tour:

It would be wrong of me to think that there have been no changes; there have, and all for the better. Courses are more comprehensive and objective; teachers and instructors are of much higher quality, and so much is provided today for your extra-mural activities. All these changes have one aim which is to give you a thorough grounding as a soldier tradesman. During my eight terms I have … removed certain restrictions and I have looked to you to decide on your way of living in the school. The response is good and a model of what is required. Keep it up.

Having seen the start of the reconstruction of the school, I very much regret that I shall not see its completion. The new buildings will go a long way towards improving life here for you and your successors.

In conclusion let me say how proud I am of you and your predecessors … I wish you every success.

There were high expectations of the improvements that the modern build would bring to the way of life of everyone at the school. The facilities would put the school at the forefront of establishments of its kind. The main difficulty was the need to continue training, living, playing and sleeping at the same time that the old buildings were being demolished and the new ones were being erected. The Chief Instructor, Lieutenant Colonel PH Brown, was given the secondary appointment of Project Liaison Officer (PLO) with the aim of minimising the disruption that would be suffered. At the outset he reported:

…it appears that there was not enough money in the national kitty three years ago to make a start. … It is still hard to believe that a start has been made. Admittedly, the amount of mud about might well give rise to the fear that the whole area was being converted into a rather nasty 'Uniacke Pudding!'

… The School Headquarters is now rising from the mud at the north-east corner of the square. This will be a two-storey building housing all the present HQ personnel plus the RSM, the district youth liaison officer and the paymaster's staff. The Commandant will have a balcony on the top floor overlooking the square, and from this vantage point he will be able to keep a sharp eye on the future ninth-term cadre courses and military training. It should also be noted that the planners' objective of reducing unnecessary movement has been achieved. The distance from the Commandant's office to the guardroom next door is but a few yards!

The three churches will be built in one complex, standing in an extensive grassed space at the east end of the parade ground. They will share a terraced area on their western side, and in keeping with the trend towards unity, a number of facilities will be shared regardless of denomination.

The Junior Ranks' Club is of novel design, being completely circular. The kitchens and service bars form the hub, while the restaurants, taverns, games rooms etc., fill various segments of the circle. The NAAFI staff are accommodated upstairs above the hub.

Apprentices' living quarters will be in five blocks, in the form of a square 'S'. Barrack rooms are designed for eight men and will have all the usual modern amenities. The ground floor contains the offices and stores of the squadron living above them and also provides accommodation for the Quartermaster, the Medical Reception Station (MRS), the Dental Centre and miniature range.

The present kitchen and dining hall will be extended to serve all living-in PS and apprentices. It will undoubtedly be a bit of a crush, as the planned extensions will not be as capacious as we should like.

The new gymnasium and the swimming pool will be built beside the indoor arena (which is one of the original buildings in the camp) and this will become the main PT area ... and changing rooms ... and above this there will be two squash courts.

The trade and education block will rise in the area south-east of the parade ground, and will consist of four three-storey blocks joined by single-storey appendages. The general intention is that two blocks will be used by Technician Wing, one by Education Wing and one by Operator Group.

... 'NAAFI break' as such will disappear in that the apprentices' wants will be provided by vending machines.

The warrant officers' and sergeants' mess will be located in the area now being excavated near School HQ and the officers' mess will be rebuilt near its present site.

The mountains of rubble and mud being bulldozed around on the north-west edge of the running track will be converted into a spectators' terrace overlooking the athletics area.

This was how the PLO described the future school in April 1965.

The school developed into becoming an efficient communications teaching environment and this coincided with changes in the Royal Signals trade structure. It became necessary to rearrange the Signals Wing organisation and restructure the programme.

Under the revised organisation there were to be two distinct branches to trade training: operators and technicians. To achieve this, Basics Group changed allegiance and left Operator Group, under Captain P Wetherill R Signals, to continue training for the 245 trainees. The group was not immediately involved in the rebuild and was able to implement the changes in their programme in an orderly fashion. Mr AK Steel was the supervising instructor and Messrs Hill, Sladdin, Ring and Strange were members of staff who saw the changes through and remained for many more years. As a result of the rearrangement of staff, Major JW Roberts, who had been OIC A Wing, moved into the HQ and became OIC Tests and Evaluation Team.

The aim of the group was to classify apprentices at AIII level but many were able to graduate at AII. This required an operator to receive Morse at 22 words per minute with 99 per cent accuracy and type at 35 words per minute with 10 corrected errors.

Technician Wing, was an amalgamation of A and B Wings, less Operator Group. It was commanded initially by Captain PA Dally R Signals (later Brigadier) and then by Captain PF Larrington R Signals (later Lieutenant Colonel). It had three groups: basics, intermediate and equipment, each of which provided training of one year for the apprentices.

Captain F Smith R Signals, whose son was to follow in his footsteps as a Troop Commander at the college twenty-eight years later, commanded Basics Group. The group, as the name implies, was in the important position of transforming the new apprentices from schoolboys into tradesmen. Such a task had its many problems. In their first year the apprentices had to pass such barriers as the Army senior telephony test.

Intermediate Group, commanded by Captain BB Postelthwaite R Signals, was immediately affected by the rebuild and had to move to a block at the edge of the square. This was regarded by the 'second term-ites' as being rather too noisy and too close to the RSM. Another member of staff was Mr Peter Sharp who was a senior instructor and had considerable Signals experience. He had joined the corps in 1946 at Catterick as a boy and moved to Harrogate with the first intake of Royal Signals. He was the first graduate of the school to return as a member of staff when, as a corporal, he arrived in March 1954. He attained the rank of staff sergeant before he retired from the Army in February 1959 and remained on the civilian staff. He served at the college until its final year, having reached the appointment of senior instructional officer in 1969, and in so doing completed forty-nine years of association with the corps of which over forty-one were at Harrogate.

At this time a secure area was created and technicians were trained to maintain the BID 60 and 200 – later the BID 610 was also introduced. The D11 replaced the 53 Set and a new range of line equipment arrived, such as the CST 1+4 No.3.

The group set about teaching the integrated syllabus for second-year apprentices in two streams: radio and radio relay technicians: telegraph, line and electronic technicians.

Equipment Group, commanded by Captain RD Willingale R Signals, made the offer to those in their final year that, 'If you fail your trade test you can come back for another term!'

The main exercise to introduce apprentices to field conditions was *Exercise Petasus*. It was designed to bring out the concept of fixed command with brigades and divisions moving around it. HQs moved and changed several times and personnel alternated with those in the 'Commcen'. Typically there were detachments at Ripon and Gandale with a relay station on Sutton Bank; fine in summer but 'bracing' in winter.

The main aim of the group was to qualify apprentices as Class III tradesmen, but about a third of them reached Class II standard. A lot of emphasis was also placed on gaining City and Guilds, ONC and HNC qualifications.

The school continued to attract its share of high-ranking visitors and in this period the ecclesiastics were well represented. On 26 January 1964 the Bishop of Knaresbrough confirmed 13 ATs. On 18 March Rev. Canon AT Begbie, Chaplain General to the Australian Forces visited. This was followed three months later on 15 June when the Bishop of

The Reverend Pastor Bethual Tunga, Congolese Army, visits the church in Hildebrand Barracks on 5 November 1964. Left to right: Reverend Arnold Page; the Chaplain General, Northern Command; Reverend JR Lamb, the School Chaplain. This building eventually became the Bate Centre.

Maidstone the Right Rev. Stanley Betts, Bishop to the Forces, confirmed a further 14 ATs and five daughters of members of staff. The Venerable F Halliwell, Archdeacon of Bombay, followed on 28 June. Amidst the usual Harrogate gales of Bonfire Night, the Rev. Pastor Bethuel Tunga, Senior Protestant Chaplain to the Congolese National Army, graced the church with his presence. This high level of visits showed the importance attached to religious education.

Throughout the history of the school, the choir 'had its moments'! This was a period when the choir was a well-supported organisation with practices being held regularly up to three times each week. The choristers wore fine scarlet cassocks and often sang at functions outside the school, their favourite venue being Dr Barnados home at Hampsthwaite. The choirmaster, Mr J Platford, invigorated the singing fraternity and was assisted by Captain C Barron and ATs such as Cawthra, Ficke, Gosling, Rees and Tyres.

The final visitor of 1963 was the Secretary of State for War, the Right Honourable James Ramsden PC MC. A year later Mr Peter Kirk, the Permanent Under Secretary for War, followed. This underlined the political importance that was still being placed on the military training of British youth.

At the graduation parade on 15 April 1964 Sergeant J Roberts was the proud recipient of his British Empire Medal, in recognition of his outstand-

ing service in Aden. The Mayor of Harrogate made the presentation on behalf of Her Majesty the Queen. Just a year later at an Investiture at Buckingham Palace, Her Majesty presented the George Medal to Captain IP Crawford, the medical officer, which was for service in Borneo. And at the same ceremony the district youth liaison officer at the school, Major BP Pryer RA, received his insignia as a member of the Most Excellent Order of the British Empire.

The ATs were also making their own contribution to history. AT RSM Cornforth commanded the August 1964 graduation parade and wore Blues for the occasion. There were 64 ATs representing the school at the Festival of Remembrance at the Albert Hall in November 1964. The editor of the *Teacher's World* reported the following day:

Watching the Festival of Remembrance at the Albert Hall, I was most impressed by the display mounted by the Army apprentices. Clearly their instructors do a magnificent job in giving these lads dignity and bearing. How this is achieved I do not know, but I suspect that a firm framework of discipline and pride in the community and its traditions plays an important part. Certainly many schools have used these factors with great effect.

Undoubtedly one of the saddest events of this period was the death in 1965 of Her Royal Highness The Princess Royal, Colonel-in-Chief of The Royal Corps of Signals and Patron of the Association of Harrogate Apprentices. She had been a regular visitor and the school was preparing for a further visit with keen anticipation.

The development of character through leadership and adventurous training was now taking a more advanced role in the school curriculum. Five-day exercises were held on a regular basis at company level commencing as early as recruit term. Favoured sites were Littondale, Plover Hill, Pen-y-Ghent and Bishopdale as well as the well-known local sites of Ripon, Nidderdale, Skipton and Bishop Monkton. In the summer of 1964 three ATs were fortunate to be selected for the Army boys' expedition to Corsica. They were ATs John Jennings, Christopher Boys and Ronald Ferguson. Amongst other things they climbed the islands highest peak of 9000 feet and spent many arduous hours navigating their way around the rocky highlands on the trip of a lifetime.

In December 1965 Major Stackhouse took a party of 24 ATs skiing to Voss during which most of them passed their 'one-star' test. Among those who took advantage of the week's adventurous training were ATs Ginge Leach, Vis Smith, John Kemp and Malcolm Palmer.

Hobbies and sports were forever being increased in number, giving ATs a wide variety and selection of interest to pursue. In addition to all the normal sports the range of hobbies now included:

AT Lance Corporal Sherlock preparing to fly solo in a Granau glider in December 1965.

Brass Band – Capt GC Speight
Judo – Capt RS Mansfield, CSgt G Evison
Field Club – Mr PM Shilton
Pipes and Drums – Maj AM Stewart
Fencing – Capt Willingale, PMaj A Yule
Model Railway – Capt J Robinson
Corps of Drums – Maj PW Hewitson
Model Cars – Mr Gustard, DMaj G Hall
Go-karting – Maj JW Roberts
Choir – Mr J Platford
Angling – Maj HO Groves
Bird Watching – Maj C Worrin
Table Tennis – Lt F Turner
Archery – Mr J Primrose
Rifle Club – Maj Stackhouse, Mr L Butterworth
Cycling – Capt JO Fisher
Sailing – Lt Col GH White
Drama – Maj BP Connors
Mountaineering – Capt A Bushell
Gym – Capt DW Gent
Radio – Lt DA Bowden
Gliding – Capt B Postelthwaite
Pottery – Lt DW Fisher
Badminton – Capt C Barron

Canoeing – Capt D Braund
Squash – Maj JK Eltringham
Photography – Capt P Gilham
Jazz – Capt JO Fisher
Woodwork – Sqn Ldr RH Smith
Art – Capt DW Fisher
Tennis – Maj RN Eley

The school musicians continued to strengthen. AT Band Sergeant Oakley was the first to fill this new appointment and in 1965 AT Holt was the first glockenspielist. The brass section played at the 1964 Royal Tournament, Redcar Youth Week, the Northern Horse Show and Menwith Independence Day. Engagements were many and varied. Three ATs entered the Army junior music and drama competition; Haggarth and Davis on cornet and Papworth on euphonium. In 1965 the Pipes and Drums won their section of the Army Festival competition and AT Cpl Thomas won his individual section. The most spectacular of events was probably the Quadrangular Games when the bands of the schools came together. For the 1964 games, Drum Major Hall wrote two bugle marches: 'Quadrangular 1964' and 'The

Apprentice'. There were 245 musicians on parade at Arborfield.

There continued to be a full programme of sports to cater for all levels of participation. In athletics the performances of AT Fenge in the pole vault overshadowed all other performances. In 1964 he had become the national junior pole vault champion. By the time he graduated he had cleared 13 feet in the inter-services match which put him in the top ten in the UK. There were other good efforts with AT Rogers also competing in the inter-services at the shot. AT Leech represented the Army in the mile, AT Wells in the triple jump, AT Andrews in the long jump and AT Drew in the pole vault.

In the Army championships on 2–3 July 1964 at Aldershot the school won 20 medals. Junior victors included AT Lance Corporal Ness (440 yards) and AT Cpl Illman (long jump). Youth victors included AT Robinson (440 and 880 yards), and the relay team of ATs Cribb, Devitt, Illman and Borden.

The 1966 Victor Ludorum was AT Pawlak for his ability in the sprints and high jump. Army champions included AT Corporal Paterson (javelin), AT Lance Corporal Smith (pole vault), AT Lance Corporal Devitt (sprints), AT Turvey (880 yards) and ATs Stanley and Brookes (2000 metres steeplechase). The junior sprint relay team of ATs Smith, Paterson, Devitt and Turvey also represented the Army in the inter-services match and won. These were fruitful times for the school's athletes.

The most successful boxer was AT Corporal Wink who was also team captain. He was the Army junior champion at light middleweight. Boxing administration took a major step in 1966 when it was declared that henceforth all boxing should be voluntary. During this season the school had two Army champions: AT Corporal Morrison at featherweight and AT Corporal Cribb at light middleweight.

The Commandant was a keen hockey player which raised the profile of the sport somewhat. In 1964 there was a momentous victory when the school beat Welbeck IIIs by 5-0. The captain of the side was AT CSM Osuagwu and ATs Wilson, Rodgers, Gbadamosi and Tracy were all awarded colours.

The era produced some good cricket performances. The quadrangular competition was won in 1964 and 1966, and the Northern Command Trophy was secured in 1964 by beating 8 Signal Regiment. Although no centuries were recorded, AT Corporal Taylor scored a 97, AT Dring hit 73 and AT Robinson 72, all in the 1965 season. With the ball, AT Lance Corporal Franks was prominent with performances of 7 for 6 and 6 for 16. AT Gipson had 7 for 24. The captain of the team was AT Sergeant Balding who, along with many of the others, went on to represent the corps later in their careers. The memorable sporting occasion of 1967 was when AT Legg took four wickets with four balls against 11 Signal Regiment.

1964 was the best year thus far for the canoeists.

Rugby Army Cup 1965. Back row: *LCpl Slater, Ats Coombs, Taylor, Whitworth, Cripps, Clark, Jordan, Ewing, Owen. Sitting: ATs Smith, Arundel, Sergeant Holloway (coach), ATs Williams, Mason, Bailey, Lumgair, McPhee, James.*

Archery in 1965. ATs K Hawke, R Philpot, M Wilde, A Jones, J Stokoe and J Kingswell.

'The problem of storing the cups, tankards and medals is becoming acute.' On 27 June 1964, at Walton-on-Thames, the school became the first Army champions. Mr Harper and Sergeant Bell were the driving force but ATs Pawlow, Irving, Harrison, Storer, Davis, Wood and Firth exhibited excellent paddling. This success had a lasting effect and by 1966 ATs Cook, Sherman and Waters were all Army trialists.

The best performance at rugby was by Penney Squadron in 1965 when they became Army junior rugby champions by beating A Company from Chepstow 6-5. The team captain on this occasion was AT Lance Corporal Williams and Sergeant Holloway was the coach. In the following season Williams went on with ATs Morley and James to play at Army youth level.

The Cycling Club made steady progress under the keen guidance of Captain JO Fisher. By 1965 the school had one of only three sets of roller-racing equipment in the country and six new cycles were purchased, all thanks to a Nuffield trust grant. Events were held in Chepstow, Oswestry, Bordon, Portsmouth, Arborfield and beyond. AT Lance Corporal Crittenden was the Army junior best all-rounder and AT Walker was runner-up. AT McNeilly also represented the Army and a year later became the ten, fifteen10, 15 and twenty-five-mile champion.

The time had come when it was inappropriate for groups of soldiers to be readily recognised in town and the Commandant made some changes to dress regulations. Colonel Piddington later recalled:

Hitherto, the apprentices had to wear flannels and a blazer when they walked out of camp. It was clear that as soon as they were down the road they all nipped behind the hedge and changed into 'scruff-order'; this defeated the original aim. The reason for this was partly because they didn't like this form of dress, (which, incidentally they had to purchase themselves) and partly so that they could not be singled out by the local yobs. To cut out all of this I ordered that they were to be allowed out in plain clothes that were 'not extreme'. I was pleased with the outcome and so were the apprentices.

I also recall that we had very untidy sports teams at the Quadrangular Games. So for the first time the school *purchased enough smart tracksuits for all of our participating sportsmen. The teams were immaculate for the remainder of my tour.*

The controlling of the consumption of alcohol was always uppermost in my mind. To start with there was no Corporals' Club and no Senior Term Bar. This resulted in much secretive drinking. To overcome this I opened two bars in the old NAAFI building in Hildebrand and from then on there was much greater control. Everyone concerned became much more sensible about drinking and were pleased to have the privilege.

Such was the school as 1966 progressed and the time came for Colonel Piddington to hand over command to Colonel Eagle. Perhaps no greater accolade could be paid than a station was named after him on the model railway! It was unfortunate that there was no farewell parade as he had contracted a serious eye infection which incapacitated him. No doubt he took some satisfaction from knowing that his final graduation parade on 10 August 1966 was the only one ever to include a fly-past of Provost jet aircraft; even if he did see it with only one eye. The officers were able to dine him out during the next term and he also returned to be dined out by the warrant officers' and sergeants' mess in October. He assumed the appointment of Chief Signals Officer, 3rd Division.

End of Term Report
"I am very pleased with him as he has been away for three weeks".

9

CHANGE OF NAME

Colonel JW Eagle MBE – September 1966 to August 1969

Colonel JW Eagle MBE ERD assumed the appointment of Commandant on 1 September 1966. He was no stranger to the work of the training organisation because, during the period 1959 to 1961, he had commanded 5th Training Regiment, 25th Signal Regiment and 24th Signal Regiment. He was obviously very aware that the final steps in completing the rebuild might cause problems. In his introductory remarks he stated:

During the next year, whilst the rebuilding is completed, we shall undoubtedly have many additional problems to face and we must all continue to tackle our duties with patience, good humour and understanding.

People can be divided into two categories: those who find everything a problem, and those who find everything an opportunity. To the apprentices I would say, be one of the latter. Seize every opportunity you have with both hands, whilst you are at the college, to enjoy and make full use of all the facilities offered to you.

He arrived to find that it had been decided to rename the school to college for the start of the September term. Members of the school were enamoured by the prospect of a change of name but as the chief instructor remarked, 'What is in a name? It seems to us that how greatness is to be achieved is perhaps of less significance than that it is achieved. In simple terms, if college is what we are to be called, then a college is what we must care to be.' The other apprentices' schools were also renamed at the same time.

It was also decided to 'brighten up the magazine.' One aspect of this was to change the name of the magazine from *The Harrogate Apprentice* to *The Gate*, and to give it a new style cover. The renaming exercise involved seeking advice far and wide and this included a census of the apprentices. Eventually, the name selected was that by which the representative sportsmen were known. This prompted OC Technicians' Wing, Major PF Larrington, to record:

The Gate. *There's an evocative title; what a variety of pictures it conjures up in the mind. Think of a gate... Five-barred, rusty, creaking, holding up progress but capable, in certain critical positions, of receiving a radio programme. The edifice that guards Uniacke Barracks, lovingly constructed by the brickies of yesteryear. I wonder what happened to the gates? Perhaps the black-smiths were posted before the gates were hung – or hung before the gates – Oh dear!*

Over on the other side of the road we have a variety of gates of our own. Logic gates: 'and', 'or', 'nand', 'nor'. There is a breath of poetry in their very names. Then we have the invertor whose function is to change something into nothing. We have the inhibit gate. This will allow nothing to pass unless the signal 'open sesame' has been given.

The progress made in the rebuilding programme was the dominant feature in the early part of Colonel Eagle's tour. The scheduled date for completion was October 1967. *The Gate* of winter 1966 reported that, 'The lavish sporting facilities were well under way.

WO1 (RSM) BR Boak, Welsh Guards had a three-year tour as College RSM to complete twenty-five years' service in 1970.

These comprised twelve full-size pitches, three cricket squares and four tennis courts. The athletics track was to be refurbished and there was to be a range of indoor facilities.'

By the spring of 1967, further buildings that had been completed were the swimming pool, squash courts, gym, sports pavilion and boiler house. By the end of summer, a trade wing, another accommodation block, the officers' mess garages, the indoor sports arena and some minor services had also been completed. As a result of the changes that were taking place in Uniacke Barracks, the graduation parades of winter 1966 and Easter 1967 were held on the Hildebrand Square.

It was at this successful juncture that WO1 (Foreman of Signals) RFA Davies departed for Singapore on commissioning. He had been the assistant project liaison officer for four years.

On 5 June 1968 the Junior Ranks Club moved from Hildebrand to its new premises in Uniacke. The

The College Choir during the Dedication of St Christopher's Church of Scotland on 7 February 1968.

final event was a Hippie Party. It was arranged by Corporals JA Clarke, KE Hall and Lance Corporal Rivett. In the same term the new WRVS Club was also opened above the hobbies block, and Mrs BA Hopper set about giving the new club a homely feeling. The club in camp complemented the WRVS Club that the Harrogate Council had provided at 1 Park View in the town. The premises were opened on 7 March 1967 by GOC Yorkshire District, Major General RH Whitworth CBE DSO MA, in the presence of the Mayor and Mayoress. This became a well-used facility when the apprentices were visiting Harrogate.

In the summer of 1968 the building of the three distinctive churches was finally completed. This had not been without the notice of the local population and Colonel Eagle recalled:

I remember the trepidation of the local citizens when the three churches began to emerge. Their unusual shape and position convinced everyone that Penny Pot was being developed as a nuclear rocket launching site.

I received a number of cranky letters about it and did my best to dispel their fears, with little success I suspect. Oddly enough the fears seemed justified in late 1968 when we had the most tremendous and terrifying storm one afternoon. The sky became pitch black, except for the searing flashes of lightning, and there was a gale-force wind that lasted only about ten minutes. In this time half the college windows had gone, and all the newly laid gravel on the parade square had blown away and scoured some 100 private cars. Of course, the owners sought compensation. Meanwhile, many of the locals had taken to the streets of Harrogate and were convinced that one of our nuclears had gone off. There was considerable correspondence in the local rag.

The first church to be dedicated was St Christopher's Church for Church of Scotland, Methodist, Baptist

Hildebrand Barracks for Confirmation of 45 candidates by the Bishop of Knaresborough, the Right Reverend H Cruse, on 4 July 1967 with the College Padre, Reverend Curwen Rawlinson, on the left.

and Congregational apprentices. The ceremony took place on 7 February 1968 in an ecumenical service taken by the Deputy Chaplain General, the Rev. DH Whiteford QCH MA BD PhD CF. Lessons were read by apprentices, SSM Philip Rainer, Lance Corporal Maurice Farquhar and John Roberts. The key to the church was presented by Lieutenant KC Robinson RAEC.

On 29 July 1968, the Roman Catholic Church of Christ the King was dedicated. The ceremony was conducted by the Right Rev. Gerard W Tickle, Bishop-in-Ordinary to the Forces. The Officiating Chaplain to the college was Father P Loftus. A framed tablet bearing the following historical note was transferred from the old church to the new:

> The Church of Christ the King was built by the Catholic Women's League in 1940 to serve the military units in Hildebrand and Uniacke Barracks. Various units have occupied the camps since that date.

The ceremony was attended by about 100 Catholic apprentices, members of staff and their families. A silver ashtray was presented to Father Loftus who had been officiating at the college for over ten years. He moved to a large parish in Sheffield.

The Church of St Alban was dedicated by the Chaplain General, the Venerable Archdeacon JR Youens OBE MC QHC, on 29 September 1968. This terminated over seventeen years' use of the wooden building in Hildebrand. Many friends of the college and local dignitaries attended the ceremony.

The spring of 1967 saw the arrival of two units in the college. The first was the Technological Warfare Investigation Team. It comprised Major FW Furlonge-Lollemache and his small staff. The function of the team was to determine the principles of technological warfare and to insert the results into the electronics teaching in the services.

The second unit to be established was the Army Youth Selection Centre. It was commanded by Major WJ Perry, Royal Signals, who had a small staff of six. The centre was opened by the Director of Army Recruiting, Brigadier AJ Wilson CBE on 28 May 1968. It carried out centralised selection for the complete range of apprentice trades available in the Army. It was located in the accommodation block at the top end of the camp. Each candidate attended a two-day selection course for which the college facilities were ideal. Within its first two years the centre had processed 4000 applicants. It remained in the college until it was disbanded in 1983.

The winter term of 1968 also saw the start of the Potential Apprentices' Scheme which was the responsibility of Captain DA Robinson RAEC. The scheme's aim was to raise the standard, in a maximum of two terms, of potential apprentices (or PAs as they became known) whose academic standard was just below requirement. The first group comprised 47 PAs.

May 1967, an apprentice technician repairs a T100 teleprinter.

In 1967 training at the Junior Leaders' Regiment, Denbury ceased. Many of the junior leaders who had not completed training were transferred to Harrogate. This move commenced on 11 September 1967 and included some members of staff; Major Hunt became OC Penney Squadron. The initial transfer included 96 junior leaders who, in the rank of junior signalmen, commenced training as communication centre operators and radio operators. The first of these tradesmen to graduate did so on 7 August 1968 under command of AT RSM Galloway. On this occasion the prize for best of the 28 communication centre operators was awarded to Junior Corporal IA Barron and that for the 13 radio operators went to Junior Corporal Kerr.

The arrival of junior leaders coincided with changes in the structure for trade training. For telegraph operators the course at the college was reduced from three to two years. The technician trade structure in Royal Signals was overhauled completely. The outcome was that there was a reduc-

August 1968, a foreman of signals explains the cord circuit of a 40/160 manual switchboard.

An apprentice is using the new 'Morse code trainer'.

tion from six trades to three. These were radio, radio relay and terminal equipment technician. To accommodate these changes it was necessary to review the courses already being taught. All trades also had to cope with the change from 7BWD to T100 teleprinter. The T100 remained in service for over twenty-five years.

The thirst for sport continued unabated and to an increasingly high standard. Some of the most successful ventures were in soccer. The 1967–68 final in the Apprentices' Challenge Cup was between the two college teams of Scott and Phillips. The full-time result was a thrilling 5-5 draw in which AT Parkhill scored a hat-trick for Scott. After a period of extra time, AT Licence scored the winning goal for Scott, and Lieutenant General Sir Anthony Reid, Chairman of the Army Football Association presented the cup and medals. During this period of football dominance ATs Parkhill, Heneghan and Harkin all played for the Corps team.

Rugby was not far behind football in quality. Penney had reached the Youth Challenge Cup final of 1967–68 and the permanent staff won the Northern Command Cup. AT Sergeant James was captain of Army junior rugby and ATs Sergeant Bailes, Corporal Bretherick and Lance Corporal Christie were all awarded their junior colours.

Boxing was as strong as ever and fiercely competitive. The team was undefeated against Carlisle, Arborfield, Bramcote and Ampleforth. ATs Potter and Dargan were individual Army junior champions. Mr Roy Cooper coached the cross-country team to win the Yorkshire Services League. Outstanding performers included ATs Campbell, Turvey and Sergeant Escott. Fencing was introduced in 1966 and, by 1968, AT Graham had become Army junior champion by winning all but one of his 25 contests. AT Nevill was the 1968 Army junior swimming champion for the 440 yards and was also awarded his Army senior colours.

The college team were 1967–68 Army junior basketball champions. AT Kelly was captain of the team that defeated Troon by 54-47, and went on to beat Junior Leader Regiment RE in the final. In judo ATs Lambe, Firth and Barkas all reached 6th Kyu. ATs Cook and Sherman were Army canoeists.

Games and hobbies continued to flourish. The Gliding Club was active at RAF Dishforth and in ATs Gay and Ware, the college had the youngest qualified glider pilots in the country at the age of only fifteen. AT Johnson received the silver cup for the most outstanding pilot at Dishforth and ATs Taylor, Todhunter, Dunne and Kirk were all soloists. The Mountaineering Club, under Captain F Smith, completed the Three Peaks in less than seven hours. The drama performances included *Reluctant Heroes*, the Brian Rix farce, and *Journey's End*.

The enthusiasm to maintain standards in the bands was typified by an advert in Part 1 Orders for a glockenspielist, 'Wanted, anyone who can play, or would like to learn to play, half a piano on a stick!' The demands for the services of the bands increased in 1967 and they performed at the Civic Sunday Parade, Butlin's Holiday Camp, Catterick, Bulford, US Base Menwith, Knaresborough and the Stray in Harrogate. For these occasions the principals were AT Band Sergeant Hughes, AT Sergeant (bugle major) Coulam and AT (lead drummer) Corporal Chesterman. The reward for many musicians came with a trip to Luchon, which is twinned with Harrogate. A year later in 1968, AT Urquhart was the individual piping section winner at the Army Junior Music and Drama Festival in London. The Pipe Band also won their section.

Adventurous training and expeditions remained popular. AT Drake joined the Army boys' expedition to the Dolomites in 1968 and AT Williams sailed around the Irish Sea with the Sail Training Association. In December 1967, Major Wilson took a party of 16 skiing in Norway. Other events included the Nijmegen Marches, sailing on the Norfolk Broads, Ten Tors and pony trekking in County Durham.

The tour of Colonel Eagle witnessed the most visible changes that had taken place in the history of Penny Pot Camps. At the same time there had been changes to the trade structure of the corps and in the structure of the apprenticeship. He departed from

AT RSM Bailes received the Army Commander's Prize for All-round Excellence on 9 December 1969 from Lieutenant General Sir Cecil Blacker.

Colonel JW Eagle and the Chief Instructor, Lieutenant Colonel M Scott, leaving the college on retirement.

the college to retire and his departing message in *The Gate* included:

The past three years at the college have been amongst the happiest of my thirty years' service... The rebuilding of the college, happily almost complete, has given us one of the finest technical colleges of its kind in the country.

There have been many changes in the college during these three years and undoubtedly there will be more to come ... be prepared... The winds of change, like the Penny Pot breezes, never stop.

How perceptive he was. The officer nominated to succeed Colonel Eagle was Colonel Clinch but he was not able to assume command immediately and there was an 'interregnum' from July 1969 to February 1970 when the Chief Instructor, Lieutenant Colonel Desmond Barry was at the helm. This occurred shortly after he had arrived at the college on promotion. In 1993 he reflected:

I must confess that I thought it was pretty good progress in peacetime to go from major to acting colonel in five months. For me it was a thoroughly enjoyable and eventful time and I have some vivid memories.

We were the first college to be inspected by the Donaldson Committee who were investigating all aspects of junior training in the Army. The DAT followed by the SOinC spent days with us in addition to the usual visits of headmasters and careers masters from schools.

AT RSM Davie with the Champion Squadron Trophy – Summer 1969.

I managed to acquire a new 105ft tower, ex 'Commcan', and with the assistance of Menwith Hill riggers it was erected beside the Amateur Radio Club in the old barracks. The following term I managed to get another one which was sited beside the Technician Training Wing thus enabling the college to maintain comms with those on exercises.

I instigated a study into reorganising the way we handled the new intakes and how best to deal with the training of non technicians – operating trades – but left the final decision to trades to await the arrival of Colonel Johnny Clinch, who had by then been selected to be the Commandant.

There were some other matters I remember very well and, in no particular order, they were:

The first young officer to ask my permission to live out of mess! The military salary had arrived.

At the winter term officers' mess meeting we agreed to sell the billiard table to the CO of Menwith Hill who wanted it to take back to the USA. With the proceeds we turned the billiard room into a snug bar which encouraged the married families to make more use of the mess in the evenings which, I believe, made the mess more lively for the single officers.

During the Christmas holiday a very long period of very heavy rain on the moor to the west of the college produced a torrent of water into the college which flooded all the heating ducts and most calorific rooms. The central boilers also became useless and, with no guarantee that there would be any heating in the college at the beginning of the spring term, steps were taken to prepare over 800 telegrams advising the ATs not to return. In the end they were not sent but it was a very close call.

Without doubt my greatest concern was the very poor standard of food provided by contract catering which failed to give the apprentice the quality, quantity and variety he needed and deserved. We were the only junior training unit not to have the ACC on establishment to provide this most vital aspect of morale and until the ACC replaced the contract caterers the problem of poor catering was our biggest worry.

It was a very great privilege to have been 'Commandant' and it was with regret that I handed over to Colonel Clinch.

Personnel Selection Officer
"Look, you just aren't cut out for the Army. If you really want catering you should try Civvy Street".
Apprentice
"OK then, can you tell me where Civvy Street is?"

10

MAKING BEST USE OF THE NEW FACILITIES

Colonel JC Clinch – February 1970 to December 1971

The new decade saw Uniacke Barracks with a new look and new buildings that were approaching completion. It also had a new Commandant because, after a short period in which Lieutenant Colonel Desmond Barry, Royal Signals, the Chief Instructor, held the reins, Colonel Johnny Clinch was welcomed on 5 February 1970. He arrived directly from 4 Signal Group in Germany, but before then he had served as Chief Signals Officer, Malaya and Commanding Officer of 17 Gurkha Signals Regiment. He recalled his arrival:

The grounds were being landscaped and things were beginning to take shape. The three pyramid-shaped churches stood out on the splendid Yorkshire landscape. I thought it was a pity that they had not joined together as the word in 1970 was 'ecumenical' and we could have got the whole college under one roof.

Shortly after arriving I looked out of my office window and saw a New Zealand type geyser spurting hot water from the central heating system, and it rose about 40 feet into the air. The contractor had laid the pipes directly into the ground and they had rusted. The complete system from the boiler house to every building had to be dug up and re-laid in ducts. We were back to thick mud again but on completion we also had a network of pathways around the college.

One of the first major changes to be made was to reorganise on the basis of five trade-affiliated squadrons. Penney and Phillips were technicians, and Rawson and Scott were A Trades. A further squadron was established for B Trades. This was named Bradley Squadron after Major General Peter Bradley CB CBE DSO, who was to be Master of Signals. The squadron motif, a cross, was part of his family crest as was the motto, 'Go to it'. Recruits were trained in the squadrons. Under the new organisation the college trained radio technicians, radio relay technicians, terminal equipment technicians, telegraph operators and radio operators.

To provide the educational support for these trades the Education Wing was divided into Operator Education, commanded by Major DA Robinson RAEC, and Technician Education, commanded by Major GW Davies RAEC. Many of the apprentices studied for GCE O-level, A-level, City and Guilds and ONC qualifications.

There was a further significant change for the good of the apprentices when the Commandant was able to announce that the catering had been taken over from the contractor by the Army Catering Corps:

It was clear to me that the contract caterers were not the most popular team. The contract was due for renewal so I decided to ask the ACC if they would take over. This resulted in a Parliamentary Question but with the support of General Sir Anthony Read, who was Quartermaster General and Colonel Commandant of the ACC, I managed to get it through. It was agreed, by all concerned, that we had never had it so good, and when I announced the change in the college theatre on graduation day the roof nearly flew off!

Colonel JC Clinch

Our Achilles' heel then was the college dining room which was a converted MT shed and for some reason had not been included in the rebuild. In no way did it match the culinary delights of the ACC. I was told that there was no more money and nothing could be done. However, there is more than one way to skin a cat and within a few months a rebuilt diner was opened by General Sir William Jackson, GOC Northern Command.

The rebuild of the college was accompanied by a new quarter for the Commandant who until then had resided at 25 Leadhall Lane in the vicinity of the Harrogate County Cricket Ground.

On 29 May 1970 I moved into my new quarter. The red brick stood out on the green landscape like a sore thumb and it leaked like a sieve. Major Fred Pavey, the QM, informed me that we had to give it a name so we held a competition. I cannot reprint all the suggestions but I settled on 'Penny Pot House' because of the local connection. Fred did not like this at all because he thought it had lavatorial connections that the apprentices would latch on to straightaway!

Perhaps Colonel Clinch's most remembered introduction into the college occurred after his departure and concerned a Shetland pony:

On my departure I discussed the possibility of a mascot for the college with Colonel Norman Butler, my successor. My next job included responsibility for the ACE High station in the Shetlands. On one of my visits there I met up with Major Leslie Prescott, the 242 Signal Squadron Commander, and together with the Lord Lieutenant, Mr Bruce, we selected a suitable Shetland pony. The transport was arranged by Leslie and the pony, together with a WRAC handler, just fitted in the back of a Land Rover. They arrived in the college safe and well and although the real name of the pony was 'Banner of Mousa', Norman Butler insisted in renaming it 'Colonel Johnny' after me. The first handler and keeper was Sergeant Lavery. To my knowledge the pony did well in the college and only once bit the Reviewing Officer on the bottom.

Other people's recollections of 'Colonel Johnny's' behaviour were not quite so complimentary. He was often referred to by senior officers of the corps, or reviewing officers, as 'possessing similar behavioural traits to the officer who presented him'. WO1 (RSM) AW Cunningham was responsible for ceremonial matters:

The pony arrived shortly before Christmas with very little time to be trained for any of the forthcoming events. However, he settled down very quickly and it was decided that he would be on the graduation parade. His performance was a great success and his most dignified performance influenced the next decision. To allow him to parade with the college band at their performance for the sergeants' mess Christmas Ball in the gymnasium.

Unfortunately this performance was not so successful and certainly was not dignified. In the confined area of the gym the first strike on the bass drum must have sounded like a clap of thunder to Colonel Johnny whose nervous system reacted with another 'clap' from his rear end. This resulted in a large 'covering' of a good area of the dance floor. This was much to the amusement of all, except the QMSI PT who was PMC!

AT SR Easter of Intake 76B, who later returned to the college as a sergeant instructor in 1991, recalls:

I well remember the continual promotion and demotion of Colonel Johnny. When I first met him he was an AT sergeant but by the end of my first pass-off parade he had been demoted to AT lance corporal for leaving 'little piles' on the square during rehearsals. He was then promoted again next term for making it through a complete set of graduation rehearsals without any little accidents. This up and down motion continued until I graduated and I think that by then he had made it to AT sergeant again for my parade.

Captain Lee Tilson R Signals (later Lieutenant Colonel) was 2IC of a Squadron in April 1974 when Her Royal Highness Princess Margaret reviewed the graduation parade:

I was a member of the college staff that went to the airport to meet the royal party. The cavalcade comprised a number of limousines and I was in the second one in which the equerry and a lady-in-waiting were travelling. Our silence was broken during the journey to the college when the cavalry officer glanced over the military-like brief that he was engaged in and asked, 'Tell me, Captain Tilson, is your mascot at the college a pony or a donkey?' Following my explanation and a short history of the animal he paused then turned purposefully to the lady-in-waiting and stuttered, 'That's me in the poop, I told her it was a donkey!'

Colonel Johnny lived a life of comparative luxury at the college. He graced graduation parades until 30 September 1987 when his handler, Corporal Glen Bedford, took him to a peaceful and contented retirement in Catterick.

There were also several other important occurrences during Colonel Clinch's tour of duty. The sub-aqua and free-fall parachute clubs were instigated to develop further the availability of pursuits for the ATs. On 18 March 1971 General Sir Geoffrey Baker, CGS, visited the college and he opened the 'Jimmy Club' for permanent staff of corporal and below. Colonel Clinch also accepted the silver polo trophy from Alderman S Hitchen, the Mayor of Harrogate. This is a replica of the Pump Rooms and was placed on loan to the officers' mess to represent the bond between college and town; it was displayed on all formal occasions.

Much to the joy of the whole college, the new 'military salary' was introduced in the summer of 1970 resulting in some significant pay rises.

The newly commissioned sports facilities brought increased determination to the college teams, none more so than in basketball and squash.

Colonel Clinch receives a silver model of the Harrogate Pump Rooms from the Mayor.

In 1971 the Pipes and Drums visited Luchon, which is twinned with Harrogate, at the request of the council.

By the spring of 1970 the college basketball team were the Army junior basketball champions under the trained eye of Captain Potts RAEC. ATs Anderson, Hughes and Jackson represented the Army juniors. The team retained the trophy a year later at Aldershot when they beat Dover by 62-61. In the same year ATs Anderson, Pritchard, Jackson and Tedby played for the Army.

Ability in the swimming pool was being nurtured by Captain Horsfall. By 1971 six members of the swimming team, ATs Marriott, Corporal Green, Lance Corporal Hodgson, Harland, Norfield and Wilson were selected for the Army junior team. AT Hodgson also represented the corps.

At squash the apprentices became the 1970 Army junior champions by beating the RAOC 3-2 and AT Burtin was the individual Army champion. The college were also Northern Command champions. AT Dean was the Northern Command soldiers' champion. Apprentice Sinclair made local news headlines when he beat Lieutenant General Blacker by 3-0 in the semi-final match. A year later AT Sergeant Sinclair became the Army junior champion when he beat AT Sommerville in the final. The college team beat Chepstow 5-0 to retain the junior award.

Badminton was also able to flourish in the gymnasium complex. A new recruit to the management team was Mr R Cooper who took on the job that he held for over twenty years. AT Corporal Sinclair, having reached the finals of the corps championship, was selected to play for the corps. AT Sergeant Sinclair and AT Wilson also contested the final of the 1971 Command championships and the college provided all of the junior doubles finalists.

Although the rugby team lost to Oswestry by 18-12 in the 1970 Army final they produced ATs Elkam, Gittoes, Thomas and Naylor who played for the Army juniors.

At hockey Major Edwards coached the apprentices to their highest standard to date. They reached the final of the Army Junior Cup for the first time and they beat the ACC by 5-0.

In the more individual sports, AT Rackham represented the Army at tennis and AT Lance Corporal Graham fenced for them at senior level. For the first time orienteering was taken up as a major sport with Major Templeman-Evans as OIC.

The cycling team continued to have success under the guidance of Captain (Retired) Green (whose second retirement was twenty-four years later!). In 1970, the senior team won the Army Inter-Unit Challenge Trophy (the Fraser Cup) by over 1000 points. ATs Watt and Muriel were two of only six competitors to complete the 100-mile race. They were supported by AT Arnold to ensure victory. In all, the team won seven major events. A year later the seniors were again successful and medals were won by AT SSM Hickling, AT Watt, Lance Corporal Muriel and Lieutenant Slorick. As such the senior team were in the unique position of holding three Army senior championship cups.

The cricket team had become dominant in the Command with their third successive successful Command finals. The Commandant presented plaques to Major Robinson, WO2 CSM Linford, Sergeant Barritt and AT Sergeant Bracey who appeared in all three finals.

Scott Squadron, ably lead by AT Sergeant Colville, carried the college colours in football when they won the 1970 Apprentices' Cup by beating C Company, Arborfield by 3-1. AT Corporal Pritchard was a fine goalkeeper who also played for the Army junior team. By the end of the 1970–71 season the college apprentices had maintained a six-year unbeaten record against all other boys' units.

Colonel Clinch departed, on promotion, in December 1971 after a tour of nearly two years. In his final remarks in *The Gate* he stated:

Together you and I have achieved much. The re-organisation of the training syllabus has gone well and the new system of recruit intake has been most successful.

The rebuild is now about complete and the new Weapon Training Wing will be complete in the spring.

Our dining hall must be the best in the country...

Our relationship with the Harrogate people has never been better and on 5 June 1972 the college will receive the Freedom of Harrogate. This is the crowning glory of twenty-five years of friendship...

He departed from the college in a sailing boat but changed his mode of transport before getting to Aldershot.

Colonel Clinch departs from the college by dinghy in December 1971.

Maths Lecturer
"Now, watch the blackboard and I'll go through it".

II

'COLONEL JOHNNY' IS ON ROYAL PARADE

Colonel NA Butler – December 1971 to March 1974

Colonel NA Butler arrived from Germany in December 1971 to assume the Commandant's appointment. His tour of duty was enlightened by three major formal events: two royal visits and the Freedom of Harrogate. He was further privileged by being the first Commandant to take care of the college mascot 'Colonel Johnny' or 'CJ' as he became known. He recalls:

The Shetland pony duly arrived in about March 1972. His accommodation was an immediate problem. This was solved by the DOE who quickly designed and built an emergency generator shed that looked amazingly like a stable. We were also fortunate to have Sergeant Paddy Lavery, an ex-jockey and stable lad, who managed the animal.

CJ was driven by spectacular sexual urges which were visibly obvious and often acutely embarrassing. This was especially the case during the two royal visits. He could smell a mare from miles away and his first parade rehearsals ended in chaos and some injury to his handler. He shot off the square dragging Lavery with him despite shouts of, 'Stand still that donkey!' from the RSM.

The first Royal visit to the college, since it had been renamed and rebuilt, took place on the Graduation Parade of 13 April 1972, which coincidentally was the Commandant's birthday. It was also the Silver Jubilee year of the college. The occasion was graced with the presence of Her Royal Highness, the

Duchess of Kent. The Commandant recollects:

The day was an enormous success thanks to the very warming presence of the Duchess. Excellent arrangements were made by the college but the preparations were fraught because of the Command arrangements and feuding between my two superior headquarters in Catterick and York. Eventually we resolved the differences.

A magical memory for me was when I looked out from my balcony just half an hour before Her Royal Highness was due to land at Leeds/Bradford Airport and I spotted the Padre, Robin Laird. The light was dim and the rain was torrential; it was a typical Harrogate spring day! I screamed abuse at him and enquired what he was doing about the weather. He simply pointed to the sky, where a tiny dot of blue appeared overhead. By the time the Royal cavalcade arrived there was not a cloud to be seen. I never again doubted the value of the connections of the Chaplain General's Department.

The parade was commanded by Apprentice RSM Turnbull, and Her Royal Highness presented Long Service and Good Conduct Medals to WOII DD Abercrombie, WOII AB Cooper and Staff Sergeant PM Charles.

There was a further royal occasion that involved the college in the spring term of 1972. On Maundy Thursday apprentices lined the streets of York for the Queen's visit.

On 5 June 1972, at precisely 1630 hours, 12 Jet Provosts from RAF Leeming flew over Harrogate to celebrate the granting of the Freedom of Harrogate to the college, in its silver jubilee year, by the council. The Mayor, Councillor FA Rotherham, presented the Freedom Scroll to Colonel Butler. The salute was taken by the Colonel Commandant, Major General Sir John Anderson KBE. Many past commandants and RSMs were present but, unfortunately, Colonel Carne could not attend as he was not fit enough to travel. He wrote an apology to the Commandant who retained the letter as one of the treasures of his tour.

During early 1972 the Government introduced the Raising of the School Leaving Age (ROSLA). This had considerable effects on recruiting youths into the Army as they were no longer eligible to attest until they were fifteen years and nine months. The

Her Royal Highness, the Duchess of Kent, presents the Champions' Cup on Graduation Day – 13 April 1972.

Lieutenant General Jackson inspects the parade on 15 December 1972.

Commandant put forth arguments against ROSLA but unfortunately he was trying to convince Mrs Margaret Thatcher; he failed!

As a result of ROSLA the apprenticeship was reduced to a two-year course. The college staff had to rewrite the course programmes and prepare for all the consequences of the changes. Recruiting remained good but the overall numbers in the college declined, mainly because of the shorter course.

One unforeseen result was the sharp fall in the number of juniors. This led to the move of the juniors from Catterick to Harrogate which went very smoothly with the initial group of 24 Junior Signalmen joining Bradley Squadron in the summer of 1972. Later intakes were spread amongst all the squadrons. The first group departed from the college in the summer of 1974 and returned to Catterick for trade training.

During this period of college history there was a considerable number of trophies and artefacts presented for various reasons. On 7 November 1971 Paul Samuel Genge, formerly an AT Sgt in Rawson Squadron, was killed whilst serving in Northern Ireland. Paul's first love was the Army, and some of his happiest moments had been spent at the college. In his memory a trophy, to be known as the Genge Cup, was presented by his parents. At their request the cup

was designated as the Inter-Squadron PT Trophy. The trophy was presented annually until the college closed.

On 25 May 1972 Apprentice Neil Cass, of Phillips Squadron, was tragically killed in a road traffic accident. Neil was an AT technician, a member of the choir and a very popular member of the squadron. A cup was purchased with money subscribed by members of the sSquadron and inscribed, 'Presented by his friends in Phillips Squadron'. It was presented each term to the apprentice who had shown the greatest improvement during the term.

On 15 July 1973, at a service in St Alban's Church, the Leeds Branch of the Royal Signals Association laid up a 'Book of Remembrance'. It contained the names of Royal Signals personnel who fell in the Second World War. A memorial stand, made from carved oak by Squadron Leader Harry Smith, was also dedicated to contain the book.

In 1972 Corporal Alan Greville Perkin was killed in a road traffic accident whilst serving with 3 Division Signal Regiment at Bulford. Alan trained at the college, in Penney Squadron, as a terminal equipment technician from April 1968 to December 1971. In December 1973 his parents presented a silver cup in memory of the happy times that he had whilst under training. Their second son also trained at the college from January 1973 until December 1975 as a data telegraphist. His son, Junior Leader Martin Perkin, is pictured in *The Gate* of Winter 1991, holding the Perkin Trophy as a proud member of the winning team of the assault course event on 23 October 1991.

Two new trophies were presented at graduation prize-giving ceremonies in 1974. The Wessex Trophy, an elegant silver rose bowl, was donated by the Bristol Branch of the Royal Signals Association. It was to be awarded to the best all-round apprentice from the West Country. The Community Service Shield was presented by Major Bob Edwards on his retirement after forty-six years' service with Royal Signals. The shield was carved in wood by Squadron Leader Harry Smith and was to be awarded to the person making the biggest contribution towards service in the community. Both trophies were still being awarded in 1995.

The excellent sporting facilities in the college were now bearing fruit. Teams were training hard under the guidance of many expert permanent staff and a very keen sportsman in the Commandant who later recalled:

The college was exceptionally strong at sport during my time winning many trophies and dominating the triangular events. The basketball, swimming, hockey, rugby and cricket were all outstanding. The PS distinguished themselves by reaching the final of the Army Minor Unit Football Cup twice in a row; they won it on the first occasion in 1972.

I especially remember the college cricket team winning the Yorkshire Under 17 Cup in 1973. I had entertained the New Zealand tourist team to a Sunday luncheon at the officers' mess on rest day of the Test Match and then persuaded them to come to St George's Road to see the match. When we arrived the college had been dismissed, by Knaresborough, for only 53 (Marshall 21) and the opposition were 35 for 1 with 10 overs remaining.

Colonel Norman Butler with the college hockey team of 1973 who were Army Junior Cup winners.

In an incredible finish, the college won by one run taking four wickets (three run out) in the last over. The Kiwi skipper, Glen Turner, who was as excited as we were, presented the Arthur Barrett Cup to AT K Evans and the Man of the Match award to AT Jordan with 5 for 29.

The ROSLA soon started to make outside junior civilian teams much stronger. Fortunately, the standards in the college had also improved and the teams were able to hold their own. The fuel crisis of 1974 had the adverse effect of preventing distant travel to away matches.

The college basketball team of 1972 performed creditably and were only narrowly defeated in the final of the Army Minor Unit's Cup. For the apprentices ATs Rudd and Evans played at Army level. The rugby squad provided ATs Williams, Birch, Vincent and Gilder for the Army. Likewise the swimming team provided ATs Sanford, Harland, Quick and Langford. The last three all swam for the Royal Signals at senior level.

The new squash courts were reaping rich rewards. In 1972 the Army junior championship was retained by ATs London, White, Holcombe, Bolt and Hardie. In 1973, AT Everest became the Army Under 19 individual champion. Not to be outdone, the college team beat 8 Signal Regiment 3-2 in the District Cup, in which Lt Col Tripp, Cpl Barker and AT Everest won their matches.

In 1972, AT SSM Graham was an Army fencing champion and AT K Jones was the Army and Inter-Services Under 20 Sabre champion.

In 1972, the athletics team won the inter-college competition for the first time in nine years. The spearheads of the team were AT Goodchild (100 and 200 metres), AT Bibby (triple jump) and AT Moore (800 metres) all of whom were Army individual champions. A year later AT Sgt Hall, the team captain, became the junior Army record holder at 200 and 400 metres. He also won the long jump and was a member of the 4 x 100 relay team who retained it for the fourth consecutive year.

In December 1973 ATs John Fisher and Alan Gill watch AT Nigel Manwell cut his birthday cake which was baked by the college chefs and was adorned by 'Jimmy' – on loan!

'Colonel Johnny' and Sergeant Paddy Lavery meet Her Royal Highness Princess Margaret at the graduation parade on 11 April 1974. AT RSM Jim Wakenshaw is the parade Commander.

Colonel Norman Butler departs from the sergeants' mess by camel on his way to Iran.

The 1973 hockey team provided five Army Under 22 players in ATs Wilson, Reece, Delaney, Reynolds and Quinn. It is no wonder that in the Army junior final they beat the RAOC by 10-0. Brigadier Clinch was there to lend his support.

The cricket team showed great promise under the captaincy of AT Knight. They took on, but were defeated by, the Commandant's team of Pioneers, who were mainly minor counties players. They were successful in winning the triangular competition with AT Knight scoring 39 and 44, Riley taking 5 for 38 and Birch taking 3 for 39.

This era also saw the best performances from the cross-country running team. The 1974 season saw them participating in over 50 races. The team won the Army junior unit final, the North-East/North-West/Scotland Senior Championship, and the triangular competition. ATs Staynings, Wakenshaw and Robinson represented the Army juniors against Wales. Club Captain AT Moore won the college championship. So successful was the season, that a special function was held at the Joiners' Arms in Hampsthwaite, at which the Commandant presented the trophies for the season.

The second royal visit to the college during Colonel Butler's term of office occurred at the graduation parade on 11 April 1974. Her Royal Highness, The Princess Margaret, Countess of Snowdon, graciously consented to review the parade and present the prizes. In bitterly cold weather Apprentice RSM J Wakenshaw

commanded an excellent parade and also collected four prizes. By this time CJ was deemed to be experienced enough to cope with a royal occasion.

Needless to say CJ did not behave, although he was moderately good whilst he was being presented to the Princess. The parade was held on the penultimate day before Colonel Butler departed to an appointment at the Iranian Army Apprentices' Training College. Appropriately he left the sergeants' mess on the back of a man-made camel. He could not have had a more fitting end to his tour or a more fitting final event. Twenty years after this day he reflected:

The second royal visit was also at the time of my birthday. These were two incredible coincidences. This time the arrangements with my superiors were much smoother and all went well.

But the things one remembers most from Harrogate days are firstly, the feelings of doing something worthwhile as one watched the splendid young men develop from some often tatty looking clay; secondly, the buildings and soggy ground at Penny Pot; and thirdly, the extraordinary and frequently ferocious weather. The worst part of the latter was undoubtedly the wind. Sometimes it was absolutely impossible to converse in Penny Pot House above the howling gale. I particularly remember the dress rehearsal for the first royal visit when, with one gust of wind, every single hat on parade, and there were over 750, except that of the RSM, blew off simultaneously and scattered in every direction; not a sight I could ever forget!

From an essay
"My friend's father is the mare of his local town".

12

MORE SPORT AND EXERCISES

Colonel WG Neilson – April 1974 to October 1975

Colonel Neilson arrived in April 1974 and was no stranger to training young people because, as a major, he had commanded the Signals Wing at the Royal Military Academy, Sandhurst. He came to Harrogate at a time of comparative stability. The lowering of the school leaving age had brought about shorter courses at the college, the new buildings were now fully operational and the complete range of sports facilities was in use. In his foreword in *The Gate* Colonel Neilson wrote:

Lastly, you will meet many differing people during your chosen career in the Army but you will always have one person with you all the time – yourself. You are made up of three things: the body, the mind and the spirit. Keep your body healthy and active; your mind alert and flexible and your spirit held high in loyalty, determination for success and of course courage. You have tremendous opportunities open to you; make sure you don't let them pass you by.

Colonel WG Neilson

The summer graduation parade of 1974 saw the Signal Officer-in-Chief (Army), Major General Sawers, present his prize to AT SJ Churchman. 175 apprentices graduated and 28 junior signalmen moved on to Catterick for trade training. This was followed by the visit of Major General Farrar-Hockley in December at the parade for a further 89 apprentices and 46 junior signalmen. The largest of the parades during Colonel Neilson's tour was on 31 July 1995 when 372 apprentices graduated under command of AT RSM S Baldwin. They left with terse advice from the Commandant, 'Don't switch off now.'

Many of the non-sporting extra-mural activities continued to flourish. They were a means of developing the interests of apprentices beyond the opportunities they had had previously. The Scientific Society had a programme of talks and visits that included the Science Museum, Tomorrow's World Exhibition and Jodrell Bank. The college Theatre Group remained very active with events almost every term. These ranged from straight plays like *The Peaceful Inn* by Dennis Ogden to *Quartet, Four One-Act Plays*.

Despite problems caused by the raising of the school leaving age, the bands were able to cope admirably with reduced numbers. BSM Singleton, Pipe Major Cross and Drum Major Baudy retained standards with, '...practice five nights a week and Wednesday and Saturday!' The SOinC(A) commended Bugle Major Fullwood's performance on the Quarter Guard.

Community service remained prominent and was based on squadron efforts. Bradley Squadron painted the home of Miss Butterwick who was a local elderly spinster. They also assisted in the WRVS shop in Harrogate. Phillips Squadron helped at the Ian Tetley Home and donated £300. Rawson Squadron gave stalwart assistance in the Pensioners' Home in Spofforth, and Scott Squadron gave help to aged people in town.

The OC of Training Wing was Major Dennis RRE. There was a series of exercises to train and test the military skills of the apprentices and junior signalmen. They included *Ex Ballista*, *Crossbow, Longbow, Fledgeling* and *Tiercel*. Otterburn featured as a prominent training area but Thetford and Catterick were also used.

There remained many opportunities for adventurous and overseas training. AT SSM Hickman, AT Lance Corporal Bain and AT Townsend went on *Ex Gleam Caribbean* in St Lucia. This was an HF exercise, with 30 Signal Regiment, operating C11s and D13s. In February 1975 Captain Charles Kemp took four apprentices to the mountains of Kenya on *Ex Avast*. They were ATs McEwan, Hughes, Davey and Murray, and during their time in Kenya they reached the peaks of Mounts Lenena, Nelion and Batian. Elsewhere over 80 people went skiing in Scotland and the sailors took the Nicholson '55' to Cherbourg.

The new sporting facilities were being used extensively except when the harsh weather prevented it. The basis of sporting competition was the Champion Squadron Trophy which ensured that all matches were keenly contested.

Under the guidance of Captain (Retired) Alan Green the cyclists continued to provide many Army champions. AT Bowers broke the Army junior '25' record by being the first person to break one hour. The college also won the Frazer Trophy at senior level.

The college Padre, Reverend PL Dodd CF, with the choir in St Alban's Church in June 1975.

Major General G de E Collin presents the Commandant's Prize to AT RSM Steve Baldwin – 31 July 1975.

At swimming AT Fred Steel was undoubtedly the talent of the time. Corporal Bell reported, 'AT "Flipper" Steel is a swimmer of some repute. Regrettably he also suffers from an inability to march, shoot, run or do anything in a reasonable military fashion. But we forgive our aquatic mascot!' The passage went on to list his many successes including his selection for the Combined Services tour of Germany. Based on his ability and the hard training of SI Dave Cherriman, the team won the triangular competition, the Army junior team event and provided 11 members of the Inter-Services junior team.

The new cricket pitches encouraged vast amounts of cricket to be played. The 1974 team won the triangular competition with AT Frape scoring 61 against Arborfield and AT Capper taking four for nine. There were matches in the Army cups, Harrogate Junior League, Arthur Barrett Cup, Harrogate Evening League and the Atkinson Cup. ATs Evans, Marshall, Cadywould, Jordan, Gunn, Capper, Frape, Ladbroke and Laurie went on to be awarded college colours.

The 1974 fencing team was very strong and was based on the PS of Captain Simmonds, Lance Corporal Goodacre, WO2 CSM Maltess and SSgt Pritchard. A year later the staff combined with special apprentice talent to produce the best season to date. They won both the Junior and Senior Inter-Unit Cups which had

never been achieved by a single unit. The three outstanding apprentices were AT Lance Corporal Tony Byrne, AT Dave Horne and AT Lance Corporal Peter Martin.

The 1974 athletics team won the triangular competition and in the Army individual championships they secured 19 medals, 10 more than any other unit. This resulted in 18 ATs being selected for the Army Under 20s against Wales. AT RSM S Hall was the pick of the team and went on to earn Combined Services colours for sprinting. In the outstanding performance of the season, the relay team, of AT Potter, AT RSM Hall, AT Sergeant Spink and AT Corporal Ypey lowered the Army record for the 4 x 100 relay.

For the fourth consecutive year the cross-country team remained unbeaten against Arborfield and Chepstow. The team had a number of stalwarts who were about to graduate, including ΛTs Jeff Warburn and Jim Richardson who between them had run 119 times. AT Sergeant John Boyes was the outstanding U18 captain and ATs Edon, McGiveron, Patterson and Little were all awarded colours. The successful season ended with the departure of the coach Sergeant Mick Gue.

The rugby team managed to win the triangular event for the first time for twelve years even though they battled out a 7-7 draw with Arborfield thanks to a highly individual try by AT RSM Jock Clark. AT Corporal Tepielow was responsible for kicking all the goals in both matches. AT Sergeant Steve Green played for the Yorkshire Colts and the coaching staff included the Combined Services player Sergeant Jock Cairns.

In March 1975 the Army Youth Selection Centre, with its 24 members of staff, registered its 25,000th candidate and continued to provide good quality recruits for the junior Army. Well before the recruiting year was finished the vacancies for junior entry into the Army were all taken. This reflected the healthy state of the junior Army.

Unfortunately for the college, in October 1975, the Commandant decided to retire early from the Army. He decided to join the Iranian Telephone Company who were expanding their business:

The college has gone from strength to strength during the eighteen months I have been here – not through anything magical I have been able to do but by a lot of hard work by apprentices in the various teams and of course the dedication of the officers in charge of the various sports...

Finally may I remind you of my regular warning that you only get out life what you put into it – put all you've got into whatever you are doing either at trade or on the sports field.

From an essay
"David Livingston founded the Niagra Falls".

13

SILVER JUBILEE

Colonel F Ramsbottom — October 1975 to June 1978

Colonel Freddie Ramsbottom arrived at the college in October 1975. He was a well-travelled officer and had served in West Africa, Sierra Leone, Hong Kong, Singapore, Germany and SHAPE. He came directly from OIC Royal Signals Manning and Records Office at Reading. He was no stranger to training young men because from 1955 to 1957 he was the Signals Representative at the Mons Officer Cadet School, Aldershot. He embarked on what was to be nearly three years as Commandant.

In a tour of three years it was inevitable that a diverse range of events would occur. One of the most memorable was the Silver Jubilee celebrations of 1977. The college's main contributions to these events were lining the route and marshalling the crowds at the Great Yorkshire Show and the Leeds United Football ground at Elland Road. In the latter the bands performed, with Colonel Johnny leading, to a capacity crowd, including Her Majesty the

Mr Robert Brown, MP, Reviewing Officer for the graduation, inspects the parade on 18 December 1975.

Queen and His Royal Highness the Duke of Edinburgh. The college gymnasts also performed an arena display. The Commandant, Lieutenant Colonel Pavey, WO2 Howells, Staff Sergeant Devlin, Corporal McNeil and Major Furse (AYSC) were all awarded Her Majesty the Queen's Jubilee Medal.

There was also the firemen's strike during the winter of 1977 when the Green Goddesses and their military units were based in the college. ATs were called out from time to time in order to make the crews complete.

There were nine graduation parades during the three years and whilst every one was important in its own way there were some noteworthy occurrences. On 8 April 1976 Major General PAM Tighe MBE was the Reviewing Officer. He was no stranger to the college as his previous appointment had been Commander of the Training Brigade. In his speech he remarked that, 'Colonel Johnny's behaviour had improved considerably since his recent "adjustment". In fact he now behaves better than his namesake!' For the parade on 12 August 1976 two members of the Bristol Branch of the Royal Signals Association travelled to present AT Sgt Anthony Rock with the Wessex Trophy for the best all-round AT from the West Country.

The Reviewing Officer on 16 December 1976 was Major General WT Macfarlane, who was Adjutant of the college (then school) from 1950–52. The parade was also attended by his RSM of the time, RSM Stan Lonsborough. This was the first graduation parade on which identical twins were Stick Orderlies. They were ATs James and Michael Boyle who were both promoted on the same day in February 1996 to the rank of Warrant Officer Class 1. The parade on 14 April 1977 was memorable because the Reviewing Officer invited Mr AC Johns, the father of AT RSM Steve Johns, to accompany them during the inspection. On 11 August 1977 an ex-apprentice, Major General Baldwin, was the Reviewing Officer. He had joined at the age of fifteen and was commissioned into Royal Signals in 1947.

Many college members reached significant milestones in their careers. Lt (Retd) Fred Cooper RN, who was an instructional officer in Telegraphist Wing made his 'final' retirement after devoting forty-

Colonel Ramsbottom makes a retirement presentation to Mr David (Jock) Tyrie for devoted service.

four years to military service; the last fourteen being at the college. The end of the summer term 1976 signalled the retirement of Major (Retd) David (Jock) Tyrie, Royal Signals. He had devoted virtually all of his serving life to the corps, having transferred from the RA in 1935 and remained in the corps until 1949. He arrived at Harrogate soon after his retirement. During his tour at the college his wife Jean had also worked in the MRS. For twenty-six years' loyal service the Commandant presented him with a silver coffee service.

May 1977 saw the departure of Squadron Leader Harry Smith after fourteen years' service to the college. He was a member of the maths department and also taught woodwork. He was a great enthusiast and was responsible for many items around the college such as the prayer-book holders and Remembrance Book cabinet in the church. A careful inspection would find his initials and date of manufacture carved on the back of the items.

Lieutenant Colonel Leif Welton, Royal Signals departed to Colchester in the spring of 1976 and the chief instructor post was assumed by Lieutenant Colonel Ralph Plant, Royal Signals. In the same term Lieutenant Colonel John Macfie RAEC took over from Lieutenant Colonel Horner who moved to the Resettlement Centre in Catterick. With these moves there was a completely new team in college HQ.

December 1975 witnessed the closure of the WRVS Room in Harrogate. At the graduation parade on 18 December the Commandant presented to Mrs Marjorie Cawood WRVS a silver-plated galleried tray. Meanwhile the WRVS newcomer at the college was Mrs Marie Auge de Rancourt. She replaced Miss Cummings after one year. At the same time the post of matron changed hands and Major Phyllis Broad QARANC moved into the MRS. She was an officer of vast experience who had served in Benghazi, Terendak, Singapore, Dhekelia, Iserlohn, Rinteln, Hong Kong and Tripoli.

The Commandant also served with three college RSMs: WO1s Forrest, Richardson and Connor. The latter returned to the college in the 1990s on the family housing and welfare staff.

The organisation within the college had not changed significantly in recent years. There were still five squadrons and on arrival recruits were assigned to Recruit Troops within the squadrons. Squadron commanders' appointments were still All Arms and not yet confined to Royal Signals.

The college ATs continued to carry out considerable charity work. In May 1975 members of Bradley Squadron held their second charity run in aid of the Ian Tetley Barnado Home in Hampsthwaite. In twenty-four hours a total of 236 miles were covered by Captain Kemp, Staff Sergeant Escott, Corporal Dalby, Lance Corporal Major and ATs Copland, Boyes, Garratt, O'Sullivan, Palfreyman, Edon, Anderson, McGiveron and Sparham. They beat their previous effort by 20 miles and raised £300 which was presented at the college summer fête. In November 1976, Rawson Squadron raised a further £54 for the same cause. The aim was to complete a section of the Lyke Wake Walk from Osmotherly to Ravenscar. The proceeds were presented at the school's Christmas party. Other charities also benefited handsomely. The Youth Club raised £80 by taking part in an organised shoot. ATs Simons, Lock, Thompson, Richardson and Holland, under the supervision of Captain Mahoney and Mrs Radcliffe, the club organiser, made presentations to the Harrogate Society for Mentally Handicapped Children and St Aiden's School Band.

The college was never short of visitors and Bradley Squadron had a special visitor on 17 March 1976 when Major General PEM Bradley CB CBE DSO, Master of Signals, visited his squadron, who were also the Champion Squadron. He inspected a very smart Quarter Guard, the Squadron Lines and visited the trade and military training wings. He was presented with a framed photograph of the Champion Squadron.

There was also a nostalgic visit on 28 October 1976 by Brigadier NC Butler, Commander of the Training Brigade, and erstwhile the Commandant. He had returned from Iran and was making his initial visit to the college in his new appointment.

Much of this was part of AT Jim Dryburgh's daily life and in the mid-1990s he recalled some of it from his Glasgow office as a major in the Manning and Career Management Division (which was AG11 and PB11 in years gone by):

At 0930 hrs on Friday, 9 May 1975, I sat in the assembly hall of Dunoon Grammar School and proceeded to work through the Scottish Certificate of Education Geography O-level examination. Twenty-four hours later I was on my hands and knees in a barrack room in Phillips Squadron applying wax polish to the already gleaming floor. So was to begin the most rewarding twenty-seven

AT Jim Dryburgh and AT Dave Stewart.

switch from left to right orientation without warning and the student would need his wits about him if he was to avoid the thwack from his free weapon which was the punishment for a bad guard position. It paid dividends; our team won many civilian competitions in all three weapons categories and we won the Army junior six-man team, the senior three-man team, countless individual titles and the inter-services junior six-man team competition in my time. This was fabulous grounding for me; I obtained the North Yorkshire under-18 foil title in 1976 and went on in 1979 to captain a three-man épée team from the Royal Military Academy, Sandhurst at St Cyr where we beat the French at their own game!

My other great memory of the college was being entered in 1976 as a competitor in the Harrogate Junior Chamber of Commerce Public Speaking Championship. This was an event open to all schools in the area and sponsored by R Ackrill Newspapers. I was coached for the competition by a man for whom I had great respect, 'Clem' Clements. Clem was a Burnham lecturer who also ran college hockey.

For a month Clem prepared me in the delivery of my script; non-verbal communication, which I had also written. To many people's surprise, not least the local education authority, we took on the schools of Harrogate and came first. The following year both Nigel Buckeridge and I entered; I came second and he took third place! With the help of Clem we had put the college on the educational map and I was spotted as having potential as a commissioning candidate.

months of my adolescent years. In that time I developed as a young man, found myself capable of things which would hitherto not even have been considered and was introduced to a wide range of experiences which have laid the foundations for many of my present interests and pursuits.

I was sixteen years old and until that point had been a schoolboy; all of a sudden, in my naive perception, I was a man and earning a wage. A wage ... in those days my wage went straight to 'credits', compulsory saving, and every Thursday I was paid £3 which was to cover washing and shaving kit and the all essential NAAFI break. Of course if you had a special requirement, Mum's birthday, then you could apply for extra money, in writing, a week in advance.

Harrogate had everything; I added three more O-levels to my existing six certificates and pursued my interest in the Pipe Band which I had brought with me from my school in Argyll. In fact under the careful coaching of the permanent staff Drum Major Lew Bandy PWO, I eventually became drum major of the college Pipe Band and later senior drum major of the combined college bands.

I had been a fencer at school and was delighted to find a thriving club at the college. The central character in this organisation was CSM Brian Matless Grenadier Guards, who was also coincidentally my squadron sergeant major. CSM Matless was a larger-than-life character who was ambidextrous. His coaching sessions were interesting in that he would fence with a weapon in each hand. He would

Apprentice Whitehead (right) is studying for his ONC qualification in December 1975.

I was not a great tradesman and I caused the odd headache for people like OC Tech Wing Major George Harrison and the TOTs Captains Cliff Webb and Tom Stoddart. It was with some irony then that eleven years later I was to sit on the Training Group Royal Signals review of technician training, as a G3 staff officer, with both Major Webb and Lieutenant Colonel Stoddart. It was in no small way due to the tenacity and perseverance of both of these officers that I had managed to scrape through all of the barrier tests and eventually graduate as a terminal equipment technician. By the time I was a staff officer in Training Group both my trade roster and my old apprentice qquadron had become part of history.

My great love was the 'green' side of life; combats, field deployment and section battle drills. This after all is what most sixteen-year-old boys join for. I was however talent spotted by the then Commandant, Colonel Freddie Ramsbottom, and it was he in the main who encouraged me through to the RCB and my eventual commissioning in April 1979. He was my guest at the commissioning parade along with my parents and I was most proud to have lived up to his faith in my abilities.

The Army Apprentices' College, Harrogate, has always been rightly recognised as the breeding ground of the supervisory ranks in the corps both in trade and at RD but I wonder how many people would be aware of the number of regular commissioned officers the college has produced. In my time alone at Sandhurst were Steve Johns (AT RSM), Rob McCallum (AT SSM), Steve Davies (AT RSM), Pat Reehal (AT sergeant) and of course myself AT sergeant and drum major. Harrogate was a wonderful place to grow up and to experience a wide variety of life's aspects. The best compliment I can pay the college is that I would not change my time were I given it again!

There were many opportunities for ATs to travel. In July 1976 ATs McInnes and Howie spent nearly three weeks on *Exercise Errant Knight* in Antigua. This was an HF radio exercise on the Caribbean island with 30 Signal Regiment and 38 Group RAF. Less dramatic but more challenging was *Exercise Summer Eagle* that won the Earl Wavell Adventure Training travel award for AT Lance Corporal Smith. He planned an exercise to Ailsa Craig which is an uninhabited island 10 miles west of Girvan in Scotland. His party comprised ATs Welham and Hill.

Exercise Pacific Spring was a task with a difference. In the spring of 1977 ATs Shield, Hugill, Leighton and Jones were dropped at Dulles Airport, Washington with only $50. Their aim was to make their way across America and join up with the main party in the Cascade Mountains of Washington State. Major Noonan, Captain Cornforth and ATs Roberts, Reader, Forse, Easter Tate and Henry were well into their skiing lessons by the time they arrived.

Not all exercises were so exotic or so adventurous. *Exercise Basic Touch* was held in York in the spring of 1978 and was the first time that most of the recruits in Phillips Squadron had slept under canvas. 'Those of us who thought it would be easier to sleep fully clothed to combat the extreme cold soon discovered that this was a bad decision. We had to get

The 1500 metre race for the Triangular Games of July 1975 between the College, Arborfield and Chepstow.

dressed in PT kit for morning "bumps and jerks",' reported AT RL Stanley.

Exercise Skye Train commenced on 17 April 1978. Captain Cornforth, Captain Isherwood and ATs Arthur, Gill, Titheridge, Hudson, McGonagle and Turner set out to tackle the Cuillen of Skye – the longest ridge in the UK. The challenge turned out to be too great and a combination of weather and dangerous climbs thwarted the team; but that was not before they had all tasted adventure and fear!

Sport and extra-mural activities thrived at the college. In one of his opening addresses the Commandant remarked that there were over 50 activities open to ATs. Boxing was resurrected and this coincided with similar revivals at the other colleges. So, in the winter of 1975 the inter-squadron boxing tournament was held for the first time since 1964. It proved a resounding success and brought the customary exciting atmosphere to the arena. The event was won by Bradley Squadron. Sergeant Constantine went on to train the college team to victory over Arborfield but could not avoid narrow defeat by Chepstow who nevertheless could not field boxers in three of the weights. Full colours were awarded to ATs Breen, Whiteford, Wilson, Oatley, Richards and Rose.

On 30 April 1976, five members of staff and 45 ATs made up the athletics team that set out to tour Germany. The main event of the tour was a match against the 7th Signal Regiment team which the regiment won by 113 points to 86. The outstanding performer from the college was AT Colin Marsden who did the double in the long and triple jumps. ATs Spence and East were successful in the discus and high hurdles respectively. For some members of the team this was their first time abroad and they were all grateful for Lieutenant Colonel M Topple's staff for making the arrangements. The tour prepared the team for better things because it went on to win the Army Junior Bowl, the inter-unit championship and the Triangular Games. 1977 was not quite so successful but there were many excellent individual performances. The club captain, AT Gerry Wilson, won the Army junior 110m and 400m hurdles gold medals and broke the 400m hurdles record. The 800m relay team knocked three seconds off the Army junior record and AT O'Hara broke the high jump record three times. AT Killen was Army junior champion in the shot. The Boyle twins performed well in the distance events being ably coached by Major David Elliott, RAEC.

Winter term was always a period of intensive activity for the canoe club and 1975 was no exception. Sergeant White, the National C1 white-water champion, had a major influence in college training methods. There were creditable performances from ATs Marsden, Pritchard and Sanders who were Army junior champions. AT Pritchard also won the junior slalom event. Captain Cornforth and Sergeant White were awarded their Army canoeing colours. In 1976 the college had considerable success. Captain

Army Minor Units Cup winners 1976–77. Back row: *WO1 Mays, Captain Rolf, Sgt McManus, Sgt Lambert, Cpl Bettson, Cpl Smith, Cpl Wood, Sgt Campbell, the Commandant.* Front row: *Sgt Mills, Sgt Ponton, Sgt Burgess (captain), Cpl McKenzie, LBdr Morrison.*

Army Junior Inter-unit Cross-country champions 1976. Back row: *Major DA Elliott, ATs Lance Corporal S Little, P McGiveron, Sergeant C Edon, R Rogers, Sergeant MT Gue.* Front row: *ATs B Hair, Sergeant J Boyes (Team Captain), Lance Corporal K Patterson, PA Cooper.*

AT Sergeant John Hunt and WO2 (SSM) Tony Curnow in the final of the Army roller championship in 1977.

Cornforth, Segeant White and SI Jamieson were selected for the Army slalom team, and ATs Marsden, Pritchard and Sanders retained their title. In 1977 the three members of staff were joined by ATs Alan Hogg and Ago Bayliss for awards of Army colours.

In 1976 the college provided three corps hockey players in ATs Bywater, Woods and Lathbury. The latter also played for the Army and Combined Services Under 22 team. A year after leaving the college he was in the full Army squad. The 1977 squad went on to win the Army Junior championship for only the second time. The final was against the RAOC ATs and with only seven minutes to go the team was 1-0 down. It took a splendid effort by the captain AT Keith Roach, with two goals, to rescue the cup from the jaws of defeat. A year later the college retained the Army junior championship. The competition started with an 11-0 victory over the RAOC of which AT Mark Hardy contributed eight!

The rugby team under Major PE Thomas RAEC had a period of honest endeavour without recording any great success. There were individual successes with AT Thwaites being awarded Combined Services colours, ATs Galbraith and Waites playing for Army juniors, AT Green playing for Yorkshire and Sergeant Beard playing for the corps. The team reached the final of the NE District Cup. But as this was for the eleventh consecutive season it did not seem very significant. The team lost to 8 Signal Regiment in the final but the try of the match was by AT RSM Clark who ran out of his own 22 to score a memorable touchdown.

The 1976 football team beat both Arborfield and Chepstow for the first time in many years. AT Rock was appointed captain of the Army youth team and ATs Pickersgill, Johnson, Morris, Edwards and Dyer were all squad members. AT Rock was also AFA (Youth) player of the year. At this time the college team coach was Staff Sergeant (F of S) Peter Smurthwaite. Some sixteen years later these two came together in the rank of major and were responsible for running the corps team. The major AT success of 1977 was in beating both of the other colleges. The PS side, managed by WO1 John Mays, won the Army Minor Unit Cup. Otherwise, it was a narrow miss for Phillips Squadron who lost in the final of the Apprentices' Challenge Cup, and for Bradley who lost in the final of the Junior Challenge Trophy. ATs Gauchi and Abbott were awarded Army youth colours.

The Army Junior Cricket Cup, first won in 1975, stayed in the college for another year. After a number of exciting matches the final was played at the Officers' Club, Aldershot, against JLR RE. The sappers scored 80 and AT Whelam took 5 for 31. The college top scorer was AT Goodhand with 33. The triangular fixtures were probably unique in that the match against Chepstow was a tie so the trophy was shared. Notable performances were AT Johns 5 for 29

Colonel and Mrs Ramsbottom are pulled out of the college by 'Colonel Johnny' in the middle of a snowstorm.

against Chepstow, and AT Groves 8 for 20 against Arborfield. AT Foster scored 29 and 25.

The college fencers, now rechristened Salle Uniacke, continued to perform well in all competitions. There was double success against the colleges in 1976 and the team prizes were taken at junior and senior level in the inter-unit competition of Zone B. A year later AT Jim Dryburgh was Yorkshire Under-20 foil champion and AT Bob Smith was Under-18 épée champion.

Colonel Ramsbottom's final graduation parade was on 13 April 1978 when the Reviewing Officer was Major General AAG Anderson, the Signal Officer-in-Chief (Army). He commended AT RSM Chris Skelton for his 'polished and self-confident performance'. The Mayor, Councillor WR Mather, presented the Borough of Harrogate Essay prize. The BBC radio reporter covering the event reported that there was a horizontal snowstorm sweeping across Penny Pot. Despite such awful weather conditions the Commandant insisted that the parade should be held outdoors. Colonel Ramsbottom remarked in his final *Gate* magazine foreword that:

I am very sad to be leaving the college at the end of this spring term. However, I can think of no better place from which to retire after some thirty years in Royal Signals. The Army Apprentices' College, Harrogate, is indeed a very special place and it has not only given me great pleasure to have served here, but I count it a great honour to have been Commandant.

Mess Secretary (the day before the Officers' Mess Summer Ball)
"Sir, the marquee has just arrived".
Major who shall remain nameless
"Good, invite him in for lunch".

14

A ROYAL VISIT AND CUT DOWN ON WASTAGE

Colonel MU Ryan – June 1978 to April 1981

In June 1978 Colonel Oulton Ryan took over as Commandant. He was born in Wokingham in 1929 and educated at Cranleigh School and the Royal Military Academy, Sandhurst. He joined the Rifle Brigade in 1947 and was commissioned into Royal Signals in 1949. He had served in Malaya, Cyprus (three times), France, Jordan and Germany and he had completed tours of duty with the Royal Marine Commando Force, the Parachute Brigade, the Royal Military Academy, Sandhurst and the School of Infantry. In his opening speech at the college he remarked that he had embarked on a military career to achieve three objectives. First, to serve with the Parachute Brigade. Second, to be an Instructor at Sandhurst. Third, to be Commandant at Harrogate. As such, this tour made his military career complete. In 1993 Colonel Ryan reflected on his days at Harrogate:

Penny Pot House 1978 and our arrival at the Apprentice's College. Weather? Raining of course. For me, a return after nineteen years when in the fifties I was seeking volunteers for the Parachute Squadron and succeeded only in recruiting one bored permanent staff NCO, one Lance Corporal Frost, later Captain Frost. That one visit ensured that perhaps one day, in the distant future, I might have the proud distinction of commanding the college.

On my return from Cyprus my visit to the Signal Officer-in-Chief remains clear in my mind for the simple reason that his words were brief and to the point, 'Enjoy yourself and cut down on the wastage.' This was a true challenge and as my wife and I walked around the sports pitches on the following day I realised how important it was to retain and develop this wonderful pool of talent from the youth of the country.

I would like to think that the ideas flowed in the immediate days that followed. Nothing could be further from the truth, but I had a superb team to help and advise me. Lieutenant Colonel Ralph Plant was my Chief Instructor, Lieutenant Colonel (later Brigadier) Tom Sherry RAEC was my Senior Educational Officer and WO1 Sammy Connor (later Captain) was a superb RSM. Our sole responsibility was to look after 800 little monsters aged sixteen to eighteen who were up to every trick in the book. A staggering number, some 65 per cent, were from broken homes, or equally sad, totally uncaring parents. It

is hardly surprising that a large percentage were low achievers with few GCEs. Many of them would go on to gain national diplomas, City and Guilds and even A-levels. But how were we to ensure that they did not walk out of the college, never to return?

After a few months we reached several conclusions. Firstly and foremost, the 'soft option' was quite obviously not the right path. These youngsters did not join for a soft life. Secondly, they loved the outdoor life of sport, adventurous training and exercises. Thirdly, the hardest problem of all to resolve was how to educate them without developing a total hatred for the classroom. Equally, we had to remember that for twenty-four hours a day, seven days a week we were not merely in loco parentis; we were in many cases their first real parents, albeit adopted.

The Guards are on parade! WO1 (RSM) Richardson and WO1 (RSM) Connor in August 1978.

*The staff, both civil and military, responded magnifi-
cently. The programmes and courses were revised and implemented gradually. We doubled the intensity of physical
training and not a single military person was left out of the
party. When the youngsters climbed, we climbed, when they
ran, we ran – in my case with my beloved dog, Judy, the most
eager participant of all. Our reward came two years later
when the wastage rate had dropped from an average of 18 per
cent to only 9 per cent, the lowest in the Army.*

The summer of 1978 also saw in the new RSM, WO1
T (Sammy) Connor, Irish Guards. He was no
stranger to the training environment as he had
served for four years as an instructor at the Guards'
Depot and two years with the infantry junior leaders
as CSM. He had served in New York, Kenya,
Germany and Hong Kong. His length of tour coincided almost exactly with that of the Commandant.
Sammy returned to the college years later in the
capacity of Estate Warden which he carried out until
the college closed.

As for all commandants, the graduation
parades held a number of surprises. The weather
also played its part in providing concern on a number of occasions. On 11 April 1979, Major General
PEM Bradley returned as the Reviewing Officer for
the third time. On this occasion the Mayor,
Councillor Angela Matthews, presented the Borough
of Harrogate prizes to ATs DP Williams and DT
Nelson. For the parade on the 9 August 1979 *The Gate*
reported, 'Anything less like a summer graduation

day would be hard to imagine. It was pelting with
rain as AT RSM Andrew Marjoribanks forded the
rivers with great aplomb.' On this occasion 108 ATs
graduated.

At the parade on the 12 December 1979, the
Reviewing Officer was Major General John Akehurst
CBE, GOC 4th Division, and it was encouragement to
those present that he and the Commandant had
enlisted together as private soldiers. The day of 10
April 1980 broke with tradition and, 'The weather
was kind, the sun shone, the parade sparkled with all
its customary verve.'

Colonel Ryan, in reflecting on his tour of duty,
remarked that:
*The highlight of my tour at the college had to be the visit of
our Colonel-in-Chief, Her Royal Highness The Princess
Royal. The tone of the day was set by RSM Sammy
Connor who, when asked by Her Royal Highness whether
they had met before, made the classic remark, 'I used to
salute you in your pram, Ma'am.' Apart from the number
of permanent staff and their wives HRH met, she spoke to
some 80 to 100 apprentices personally and many more saw
her at close quarters all under the eye of the cameras and
harsh lights. Many of them would star, in due course, in
the film 'A Day in the Life of a Princess'.*

The 'royal' day of 10 March 1981 started in true
Yorkshire fashion. The royal helicopter was diverted
to RAF Leeming and the wet-weather programme
was running. From Leeming the Princess was driven
to the college. The day comprised a full programme

Major General Sturge inspecting the parade.

Above and below: *Major General Ward-Booth inspects the graduation arade on 14 December 1978. At RSM P Cahill, the parade Commander, looks on. Chin straps are fitted to combat the bitter but familiar 'Penny Pot' wind.*

Major General Baker inspects the apprentices on the graduation parade, 7 August 1980.

Major General Baker talks to AT RSM Bingam, the Commander of the graduation parade on 7 August 1980.

The Colonel-in-Chief pays her first visit to the college on 10 March 1981. AT Sergeant Gill in conversation whilst Lieutenant Colonel Stoddart and Mr Shrimpton look on.

with visits to many of the educational, trade and military training departments. Sergeant John Hatch had the honour of being presented with his Long Service and Good Conduct medal before lunch. The afternoon included visits to the Community Centre, Cubs, Brownies, hobbies and the Jimmy Club. Finally, the Princess was driven behind the College Band to the officers' mess and the road was lined with every member of the college. To commemorate the occasion *The Gate* was published with its first photograph on the front cover. It depicted AT Sergeant Gill in conversation with the Colonel in Chief in Electronics Wing; Major Tom Stoddart and Mr Shrimpton were looking on.

Apprentices tuning D11 radios.

THE COLLEGE ORGANISATION FOR THE NEW DECADE

As the new decade was under way it is appropriate to review the organisation of the college that existed as a result of the changes of the 1970s. The charter was to train up to 825 male ATs – 255 technicians, 510 telegraphist and 60 telecommunications mechanics. The average annual intake was 425 ATs; 25 in January, 100 in June and 300 in September. Age entry was between sixteen and seventeen.

Keyboard skills on the T100 teleprinter, c.1978.

The Squadrons
There were five squadrons – HQ, Bradley, Penney, Rawson and Scott. HQ provided only administrative support. Phillips Squadron ceased in 1978.

Military Training Wing
Responsible for drill, weapon training, fieldcraft, external leadership and adventurous training. On average at least two complete weeks were spent in the field each term.

Military Training Wing staff 1981. Back Row: *Sgts Hardy, Hanlon, Eady, Prinn, Gregory, Blood.* Front Row: *Sgt Cox, WO2 Wilson, Capt R Adamson R Signals, Major LN Barron WFR, Lt CW Lockwood R Signals, WO2 Gue, SSgt Allen.*

Electronics Wing
Taught technicians and telecommunications mechanics the principles of telecommunications and the various equipment used by Royal Signals.

Telegraphist Wing
Taught telegraphists their duties and manipulative skills including message handling, voice procedure and Morse code. Practical skills were gained with Tactical Exercise Troop.

Education Wing
Provided instruction in science, mathematics, English and general studies to support trade training.

Technician ATs
The course for every one was common for four terms. At this stage selection was made for radio, radio relay and terminal equipment technician. The 'continuous assessment' method of monitoring was adopted and the courses were accepted by the Technical Education Council (TEC) for the award of their certificate.

Telegraphist ATs
Radio and special telegraphists followed a two-year course and data telegraphists completed their course in four terms. All telegraphists took the City and Guilds 777 Communication Operator's Certificate. Special telegraphists were selected from the radio

telegraphists in term three and followed a more intensive course.

Telecommunications Mechanic ATs

The mechanics graduated after four terms and then attended a driving and plant operating course. They were taught to construct, maintain and repair lead and plastic-sheathed multi-core cable routes. In addition they had to build and maintain telephone systems.

Hobbies and Sports

The college offered 53 hobbies and sports. This included the College Band and Pipes and Drums which numbered about 65 members.

Many members of the permanent staff reached significant milestones. Geoff Handley retired early in 1977 after twelve years service to the college. At the same time Jack Tyler received his Imperial Service Medal from the Commandant. The summer of 1979 also brought Imperial Service Medals to Mr Alec Henderson and Mr Jack Cowan. The latter served the college until its closure. After retirement he remained to operate the carbon arc projector in the cinema and by doing so he brought much pleasure to the college for many years.

It was a memorable day on 14 September 1979 when Lieutenant Colonel Stan Pavey and his brother Major Fred Pavey visited the sergeants' mess to bid a final farewell. Stan, and Fred before him, had occupied the QM's hot seat since 1970. They presented jointly a superb dining chair, which was for the exclusive use of the RSM.

In August 1979 the Commandant said farewell to Mr Les Strange; one of the longest serving civilians of his era. Les had joined the Somerset Light Infantry in 1935. He served in India for the next seven years without break. He then returned to the UK and transferred to the corps. He went on to serve in *Operation Overlord*, HQ BAOR Bad Oeyenhausen, the Berlin Airlift, Catterick and finally Harrogate until 1959. As such he had served the nation for forty-four years. His retirement party resulted in a photograph of Bill Bevan, Les Strange, 'Sailor' Dutton, Eric Sladdin (retired 1977) and Dave Tyrie (retired 1976); a total of 118 years' service at the college.

Sadly the spring 1981 *Gate* edition recorded the death of Mr GF 'Sailor' Dutton at his home on 27 January. Mr Dutton had enlisted in the Royal Navy in 1936 and saw action with HMS *Berwick* and HMS *Indefatigable* throughout the war. He joined the college in 1950 and received the Imperial Service Medal from the Commandant in 1980 after thirty years' devoted service to the corps and countless numbers of ATs had benefited from his diligence and dedication.

The summer term of 1980 brought the retirement of Mr Bill Bevan who was another long-serving civilian of the college. Born in 1915, he joined the Royal Signals in 1936 as an operator. In 1941 he was captured by the Japanese in Hong Kong and remained a prisoner of war for three years. After the war he continued to serve until 1958 when he retired from the college as a warrant officer and took up a civilian post. He was a staunch Association member, ran the Amateur Radio Society and was Treasurer of the Hong Kong Signal Company Branch. He had given a total of forty-six years to the corps.

In early 1981 it was the turn of Mr Norman Ledger to retire. He joined the corps in 1938 as an electrician. He was a member of the British Expeditionary Force and returned from Dunkirk in a coal barge. He went on to serve in India and the North Africa campaign. As a Foreman of Signals he landed in Normandy and fought all the way to the Wesel and beyond. At the college he became well known for his *Gate* cartoons and dialect poems.

There were also changes in the organisation of the squadrons as WO2 Ruddock recalled in the mid-1990s when he returned on the permanent staff:

I arrived at the college on Tuesday, 10 January 1978. and in true North Yorkshire tradition, it was a bitterly cold day; not at all the weather for changing into Army issue PT kit. Undoubtedly, as far as the historical events of the college go, the most significant event was the closure of Phillips Squadron. The squadron disbanded at the end of my first term which, as most who have served their apprenticeship at the college will know, it's primarily an 'individual survival' term. Allegiances and loyalties to the squadron were not very strong amongst the 'new boys'. There was, however, strong resentment within the rest of the squadron which, at the time, played a significant part in college life on both the sporting and military fronts. There was, I remember, a strong underlying feeling that Bradley Squadron should have gone under the cosh. The members of the squadron were split between the four remaining squadrons: Scott, Rawson, Penney and Bradley. The strong case for Phillips remaining may well have been justified, retrospectively, by the fact that several ex-members of the squadron went on to become AT RSM over the subsequent years (Lobb, Bingham et al).

I went to Scott Squadron under Major Dransfield R Signals and WO2 (SSM) Alex Kubbu, the latter being one of the Fijian fraternity seconded into the British Army (in the late fifties); with a passion for rugby and a physical presence that ensured 'good order and military discipline', whilst still maintaining a congenial manner at every level. I remember him well.

It was evident that the Commandant's policy to cut down wastage would include a lot of sport. The hockey team, under the training of Major Tom Stoddart, had three successful years. The team won the Army Junior Cup in 1977 and went on to retain it a year later. There were seven college players in the Yorkshire Under-19s and there were such victories as 11-0 against the RAOC (AT Mark Hardy scoring 8) and a well-earned 1-0 victory against the sappers.

Army junior hockey champions. Back row: *Sgt Le-Floch, Mr Clements (OIC), ATs Sgt Johnson, Durban, Cpl Hardy, Holden, Sgt Butcher.* Front row: *ATs Cpl Massey, Lowes, Miles, Carter, LCpl Davies, Cpl Wicking, Cpl Packwood, Sgt Oakman.* Front: *AT Sgt Moye (Captain).*

AT Saun Carter was a goalkeeper of some repute who played Yorkshire County, Army Under 21s and Combined Services. AT Andy Marston-Weston played corps hockey; an achievement that would continue into the late 1990s in senior service. ATs Oakman, Wicking, Massey, Howe, Lowes, Carter, Marston-Weston, Hardy, Davies and Moye were all awarded colours and ATs Pothecary and Marston-Weston scored four goals in successive matches.

The cricket team went through lean times but AT Jarvis represented the corps. Most contests were keenly fought but the college were not strong enough to bring trophies to Harrogate. There were solid performances by AT Miles, Wade, Wilkerson, Lidstone, Watton Sullivan Steele and Blight all of whom gained colours in their respective seasons. The main success was in 1980 when the PS side won the Minor Units Army Cup with a defeat of the Royal Engineers Depot Regiment by 103 runs. The college amassed 171 runs in their 40 overs thanks to 42 from Sergeant B Sutherland and 30 from Sergeant P Shepherd. The bowling was dominated by Sergeant Lancaster (3 for 30) and Sergeant Shepherd (4 for 14) who restricted the sappers to 68.

The overriding feature of the 1978–79 rugby season was, of course, the weather, '…which cancelled so many matches and put the college at a severe disadvantage when playing teams from the south.' Nevertheless, individuals performed well and a sound base was set for progressive success. In 1980 the team were Army Junior Cup runners-up with AT Wordsworth representing the Army juniors and the

corps, and ATs Ford, Stewart and Charman also playing for the corps. Then in winter 1980 came the best result for many years when the college beat Arborfield 9-6 to win the Army Youth Challenge Cup. ATs Dent and Munson went on to play for the Combined Services Under 19s and AT Graham played Army Under 19s.

During Easter 1979 the college football team, managed by Mr Ken Purnell and Mr Ken Backett, toured BAOR for the first time where they were hosted in Herford by 7th Signal Regiment and 4th Division Signal Regiment. The outstanding player of the season was AT Corporal Billy Freear. He was selected as captain of the England FA colts team, was Player of the Year for the Army youth team and at the end of the season he held the Harrogate and District Youth Cup aloft for the college. He was well supported by ATs Adrian Payne, Tony, Redman, Slaney and Skeith.

Golf has always featured as a well-supported sport especially amongst the PS. The ATs were also well catered for and had four members' passes for the Oakdale Golf Club and many of them went on to represent the corps at later stages in their careers. Tuition was arranged with Donald Stirling at the Harrogate Golf Club. The Quartermaster Stan Pavey was classified as a bandit on one occasion when turning in with a 75 (nett 57). AT Pat Wood became the college champion with a 79. In spring 1980 the PS team won the Catterick Scratch Team Trophy with Chris Barron, Benny Newall, Bruce Graham and Jim Briggs. At this time Alex Kubu, Don Robinson and Bill Dunbar were also prominent players.

Under the watchful eye of WO2 (Y of S) 'Chippy' Wood, the swimming team were well trained and very successful. In 1979 the team won

Army junior swimming champions – 1981. Back row: *ATs O'Brien, LCpl Churchwood, Young, LCpl Noble, Morley, Campbell, Argust.* Middle row: *AT Curley, Stringfellow, LCpl Hitchens, Murphy.* Front row: *AT Needham, Mr Purcell, WO2 Wood, Cpl Tibble, AT Richmond.*

the Army junior swimming championships by winning all but two events. ATs Richmond, Young, Noble, Needham and Morley were all selected for the inter-services youth team which beat the Royal Navy by 75-65. The team was also victorious in the triangular event at Arborfield. Lieutenant Dianne Willcox WRAC and AT Richmond also represented the Army senior squad.

The college cyclists continued to be successful at all levels. The triangular event was won narrowly from AAC Arborfield. AT Ginger Beattie was the main stay of the team and became the Army junior record holder for the 10-mile event with a time of twenty-three minutes six seconds. AT Beattie, AT Pinkney and WO2 Curnow won the Army senior 100-mile race and the college were awarded the Best All-round Team Trophy. Lieutenant Dianne Willcox was also the Army Ladies' champion. AT Rob Young capped his successes by being selected to represent UKLF in BAOR where he was top rider. In 1980 he also became the Army Two-Day champion and went on with ATs Smith and Binns to ride for the Army. In the inaugural Army junior and senior roller championships the college riders lifted 12 of the 18 trophies and not one college rider was beaten by an outside rider. The riders went on to further successes in 1981. AT Gary Haslam was the reigning Army junior best all-round champion. The new squad comprised novice riders AT Tommy Steele, Dave Jones, Dave Rowe and Terry Adams who went on to defend the junior championship for the third year running. There is no doubt that the driving force behind this success was Captain (Retired) Alan Green who also rode in the senior event.

The tennis team had a considerable uplift when six new courts were built near the gymnasium for the 1978 season. This obviously inspired them for in 1979 they won the triangular competition at Chepstow by winning eight of the twelve matches. In the Junior Army championships the doubles was an all Royal Signals match in which ATs Freear and McLellan defeated Clark and Howse. A season later ATs Freear and Lamplough represented the corps.

The artificial ski slope at Catterick encouraged many ATs to take up the sport and in 1978 ten of them went to Bavaria with Captain Nigel Cory with 2 Armoured Division Signal Regiment on *Exercise Snowstorm*. The exercise was repeated a year later when AT Halliwell was most improved skier, AT Fisher was best all-round and AT 'Radar' Marsh got the wooden spoon.

There were many other minority sports which also thrived. The Judo Club mustered 46 members in 1979 and AT Marjoribanks was a karate blue belt. Squash was well supported. The cross-country runners had many good performers, including ATs Laycock, Webb and Delaney, who were all selected to run for the Army Under-20s against Wales. Corporal Robertson won the inter-services marathon and went

on to represent Britain in Spain. SI Rafferty ran in the New York marathon in the autumn. At basketball Lance Corporal Mullholland was awarded Army colours and two years running the PS team were Army Minor Unit runners-up with Staff Sergeant Greef APTC and Sergeants Sutherland and Matthews playing prominent roles. Canoeing was strong and AT Dobson was second in the Army slalom championships at Llandysul. The team won the 1978 triangular match by a comfortable margin with six in the first eight paddlers.

Adventurous training featured high on the Commandant's priority list and there were many exercises and expeditions. *Exercise Sea Legs* in August 1978 was a two-week Baltic cruise aboard the 53ft sloop *Ragnar* in which Captain SG Townsend showed the ropes to ATs Cable, Carter, Mitchell, Morris, Black and Newman. A visit to a Danish Signal Regiment was included and the nightlife of Aarhus Bay was sampled.

Exercise High Fell in 1978 was a week in the Ullswater area of the Lake District during which Captain Cornforth nearly managed to drown AT Orchard. In May, 30 ATs completed the Lyke Wake Sponsored Walk. External leadership training in early 1979 comprised skiing at Aviemore with the ATs staying at Granton-on-Spey. There was also more arduous training in the Derwent Water area. Easter 1979 saw *Exercise Sea Games* in which 10 ATs spent nearly three weeks in Cyprus. The visit included a wide range of activities and cultural visits across the whole of the island arranged by 9 Signal Regiment and 259 Signal Squadron.

In 1980 Captains Cornforth and Whitely took ATs Smith, Roose, Brayley and Vass to Morocco on *Exercise Atlas Overlord*. They reached their destination via Gibraltar and Tangier. The main aim was to reach the summit of Jebel Toubkal in the High Atlas range. Despite some members being affected by altitude sickness the aim was achieved. Whilst on the Jebel, the party were nearly involved in the search for a murderer in the local village .

Whilst the sport and adventurous training programmes were achieving the desired aim in reducing wastage, there was still much work to be done at military and trade training. Lieutenant Colonel Ralph Plant was eased out of the chief instructor's post to make way for Lieutenant Colonel Colin Grundy MBE in summer 1979. He came from MOD but he had held a wide variety of appointments in BAOR, Cyprus, Hong Kong and the UK. Since commissioning in 1955 he had also served with the RAF and Royal Navy. Ralph moved on to Catterick so he did not have far for his MFO to move.

In the trade wings there were steps taken to enhance the technical equipment. In 1978 'Tarif' arrived at Catterick and the college, '…have two channels into the beast for training our apprentices. We also have a new toy in the C141 tape comparator

which is used for City and Guilds test checks.' The following year saw the introduction of Clansman radio into D Block. VRCs 353 and 321 were installed in the classrooms and in the winter term they were introduced into the syllabus. By the summer term 1980 all traces of 'Larkspur' equipment had gone and the college also had its full scaling of PRC 350/351s. Major LN Barron was OC Military Training Wing from 1978 to 1982. He was the only infantry officer in the college and in the nineties he reflected:

My first impressions were unfavourable – military skills being accorded too low a priority compared with technical training and sport; particularly the latter. Standards of instructional ability and professionalism in general amongst my staff also left a lot to be desired. In fact I would cheerfully have gone elsewhere after my first term.

In time I began to understand exactly what the college as a whole was trying to achieve and I began to undergo a change of heart. As standards within the wing improved so did appreciation of what we had to offer, thus lessening reluctance to sample it. Watching the apprentices literally growing up in every respect was rewarding proof of what can be done with the dreaded teenager when properly handled. The times at which this was particularly apparent were the occasions when parents were present such as at Recruits' Pass-Off and Graduation Day. Many of them expressed their gratitude, and often amazement, for what we had achieved.

This page and opposite: *The assault course competition for the Champions' Cup in November 1978.*

Some particular memories to me were recruit camps in near monsoon conditions, the high standards at drill competitions, the enthusiasm and dedication with which all competitions were tackled, high level navigation in the Cairngorms, the officer who did not like the Commandant's red-ink corrections in the float file and the AT RSM who commanded the graduation parade with his wife and baby amongst the spectators.

In common with several thousand others, I will not forget AAC Harrogate.

AT Best recalls his arrival at the college on 6 January 1981 as a member of Intake 81A:

The first sight of the place was enough to put anybody off. It was cold, wet and shrouded in mist. We then made our way to our squadron rooms after which we went to the stores to collect our kit. Everybody looked forward to trying their kit on; at least we were real soldiers. We were taught how to dress by Sergeant Morgan. For the next few days we were getting jabs, haircuts and getting to know the camp. By this time Meakin and Allen had decided that they didn't like it at all. The next week we started Ex Fist, learning about the SLR and SMG and running around in our 'Action Man' kit. Week four was Ex Fledgling which we were dreading from what we had heard of it. But it turned out to be enjoyable. By week six we were allowed 'walk off' and a few of us went down town. We then settled down to trade until week twelve when we had 'pass-off'. As the day approached we all dreaded it. On the morning we all went for a run. We threw most of the PS, Sergeants Aldous and Morgan and the corporals, in the river except for Lieutenant Fletcher who had had a good night out and was not fit to come on the run! Pass-off went well and we then went down town with our parents and had a meal. On Sunday we all moved to our respective troops and so ended Recruit Troop.

Features of the college curriculum that were never forgotten by ATs include the termly drill competitions which were held at junior and senior level. Practice always commenced weeks before the event and 'bull nights' were a regular feature of the pre-event ritual. Doing well was important and AT Sergeant Webb of Scott Squadron recalled in 1979:

A couple of things went wrong. Corporal Loz Middleton forgot to put his gloves back on and Lance Corporal Brown didn't seem to want to perform an eyes right. But the judges declared us winners. We would like to thank Sergeants Burton and Hatch for their help. It turned out to be an eventful day as the Scott juniors won as well. This was the first time the Scott had done the double and it had only ever been done once before.

Mention should also be made of the Army Youth Selection Centre (North), under Major Pip Furse, which was a lodger unit in the college. In early 1980 the unit had its 50,000th candidate for whom they found a place as Junior Leader in the Royal Armoured corps; this occurred during the 10th anniversary year of the unit. 'After ten years we are looking to replace our internal displays which are looking distinctly tired,' noted the OC.

Colonel Ryan's reflections of 1993 ended: 'For me my final graduation parade was followed by my decision of three years earlier to leave the Army. The thought of returning to a vast headquarters after Harrogate was all too much. My wife and I left on a high, and for us, an extremely happy note, our final two weeks never to be forgotten'.

1st Term Test.
Q. *What is the Audio Frequency hearing range?*
A. *About 400 yards.*

15

REVIEW OF COLLEGE TRAINING

Colonel GC Verdon OBE – April 1981 to April 1984

Colonel GC (Paddy) Verdon OBE arrived at the college in April 1981 from his appointment at the School of Signals in Blandford where he had been the GSO1. He was born in Dublin, joined the REME as a soldier in 1953 and went on to pass the Regular Commissions Board. He entered Sandhurst from where he was commissioned into the Royal Signals. He went on to serve in Germany, Aden, Hong Kong and Malaya. He commanded 20 Armoured Brigade Signal Squadron, Burma Company RMAS and Queen's Gurkha Signals where he was appointed OBE. He was an accomplished sportsman at hockey, tennis, squash and off-shore sailing. His interests included .22 shooting, gardening, fishing, DIY and model railways. In his opening remarks he stated:

May I say on taking over how proud I am of being selected to command a college which is held in such high esteem by those within and without the corps, and which for many years has successfully provided a foundation of highly trained young men from which a high proportion of our technical officers telecommunications, traffic officers, foremen of Signals and yeomen of Signals have emerged in later years. My aim is to continue to foster the spirit of professional excellence which exists in the college so that we may continue to produce the highly skilled tradesmen which the corps requires both now and in the future and to ensure that both permanent staff and apprentice tradesmen thoroughly enjoy their time at the college. Also, I extend my best wishes, and those of everyone at the college to Colonel Ryan and wish him good fortune in the future.

WO1 (RSM) LFA Bailey arrived in April 1981 from his battalion in Germany. He was a Yorkshireman and a Coldstream Guardsman. He had served in British Guinea, Northern Ireland, Germany and the UK. He had considerable experience of junior soldiers from his time as drill sergeant major with the Royal Armoured corps Junior Leaders' Regiment. His main sports were boxing and rugby.

The changes in appointments in college HQ continued when Lieutenant Colonel E (Eddie) Pickup assumed the appointment of Deputy Commandant. It was often stated that the Commandant and his Deputy were on the same wavelength because they both originated from over the water. He left Dublin to enter

Major General Badcock makes a presentation to Mr 'Taff' Steel for his service to the college on 5 August 1983.

The Master of Signals, Major General Badcock talks to AT M Pullin whilst AT RSM S Norris and AT SSM M Maloney provide escort on the graduation parade of 5 August 1983.

Sandhurst in 1955 to be commissioned into Royal Signals two years later. He had served in Germany, Cyprus, Bahrain, Northern Ireland and Malta. He was a great mountaineering, skiing and tennis enthusiast.

An unusual feature of the graduation prize-giving of 30 March 1980 was that AT CMG Thompson was the only telegraphist to graduate and,

Field Marshal Bramall inspects the senior term on the graduation parade of 14 April 1984.

as the Director of Studies remarked, 'He was literally in a class of his own.' The graduation parades during this period were up to their 'climatic normal'. On 17 December 1981 Major General DM Woodford CBE inspected in Arctic conditions with a foot of snow on the ground; a thaw-out period was ordered before prize giving could commence. The Reviewing Officer on 14 April 1984 was Field Marshal Sir Edwin Bramall GCB OBE MC, the Chief of the Defence Staff. On arrival he cut a ribbon in Royal Signals colours to declare formally open the college's new imposing Yorkshire stonewall entrance which was inset with the corps badge and the Borough of Harrogate coat of arms. The first arrivals through the gates were the triumphant college cyclists from their round Britain exertions.

Major General PEM Bradley CB CBE DSO, Master of Signals, made his farewell visit to the college on 5 July 1982. The Bradley Squadron representation was provided by ATs Bridgewood, Marritt, Beverly and Mann. The Master of Signals went on to present WO2 (SSM) J Hodge BEM with a GOC's Northern Ireland Commendation. The finale comprised a presentation to the Master before the whole college lined the route whilst the junior Bradley Squadron entrants towed the Master in an open topped Land Rover behind the College Band.

The college continued to attract its share of high ranking visitors. On 24 April 1983 the Right Rev.

Francis Walmsley CBE, the Roman Catholic Bishop-in-Ordinary to the Forces, celebrated Mass in the Church of Christ the King. Brigadier IOJ Sprackling, Commander Catterick Garrison, made his final visit on 13 December 1983. It was a busy and physically testing day for the ATs which culminated in a senior term buffet. The finale was a traditional midnight send off when he was ceremoniously towed through the college gates on a Land Rover behind the Pipes and Drums. Lieutenant General Sir Charles Huxtable, head of training establishments, visited on 9 February 1984 and saw the full range of training facilities.

One embarrassing incident occurred when the Mayor visited the college and Colonel Verdon invited him to see some military training. The Mayor was very impressed by the standard of fitness and decided that he would like to leopard crawl underneath the camouflage net tunnel. Unfortunately when he appeared at the far end he was without his toupé and the sergeant on duty had to crawl back and unhook it from the net.

Monday, 5 July 1982 saw the culmination of one of the Commandant's projects. Mrs Pat Bate, wife of the late Signal Officer-in-Chief (Army), officially opened the Bate Centre in the converted NAAFI/church building in Hildebrand Barracks. This was to provide a much needed recreational facility for families, Wives' Club, Thrift Shop, Brownies, Play Group and Pottery Club. The project had been masterminded by Major Jack Boyle and was named in memory of the late Signal Officer-in-Chief, Major General AC Bate OBE, who had died suddenly after only three months in office. The occasion was attended by the Master of Signals and Mrs Bradley and many dignitaries. The community cccentre remained a focal point of college life until the college finally closed.

The Commandant made a number of Imperial Service Medal presentations to long-serving members of the college. Mr Jack Lupton was awarded on

On 5 July 1982, Mrs Pat Bate opens the Bate Community Centre, Hildebrand Barracks, in memory of her late husband Major General Bate.

ON 30 JULY 1982 OVER 350 APPRENTICES MARCHED THROUGH HARROGATE TO COMMEMORATE
THE FREEDOM OF THE TOWN. THEY DISPLAYED A WIDE RANGE OF COLLEGE ACTIVITIES.

'Colonel Johnnie' marches past
the Mayor and the Commandant.

Lieutenant Colonel Pickup leads the parade.

Bradley Squadron follow.

Major Price and Penney Squadron.

The unknown soldier in NBC kit.

Major Bowles and Scott Squadron.

The sporting theme.

Major Hoyle and Rawson Squadron.

3 March 1981. He had joined the college in 1947 after wartime service with the RAF. Mr Henry Clough received his medal at the winter 1981 graduation parade after spending the whole of his career teaching Royal Signals soldiers. Mr Herbert Fox received his medal from Major General Benbow at the winter 1983 graduation parade. He came to Harrogate in 1965 to teach electronics theory after wartime service with the RAF, the General Post Office and REME.

Other long-service departures included Mr Geoff White who spent fifteen years in Telegraphist Wing. Mr Jack Cowen served thirty-two years up to 9 December 1983. In December 1981 Mr Jim Purcell transferred to Princess Marina College, Arborfield on promotion to Senior Instructional Officer. Jim was an Airborne Signaller who, over a period of twenty-three years at the college, had conscientiously looked after angling, swimming and water polo.

At this point it is appropriate to review what the Commandant stated on his departure, because by doing so it shows what the main restructuring activities were during his time at the college. He stated in early 1984:

The last two years have seen a number of quite drastic changes in the role, organisation and development of the apprenticeship. These changes are now complete ... and the role of the college has been redefined, 'To give apprentice tradesmen a broad foundation of military, education, trade and leadership training so that they have a better than average chance of achieving selection for Foreman and Yeoman of Signals training at an early stage in their careers.' In line with the changing role of the college, a comprehensive review of training and the individual apprenticeships has been carried out over the past two years... The data telegraphist apprenticeship has been dropped and plans are being made to introduce full special telegraphist and electronic warfare apprenticeships in September 1984 and 1985 respectively. Technician apprentices will undergo common training for two years at the college and will only specialise into one of the three technician trades when they move to 8 Signal Regiment for their equipment training module. All apprenticeships with the exception of the tele mech, which is still under review, have been standardised on two years.

The organisation of the college has also been changed to cope with an overall 25 per cent reduction of staff caused by the MOD inspection of January 1981... The main changes in the organisation are that the Deputy Commandant assumes command of the four apprentice squadrons and all outdoor training. The Senior Education Officer, retitled Director of Studies, assumes responsibility for all trade training, trade related education, and general education. It is also hoped to introduce computer aided management with a link to the Monarch computer system, to enable us to identify apprentices' weaknesses more quickly.

Following on from these changes responsibility was given to the Deputy Commandant for the AT Squadrons, Military Training Troop, gymnasium staff, external leadership staff, sport and hobbies. By this time there were four squadrons – Bradley, Scott, Rawson and Penney. The director of studies (chief instructor) was responsible for Electronics Wing, Telegraphist Wing, Tactical Exercise Troop and Education Wing. Radio, terminal and radio relay technicians would gain BTEC qualifications. Radio telegraphists, special telegraphists and EW operators would gain City and Guilds Certificate 777. Telecommunications mechanics would gain City and Guilds Certificate 534.

Education Wing set about ensuring that the educational needs of the new changes were met. Lieutenant Colonel Brian McMahon RAEC set matters under way and handed over the post of Director of Studies to Lieutenant Colonel Jack Wishart RAEC in summer 1983. The BTEC qualification required that a new TEC submission was compiled and this was completed in Education Wing by Tim Bevan and Bob Horton in 1982. By mid-1983 the college was still not very computer orientated. 'We are still touching wood with crossed fingers but believe we shall have a fully-equipped computer lab before long. This will be of enormous benefit to all ATs. If we can convince

Lord Trefgarne erects an elevated antenna during his visit in June 1984.

the "moneybags" that we need another dozen – one for each classroom – to take care of teaching, then we will all be able to go on extended leave.' It was also decided that ATs could pass elements of their Education Proficiency Certificate (EPC) whilst they were at the college. The first candidates for maths and current affairs passed in early 1981.

Lieutenant Colonel Tom Stoddart was promoted and soon afterwards passed over command of Electronics Wing to Captain (TOT) Jim Jenkins. Tom had entered the Army Apprentices' School first time round in September 1949. He had departed three years later as a line mechanic. This final move therefore represented a total of thirty-two years. He went on to Catterick where he would be a main stay in the 'Ptarmigan' project. Jim handed over to one of the genuine characters of the corps, Major Dicky Dyer MBE. There was a lot of work to be done in the wing to train to both the old and new syllabus at the same time. 'Ptarmigan' training had commenced by summer 1983.

There was also promotion for Lieutenant Colonel AMP Howie BEM of Telegraphist Wing before he handed on to Major Les Waulmsley. The wing were operating Clansman VRC 321/322 and carrying out HF exercises on an international basis and with a half-wave dipole the ATs were communicating to America. ATs Newman, Heap, Morgan and Liddle were learning how to change frequency on a dark, wet and windy Penny Pot night. They also used RATT to the TA in Scotland. The last of the D11/R234 HF stations was replaced by the summer term 1982, much to the delight of the ATs and staff alike. One of the genuine privileges for the wing was the provision of 12 ATs to assist 10 Signal Regiment with the communications commitment for the Royal Wedding in July 1981. The party comprised ATs Bolam, Ball, Barry, Malvern, Brudenall, Bunce, Hamer, Hornsby, Allen, Sparks, Rowe and Allen.

Around the college the 'extra-mural' programme was busy. On 30 July 1982 the college commemorated the Freedom of Harrogate with a full parade through the streets of the town. Mayor Frank Pickles took the salute on the Queen Victoria Monument and was evidently impressed by all the ATs and the abilities of the musicians. The day after attracted a good crowd to the annual Open Day despite poor weather. In the same term over 2000 books were despatched to soldiers in the Falklands. In November 1983 new recruits of Rawson Troop set out to build a keep-fit course in Harrogate as part of their Duke of Edinburgh Award Scheme. On 2 November 1983 the ATs of Bradley Squadron presented Mr Leslie Bell, one of the more disabled members of Leeds BLESMA Branch, with a wheelchair. This was from the proceeds of a sponsored shoot and AT (SSM) David Rook made the presentation. The efforts of the ATs enabled the

A gymnastics display during Open Day.

YMCA to open a coffee bar in Harrogate in September 1982; it was at 20 Cheltenham Terrace.

Rawson Squadron established a close relationship with the Ian Tetley Memorial Home near Killinghall. Visits were arranged to the college for their Scouts and Guides. They saw the White Helmets and were presented with a cheque towards

'Going Over The Top' – external leadership training.

the Disabled Students Unit. This relationship continued until the college closed.

There were a number of incidents in the early 1980s that demonstrated how well former ATs were doing in their military careers. AT Jerry Peck (Intake 73B) was commissioned into the Royal Signals on 8 April 1983 and was awarded the Agar Memorial Prize for the best Royal Signals Officer of his Sandhurst intake; he went on to reach Lieutenant Colonel before his retirement in 1997. The photograph of 16 June 1983 Quartermasters' Convention at Blandford made its way to Harrogate. No less than 12 of the 15 had junior service. Number 48 Foreman of Signals Course of 30 November 1983 comprised five successful ATs. On 17 February 1984, WO1 (RSM) Mike Stevenson (later Lieutenant Colonel) arranged a reunion in Catterick for 31 members of Intake 61C. Those present ranged from sergeant to captain and there was one civilian – Mr Gats Gatenby of British Telecom.

Military and leadership training were both demanding and rewarding. Each new recruit went on the Recruit Weekend Camp held in the area around Malham. External leadership exercises were held annually in Granton-on-Spey and included hill-walking and skiing. *Exercise Tiercel* was held on a termly basis and introduced ATs to the Lake District. There was usually a variety of command tasks to be performed, much hiking and the occasional visit to Helvellyn. In 1983 Major Bowles took a party of skiers to Obergurgl in Austria.

Horse riding became popular again when the college acquired a horse which was stabled at Catterick. Major Harrison and Mrs Sue Filer provided the expertise and 2nd Lieutenant Hodges provided the entertainment by being unsaddled on more than one occasion.

In the winter term 1980 AT John Page was tragically killed on his motorcycle. His father presented a trophy in his memory that was to be competed for at squadron level as the award for a safe driving competition. The inaugural event was won by Bradley Squadron but a year later AT 'Spock' Bolom received the trophy from the Mayor for Penney Squadron.

The newly opened Bate Centre provided accommodation for many activities including the 1st Penny Pot Scout Troop which in July 1982 took 30 scouts to the Ardennes. The Senior Youth Club, lead by Mr Bill Dunbar and ably assisted by Mrs Moira Graham, were also very active with about 50 youths attending activity evenings. On 11 December 1981 the Club presented £223 to the Commandant for 'Save the Children Fund'.

Sailing was an active sport which was held at Thruscross Reservoir with regular competitions against the Leeds Sailing Club. Such was the success that the Commandant took a team to the corps Regatta and ATs Doug Hassal and Martin Hayter

Army Youth Cup winners – Rugby 1981/82. Standing: *SSgt Rumble, As Lazenby, Richmond, Thompson, Norris, Amos, Markham, Daniels, Jennings, Sgt Jewell.* Sitting: *ATs McKissock, May, Longley, Hood, Dent, Phillips, Neighbour, Kimber, Lazenby.*

The Royal Signals Colts team 1984. Back row: *Major Horne RAEC, ATs Corporal Allen, Lance Corporal Swanston, Eyton, McTavish, Lane, Major Robinson.* Middle row: *ATs McWilliam, Lowe, Sergeant Barrow, Bishop, Brudenall.* Front row: *ATs Sergeant Sheppard, Corporal Sturley, Lance Corporal Challiner, Phillips.*

were invited to sail for the corps against the RAF. They went on to become Army Under 21 champions. In 1981 the college cyclists organised the Army Festival of Cycling with riders from the UK, BAOR, Cyprus, the RAF, the RN and civilian clubs. There were 11 events in eight days which included the Triangular Games. AT Gerry Haslam was outstanding and a year later AT Dallas was the Combined Services junior best all-rounder. In 1984 ATs Chatfield and Wilkinson both performed superbly to win the major prizes.

In 1982 both the AT and PS cricket teams were very strong. ATs Dixon, Jackson, Jones, Jennings and Evans all played for the corps. Major Price, WO2 Palmer and Sergeants Aldous, Cottle, Lancaster and Shepherd were prominent staff team members. In 1983 the college won the Triangular Games with fine bowling from the AT Matless twins. The team also won the Junior Army cricket championship by beating the RE, RA and RAC teams. ATs Barnett and Bain were consistent bowlers and ATs Bain and Campbell batted well.

There was moderate success at tennis. Most notably in 1983 Captains Ibbotson and Dixon won the female Army doubles competition and the staff won the NE District League. AT Pearson won the Army junior championships and he then partnered AT Edge to win the doubles. ATs Hill, Rogers and Pearson all represented the corps.

In 1982 the college team retained the Army Rugby Youth Cup in a pulsating final at Aldershot against REME. AT Dent was captain, AT Neighbour lead the pack and AT Hood scored two tries in the 17-0 win. A year later, under coach Captain Gareth Davies RAOC, ATs Phillips, Matthews, Halliday and Billsborough all played for the Army.

College soccer remained strong and well supported under the eagle eye of Ken Purnell. In March 1982 the team defeated York Garrison 3-1 which secured both the Yorkshire Services Division 2 championship and the Cup competition. AT Evans made two superb saves and ATs Bruce Smith and Tommy Steele provided the goals. In the season, the team won 10 of its 12 matches and then toured Germany being hosted by 4 Armoured Division Signal Regiment. In 1983 Penney Squadron lost by the narrow 2-1 margin in the final of the ATs Challenge Cup having defeated Bradley Squadron 2-0, RE D Company 3-0, ACC 4-1 and RE C Company. ATs Ross and Johnson were the main goal scorers.

In 1982 the hockey team were runners-up in the Army Junior Cup; narrowly defeated by the REME 2-1. ATs Bridgwood, Marshall, Howes, Hodkinson and Wood went on to play for the corps and the latter two played for the Combined Services. A year later the college won the Army Junior Hockey Cup with victories against RCT, ACC, REME and RAC totalling 21 goals for, and only two against. AT Mamos was a devastating striker with eight goals. ATs Baughan,

Crabtree, Swain and Mamos played for North Yorkshire. WO2 Eames (later Major) was the successful coach.

The staff squash team won the NE District League in 1982 with SSI Ray Surgeon, Sergeant Dave Heinaru, WO2 Sharp and Sergeant Bob Genge being the mainstays. The act was repeated a year later this time strengthened by Captain Paul Robertshaw (ex-AT of 67C) who also went on to win the corps championships.

The college had some very high-calibre cross-country runners. Sergeant Cain was undefeated in every race in the league. He represented Great Britain in the half marathon in Puerto Rico and was the Army champion. The college won the league, in which the other main runners were Corporal Carr, Major Arnold, Lance Corporal Freeman and AT Mason.

The college canoeists had excellent results in 1983 when the junior team were Army white-water, sprint, marathon and slalom champions and Triangular Games winners. The seniors were sprint runners-up. Eight college members were selected to represent the Army: Captain Robertshaw (Army Team Captain), Sergeant Tubman, Lance Corporal Eaton and ATs Reed, Dobson, Sharpe and Collins. Other Army champions included ATs Moloney, Anderson and Corporal Speck.

There were also some notable successes in 'minority' sports. The volleyball team beat six other teams to become Army junior champions in 1983. AT Pearson was the Army junior singles badminton champion of 1983 and he joined with AT Baugham to win the doubles title. ATs Pearson, Powell, Edlin and Matthews all had excellent performances at athletics. The latter two set new Army records. In 1982 five members of the college represented the corps in orienteering: ATs Rowland, Rutherford, Bailey, Davis and Rogerson.

Sport at the college was of a high standard in the early 1980s. This was supported by the award of the Birtwistle Pennant for Sport for the 1983–1984 season. The award was made by the Signal Officer-in-Chief to the corps unit which was deemed to have enhanced the reputation of the corps through its sporting prowess. The pennant flew below the unit flag at the guardroom for one year and was a fitting reminder of the importance of sport in the corps and specifically at the college.

These were also busy days in the WRVS lounge which was under the supervision of Mrs Kathy Clarke. The seriousness of the activities was raised when the Len Lee Snooker Trophy was introduced. Len represented the company that printed *The Gate* and he presented the trophy in 1982. Thereafter it was competed for twice each year with ATs Rutherford, Murray, Leigh and Boughey being among the first names to be engraved on it. By the time Miss Ann Dawson had taken over there were also competitions for darts and games evenings.

This era brought about the demise of the Army Youth Selection Centre (North). The OC, Major Edinger Royal Signals, retired from the Army and reported in the spring 1983 *Gate*, 'Our small establishment is slowly but surely shrinking. By the time these notes have been printed we shall have reduced to a total of five officers, ten NCOs and two civilians. In the past year we have interviewed over 3000 applicants to join the junior Army of whom 1700 were accepted. The threat of final closure still hangs over us although the letter of doom has not arrived in irrevocable form.' However, the report one term later was terminal, 'Major York takes over as OC and … despite our even more impending closure we continue to try to work on. We are still trying to locate the thousand and one bits and pieces of supposedly necessary equipment that were taken on charge in 196… or was it 186…? This article is (regrettably) our last contribution to *The Gate*.' So ended another chapter in the recruitment of junior soldiers.

The closure of the Selection Centre made it free for conversion into a new Hobbies Centre. In a small ceremony the centre was opened on 4 March 1984 as the Forge Hobbies Centre. This was in memory of Major Michael Forge, Royal Signals, who was tragically killed in action on 5/6 June 1982 in the Falkland Islands. The ceremony was performed by Mr Edward Forge, his father, who unveiled a plaque to his son's memory, and spoke of the pride and pleasure that Michael had felt in serving the college as OC Tactical Exercise Troop, OIC Adventurous Training, 2IC and later OC Rawson Squadron. Also present was Major Forge's mother.

Hobbies remained an important element of the AT development programme and the availability of its own centre was an important enhancement. The activities waxed and waned somewhat according to the availability and expertise of PS. For instance, the Car Maintenance Club commenced in September 1982 with Staff Sergeant BJ Parsons in charge. By its second term there were over 30 members. The club provided an excellent course on engine theory, car maintenance and servicing.

One other important innovation of the early 1980s was the Commandant's Walk. WO2 RQMS Gerge Firth recalled in 1994:

In 1982 the RSM held a walk for sergeants' mess members. The Commandant, Colonel GC Verdon OBE, decided that this was a good idea and should be held every

Councillor Fred Pickles, the Mayor of Harrogate, presenting Pipe Sergeant Major Burns with the Yorkshire Banner at the Yorkshire Show.

term and extended to all staff both military and civilian. The Deputy Commandant, Lieutenant Colonel Pickup, was 'volunteered' as the organiser. As a keen mountaineer his walks somehow always managed to contain a fair amount of ascent, normally 300–400 feet of steep ground. Early walks were held in the Haworth area, one even took in the Three Peaks of Yorkshire.

When Lieutenant Colonel Pickup was replaced by Lieutenant Colonel Hills as Deputy Commandant he 'Pickup-ed' the job of organising the walk. He came up with a number of interesting routes in the surrounding Yorkshire Dales – the product of many hours spent on foot ensuring that his routes were over Rights of Way etc. A number of the walks were graced by the presence of Brigadier Maynard when he was Commander Training Group.

In 1988 when Lieutenant Colonel Hills retired he was replaced as walk organiser by the present team, myself and Mr Mike Wilson. I am the 'safety man' and coordinator and Mike, a keen Dales man, the route planner. Over 30 new routes have resulted from the hours that Mike spends both studying maps and walking the Dales.

Over the period, walks have been held in Wharfedale, Nidderdale, Malhamdale, Swaledale and Wensleydale. In the early days two routes used to be planned; one of 12 miles for men and a 6-mile option for the ladies. By the time the organisation passed to the present team it had been found that the majority of walkers opted for the 12-mile route so the 6-mile option was discarded. Walks now are 12 miles in length usually with one or two 'short cuts' to enable walkers to reduce the distance by a mile or two. A number of civilian staff members have completed all but one or two walks since they started.

The walks enable people to get to know each other as they cover a broad range of the rank structure both military and civilian; many a problem has been solved by a chat on a wind blown moor top.

The Commandant's Walk continued until the college closed.

Colonel Verdon departed from the college in April 1984 but there was a six-month gap before the next Commandant was available to take up his appointment from Staff College Camberley. The void was ably filled by the Deputy Commandant, Lieutenant Colonel Eddie Pickup.

Gate Magazine
"Compulsory judo lessons have been introduced as
part of the leisure activities programme at
Queen Ethelburga's School for Girls. We wonder why?"

16

JUNIOR LEADERS ARRIVE

Colonel SR Carr-Smith — September 1984 to October 1986

Colonel Stephen Carr-Smith assumed his two-year appointment in September 1984 on promotion. He was an Old Welbexian (the first of four who would be Commandant) who after commissioning had served in Germany, Aden and the UK. His regimental service had included being Regimental Signal Officer of 1st Battalion Coldstream Guards in Iserlohn, Officer Commanding 6th Armoured Brigade Signal Squadron and Commanding Officer of 1st Armoured Division HQ and Signal Regiment. He had been a member of staff at Mons Officer Cadet School and the Army Staff College. Staff appointments had included Military Secretary's Staff and Operational Requirements in MOD. He was an extremely competent all-round sportsman and had represented the Army at hockey and cricket. In his initial message to the college he stated:

May I say, on taking over, how proud I am of being selected to command a college which is held in such high esteem by those inside and outside the corps... With the recent requirement to produce a strict six-term apprenticeship, and the impending arrival of 180 junior leaders during 1985, there are bound to be changes... There is much planning and hard work to be done; I look to you all to help me.

There was also a change of Director of Studies with the arrival of Lieutenant Colonel R Kirkwood BSc MA RAEC. He had served in Singapore, Germany and the UK. His UK tours included Sandhurst and MOD. His main interests were in music, computers, shooting and amateur dramatics.

The new Regimental Sergeant Major WO1 (RSM) Eddie Lyne, Coldstream Guards, arrived at the start of the spring term 1984. He was widely travelled having served in Munster, Cyprus, Kenya, Aden, Northern Ireland and Canada. He had, of course, completed a number of public duty tours. He was familiar with junior traits having served with the Royal Artillery Junior Leaders at Bramcote. He was a keen sailor. WO1 Lyne was succeeded by WO1

(RSM) JFP Faloone, Irish Guards, in 1986. He had served in Aden, Hong Kong, Germany and the UK. He had been a junior soldier himself and was a junior boxer, soccer goalkeeper and battalion shooting team. He had also been an instructor at the Junior Leader's Battalion, Oswestry.

The changes mentioned by the Commandant in his opening remarks soon started to take place. The first intake of 45 junior leaders arrived in Penney Squadron on 27 February 1985. Their course comprised mainly military, educational and leadership training. Their graduation parade was on 20 December 1995 when 37 of them moved on to Catterick to commence trade training. The Reviewing Officer was Major General GR Oehlers and he remarked on the sense of pride that both JLs and ATs should feel on this historic occasion. During the course of the first year 180 junior leaders commenced training.

There were a number of important external exercises at this time. First, the college had the responsibility to man No.15 Reinforcement Drafting Unit (RDU). The unit was mobilised annually and members of the college had to move to Lancashire and distribute equipment from pallets to the TA who were the 'players'. This involved PS and ATs. Although VIPs enhanced the excitement there was nothing quite so dramatic as when one of the returning coaches caught fire on the way into camp.

Second, the college also supported *Exercise Lionheart* in summer 1984. Specifically, Telegraphist Wing provided a communications and security monitoring group. Many of the wing also joined their TA units including Messrs Newall, Skinner, Graham, Howells and Buss.

Military and external leadership exercises remained challenging. The aim of *Exercise Bradley Basha IV* in May 1984 was to scale the Three Peaks over a two-day period. *Exercise Cold Comfort* in January and February 1985 was aptly named. The aim of this annual exercise was to introduce ATs to some of the outdoor physical pursuits that are under-

The college Regimental Sergeant Major, WO1 (RSM) RE Lyne, Coldstream Guards.

Junior Leaders Johnston and Rowan on command task training at Catterick in 1985.

taken in the Cairngorms during the winter months. Over a four-week period 223 ATs were able to experience downhill skiing, cross-country skiing, snow climbing and snow navigation.

In the Trade and Educational wings much work was carried out to standardise the apprenticeship, to cater for the junior leader syllabus and to accept a new apprentice trade. In the winter term 1984 the electronic warfare (EW) apprenticeship commenced with an initial intake of 20 ATs. Computer courses were also run for City and Guilds examinations in computer literacy.

A number of college stalwarts retired after many years of dedicated service. On 29 March 1985 the Commandant said farewell to Mr Eric Hill and Mr Fred Craven, both of whom had served at the college for thirty-seven years, having arrived in 1948. Mr Hill had served with the Air Ministry, the Post Office and as a radio mechanic in Royal Signals. He taught the first ATs to arrive at the school. Mr Craven was ex-REME and had served in Egypt and as an instructor.

Mr Harry Clough retired in early 1986 and was then the longest-serving member of the college. He had served with the Post Office and during the war was a technician on the defence telecommunications network. He joined the college in 1951 and had been a member of Technician Wing. In the same term

Major (Retired) Pat Watts also made his 'final' retirement as a Burnham Lecturer. He had joined the college in 1961 as a serving RAEC officer and he remained on the staff after his retirement. His contribution to college life included public relations officer, OIC drama, *Gate* editor and founder of the Saddle Club. He was also a keen hockey and squash player.

Sport, character development and extra-mural activities all remained important aspects of the college programme. The 'Review of the Term' published in the spring and summer 1985 *Gate* magazines illustrate the point well:

Basketball. The team heads the Catterick Garrison League.

Cycling. Winners of the Army Senior and Junior Roller Cycling Championship League.

Canoeing. Winners of the Army Junior Wild Water Canoeing.

Cross Country. Currently second in the NE District Services League.

Rugby. Winners of the Army Youth Cup.

Soccer. Seven points clear at the top of the league.

AT Williams. corps Basketball.

AT Chatfield. Army Senior Roller-cycling Champion.

AT Sole. Combined Services Best All-rounder Cycling.

AT Souter. Army Under-21 Hockey.

ATs Maul, Campbell, Roberts. North Yorkshire Schools Hockey.

ATs Welsh, MacMillan, Swanston. Army Youth Soccer.

ATs Williams, Jakins, Pickersgill, Vowles. Army Colts Rugby.

ATs Swift, Humphreys. Army Junior Squash Team.

AT Solomons. Combined Services Athletics.

The college has maintained its usual high standard in the world of sport. The basketball team has won four major competitions: the Junior Championships, the NE District Senior Competition, the Harrogate and District League and the Catterick Garrison League.

The college hockey team has included players who have achieved individual distinction; AT Souter has played in the Army Under-21 and the corps teams. ATs Campbell and Eldridge represented North Yorkshire Schools and AT Metcalf also played for the corps.

The rugby team won the Army Youth Cup (Under-19) and were finalists in the Junior Cup (Under-17). The soccer team won 11 of their 13 matches and are currently top of their league. A combined group of 50 members of the soccer and rugby teams are going to BAOR over Easter.

The squash team won the Army Junior Championships and AT Smith won the corps Junior Championship.

ATs Turner and Mathis have gained Royal Yachting Association Competent Crew certificates; the former also achieved qualification as Day Skipper.

During the term 26 ATs took part in an enjoyable skiing trip to Austria.

Once again the college has been particularly active in community service. £1000 has been raised for the training of guide dogs for the blind and a recent twenty four-hour sponsored run raised £2000 towards sending 12 local handicapped children for a once in a lifetime diving expedition to the Red Sea.

The college cricket team won the 1984 Triangular Games with competent efforts by AT Barnett who scored 46 and 69 and took 6 for 33. He was supported by AT Williams with 4 for 18.

The soccer teams went through a very successful period. On 3 April 1985 the ATs won the League Cup final by beating 210 Signal Squadron 3-1 at Catterick. ATs Jacko Jackson, Craig Shrive and Scotty Scott scored the goals. Jackson went on to score 29 in the season. ATs Shrive, McWilliam, Cheetham and Welch represented the Army and the last two went on to play for professional league teams. In 1985 Penney Squadron won the Apprentices Challenge Cup. They defeated Bradley Squadron 1-0, Scott Squadron 3-2, E Company RE 6-1 and A Company REME 3-1 in the final. The very successful trainer-coach was Sergeant Thomas.

The Army Rugby Cup win was achieved with sound victories in the semi-final against the RE by 22-0 and in the final 15-0 against the REME. The juniors beat the RA junior leaders, the REME 13-7 and the RE 21-11. ATs Andy Williams, Bob Vowles, Tom Pickersgill, Jake Jakins and Martin Tombs represented the Army Colts and went on to win the inter-services competition.

The Rawson Squadron boxing team 1985. Back row: Sergeant Griffin, ATs Woodfine, Lance Corporal Bond, Lance Corporal Philip, Coussons, Protheroe, Lance Corporal Pryme, Atkinson, Sergeant Clifford. Front row: ATs Corporal Pugh, Starr, Corporal McInnes, Captain BP Neillings, Major GA Allen, ATs Lance Corporal Haigh, Lance Corporal Abel.

Rawson Squadron giving the residents of Dene Park a hearty Christmas party.

The Rawson Squadron management – 1985. Back row: *Sergeants Griffin, Clifford, Tedby, Sear, Corporal Patterson.* Front row: *Lieutenant Llewellyn, Captain Neillings, Major Allen, WO2 Matthews.*

The inter-squadron boxing competition was revived in 1985 after ten years in the dark. The responsibility lay with Captain Bernie Neillimp who divided the boxers into senior and junior divisions. This was an extremely popular event and Scott won the inaugural senior competition.

The college canoeists won the 1985 Junior Army surf canoe championships with AT Manson being the individual champion. Mr Archie Miles trained the team of JLs Welch and Ridgway, and ATs Hyde, Haigh and Monson. He provided another ten years of dedicated support to the sport.

After considerable effort WO2 (SSM) Warren and Staff Sergeant Figura managed to get volleyball off the ground. JL Haggart was the best of the initial players but he was closely followed by ATs Bundy, Dexter and Ruxton. Volleyball remained a popular sport.

The ATs golf trophy went to AT Martin Flather in 1985 with an outstanding net 66; AT Mike Cowie was second. A year later AT Colin Stroud was the winner. Many of the PS were keen golfers and Major

Bill Price became the corps individual champion in 1985. College prizes were won by Jim Briggs, Ron Light and Peter Root.

Other worthy performances in 1986 included college victories in both the NE District Minor Unit Hockey Cup and the Army Team Orienteering Championship in which AT Rowlinson-Bates became the junior Army champion.

There were also many fun events such as the annual Knaresborough bed race of 9 June 1984. This was not to be taken lightly and involved pre-season training to steer the bed which on the day would be occupied by Lieutenant Elspeth Mollison. Bradley Squadron represented the college and the team comprised Sergeants Lund and Oliver, Corporal O'Rourke and AT Bruce Newton. They completed the course in eighteen minutes. For this race Telegraphist Wing also provided all of the communications for the organisers.

There were charity events galore. ATs Iverney and Eldridge deserve special mention for having completed the Westminster Charity Run from John O'Groats to Land's End. The route must have been infectious as on 17 April 1986 the college cycling team set off on its second marathon ride to Land's End, thence to John O'Groats and back to Harrogate by the 21st. A total of 14 riders completed the course.

Rawson Squadron entered the York half-marathon which ATs Walker and Brebner completed in 1 hour 26 minutes. ATs Sommerville, Morris, Dobson, Cowan and Stebbing all finished within a further twelve minutes.

The 3 May 1986 was the thirtieth anniversary of the college's adoption by the former Harrogate Borough Council and it was celebrated with a commemorative march. Over 300 members of the college marched through the town centre in keeping with the right to exercise the Freedom. The march was led by the Commandant with accompaniment from the College and corps Bands. The Mayor of Harrogate,

The Mayor, Mrs Brenda Tyler, inspects the apprentices with the Commandant.

ON 3RD MAY 1986, 300 MEMBERS OF THE COLLEGE COMMEMORATED THE ADOPTION.

Marching through the streets of Harrogate.

The Commandant leads the march past.

The start of the Summer 1985 Junior Assault Course Race.

Mrs Brenda Towler, took the salute with Major General AC Birtwistle CB CBE present as the Representative Colonel Commandant. To mark the occasion the Mayor presented the ceremonial Harrogate Sword which was worn by the AT RSM on all future ceremonial occasions. In return, the Commandant presented the Mayor with an embroidered Pipe Banner which would be paraded whenever the Mayor was present. The day ended with a celebratory dinner in the Mayor's Parlour.

In his departing statement the Commandant wrote:

The JLs have been assimilated into the college without any 'aggro'; integration rather than segregation has proved to be the right answer ... the JL Development Organisation has been set up ... and a JL is regarded as a first-year AT who does not do trade.

All the apprenticeships have been rewritten and in January 1986 all AT Intakes were on the new six-term course. The days of the 'fast/slow' AT are over. The early predictions about the reduction in BTEC and C & G passes have not come about ... and with the first intake of EW operators about to graduate the AT situation looks rosy.

One of the saddest notes is that the college now is responsible for the complete training of only one trade – the radio telegraphist. It is, of course, a function of money and resources, but every effort must be made to stop Harrogate from becoming a non-equipment orientated college.

Perhaps belatedly, the college appears to be getting into the twentieth century. 'Comet' – our computer assisted management system – has arrived and is now being installed. We also have, at last, a course development officer, and our quality control team is up to strength.

I am very sad indeed to be leaving the college... It has been a privilege to have been part of a first-class team of permanent staff, both military and civilian, dedicated to the task of producing a large proportion of the supervisory ranks of Royal Signals. To all PS I give my heartfelt thanks. To the apprentices and junior leaders, I wish you all every good fortune and hope we meet again.

> From a test:
> Q. *What are the positive and negative terminals for on a 300 watt charging engine?*
> A. *They stop the control box from falling off the generator.*

17

THE DEMISE OF 'COLONEL JOHNNY'

Colonel CT Garton – October 1986 to January 1989

Colonel CT Garton (Conrad) assumed his appointment as Commandant in October 1986. He had previously served in Germany, Northern Ireland, the Netherlands and the UK. He commenced his military career as a national serviceman and shortly after commissioning he had commanded a troop in the Junior Leaders' Regiment, Denbury, so he was no stranger to junior soldiers. He had also commanded a squadron of 16 Signal Regiment, 39 Infantry Brigade HQ and Signal Squadron and 13 Signal Regiment. He had served staff appointments with the Junior Division of the Staff College, NATO, and the Royal Signals Directorate. His main interests were sport including rugby, cricket, squash and golf. He enjoyed music and gardening. In 1994 his reflections about his tour at Harrogate included the following:

Colonel C Garton

It was exceptional for the college to be involved in military exercises. But shortly after my arrival we provided 800 apprentices and PS on Exercise Brave Defender. They were organised into Home Defence Companies and flew in Chinooks to defend key points. They all performed admirably.

I was also surprised to find that Her Majesty's Inspectors of Schools sent a team of 12 for a full week to check on our standards. The report was very complimentary on most areas but there were some adverse comments on our laboratories.

Sport played an important part in our training. John Conteh, the world champion, attended our boxing competition. We won most of the judo contests that we entered, and to my delight we won the Army Cricket Cup with myself scoring a 50 in the final.

I had never liked the cross in our church. In my view it was a rather inappropriate glass object. When the padre advised me of his own similar feelings I was the first to support his view that we should replace it. The cost was about £1500 and the original was repositioned near the exit door.

I have to admit that I was the Commandant responsible for the demise of Colonel Johnny, the college mascot pony. On my initial interview with the Signal

Officer-in-Chief he remarked that during a graduation parade he had found the pony to be, 'bad tempered and behaving inappropriately. Perhaps the time had come to retire the pony.' Added to this the pony had developed problems with his hooves so I found a stable for him in Catterick for his retirement. No sooner had this happened than Brigadier Johnny Clinch, the donator of the mascot, rang the Master of Signals to complain of the treatment that I had meted out. It was decided that, in turn, the Master would discuss this important matter with the Signal Officer-in-Chief. So, I knew I was on a solid foundation.

Our relationship with the local community remained important. We provided significant assistance and funds for local charities and signed a Memorandum of Understanding with the American station at Menwith Hill.

The other two senior staff officers of the college changed almost simultaneously. The new Chief Instructor, Lieutenant Colonel Jimmy Blake arrived in summer 1987. He had served several tours in Germany, Northern Ireland, the UK and had commanded the White Helmets. He was a keen sportsman with special interest in rugby, rallying, golf, squash, sailboarding and sailing as well as music and reading. His tour was planned to be short before he moved on to HQ Northern Army Group later in the year when he was replaced by Lieutenant Colonel Chris Melhuish who had served with an Army Youth Team and extensively in BAOR. He had commanded 244 Signal Squadron (Air Support) and was a corps standard rugby player.

The new Senior Education Officer, Lieutenant Colonel Denis Aitken MSc RAEC, was an Old Welbexian who had originally been commissioned into the Royal Artillery. He had transferred into the RAEC and amongst other posts had served with the Junior Infantry Battalion, Shorncliffe. He was a keen sportsman.

Lieutenant Colonel Felix (Frank) Rogers came to the college as Quartermaster in spring 1988 on promotion. Thirty-seven years earlier in September

Band Sergeant Major Catterall leads the Pipes and Drums at the Harrogate Remembrance parade on 9 November 1986.

1950 he had arrived at Harrogate for the first time as an apprentice. Since then he had seen service in Hong Kong, Aden, Singapore, Malaya, Aden and BAOR. Frank was one of a few ATs to have made progress through all the ranks up to Lieutenant Colonel.

A warm welcome was extended to WO1 (RSM) R Ritchie, Scots Guards, during the summer term 1988. He had served in Northern Ireland, British Honduras, BAOR, Cyprus, and Kenya. Previously (1982 to 1984) he had been SSM of Bradley Squadron. He was a keen boxer, athlete and cyclist and stated that he was, 'Delighted to be back.'

The graduation parade on 3 June 1988 was of particular note because the Reviewing Officer was Major General WT Macfarlane CB who was the School Adjutant from 1950 to 1954.

During the summer term 1986 the first inter-squadron pace stick competition was held and won by Rawson Squadron. From this event the college team of WO2 Gordon Townsley, Sergeant Pete Griffin, Sergeant Lawler and Sergeant Rixon was selected to enter the 1986 world championships in which they came fifth. The delight was in beating the Irish Guards.

On 27 January 1987 three members of the college RAMC staff were outstanding when they were able to save the life of a young lady who was in a traffic accident on Penny Pot Lane. Lance Corporal John Williams was first to the scene of the accident, quickly followed by Staff Sergeant David Garbutt and Sergeant Peter Tyers.

The demise of Colonel Johnny came about on 30 September 1987 when he was put out to graze in Catterick. His handler, Corporal Glen Bedford, was delighted as he often finished important parades with bitten fingers and bruised legs. On one occasion his finger was fractured.

On 1 September 1986 Bradley Squadron became the Junior Leader Squadron and remained so until junior leaders ceased training at Harrogate. Troops of the squadron were associated with regiments of the corps and had appropriate insignia; Lightning Troop with 13 Signal Regiment, Quadrant Troop with 4th Division HQ and Signal Regiment, Rapier Troop with 22 Signal Regiment and Whitespear Troop with 7 Signal Regiment. The Squadron Commander was Major Rollo Rumford and WO2 (SSM) DJ Williams Scots Guards upheld discipline. Intakes 86B and 86C comprised 138 junior leaders and 78 junior leaders graduated in July 1987; so there was no shortage of willing volunteers. Bradley Squadron went on to win the Champion Squadron Trophy twice within its first year of existence.

The Adjutant, Captain WT McFarlane, and RSM, WO1 (RSM) S Lonsborough in 1952.

Major General WT McFarlane CB, the Reviewing Officer in June 1988 with WO1 (RSM) Stan Lonsborough who was a guest at the parade.

The college pace stick team that won the non-Household Division World Championships at Pirbright on 3 June 1988. WO2 (CSM) Mal Pearson, Sergeants Tom Dooley, Ken Shepherd, Jeff Watts and WO2 (SSM) Tony Spray.

The Mayor, Councillor John Marshall, presents the 'Helping Hand' for services to the community to AT J Osborne 3 June 1988.

By 1986 the Champion Squadron competition was decided on one day except for the drill competition. The format was designed to test the whole squadron with a range of tests that required most of the ATs to participate. It included NBC, first aid, swimming, obstacle course, shooting and a log race.

There were a number of charity events to maintain the college ethos for supporting less fortunate people. Rawson Squadron took the Dene Park Luncheon Club of elderly people on an all expenses paid day out to Blackpool. There was also a marathon darts event of twenty six hours six minutes and forty-one seconds on 12 July 1986 which raised over £600 for the Cheshire Home at Spoforth. In all, Sorbie, Prior, Bentley, Bingham, Chapman, Thomasson, Green and Hollamby scored over half a million points with AT Bingham being top scorer at 99,720.

The Catterick-to-Harrogate fun run by the PS in October 1986 was for the Harrogate Lourdes Fund.

This was in support of the wife of Sergeant Kingston who had recently benefited from the fund. In the same month Corporal Vivian and 9 ATs went to Leadhall Grange to build a playground area for the handicapped children.

One of the most challenging charity events was organised by Alan Green and his cyclists. *Exercise Long Haul* was a round trip from Harrogate to Land's End and John O'Groats covering 1856 miles. The event was to support the Oxfam 'Eritrea Agricultural College' and over £500 was raised. *Exercise Warrior* was a newly designed military training exercise to test ATs and JLs in range work and weapon handling. It was held at Wathgill Camp.

Telegraphist Wing also redesigned its exercises to meet trade requirements. The *Mercury* series of exercises were to practise VHF, HF and operator skills. Much of the exercise was carried out at Bishop Monkton which had been recently set up as a training area. Nearly 400 ATs went through the exercise in 1986. *Exercise Darb Zubaydah* 9 in November 1986 was to provide rear link communications to an expedition base camp in Riyadh, Saudi Arabia. This resulted in a training schedule being set up every Wednesday. There were also opportunities to provide local events with communications such as the Ripon 900 Diocesan Jubilee. Yeoman of Signals Bowden and 16 ATs provided communications with PYE pocket

An advert for the charity fund-raising Duck Race.

phones. The reward was a barrel of beer delivered to the guardroom by the Bishop.

Major Brian Kerslake RAEC led an adventurous training expedition to the Isle of Skye in June 1987 – *Exercise Skye Venture 1*. A total of nine personnel were given the opportunity to be introduced to mountaineering skills in the Cullin Mountains – the most challenging mountain environment in Great Britain. The week was a great success and a good time was had by ATs Alexander-High, Duffy, Thompson, Townsend, Firth and Adamson.

Adventure also came for the sub-aqua participants in the form of *Exercise Sea Scape* who were meant to go to Cyprus in Summer 1987. However, due to the unavailability of RAF flights, the location was eventually Oban. There were seven ATs and five instructors headed by Lieutenant Wilson RAEC. The lucky ATs were Christie, Osborne, Young, Millert, Collins, Newall and McCarter.

The Commandant's speech at the graduation on 19 December 1986 highlighted some of the successes of the year:

Cricket. A mention here of the college PS. They did very well to reach this year's Army finals on 3 September, but were narrowly defeated.

Football. The Penney Squadron football team retained the Army Apprentices' Cup by beating A Company of Princess Marina College, Arborfield. We have this season provided the captain and six regular players of the Army Youth Squad.

Hockey. The college beat the King's Division Depot last Saturday to win the district hockey championship and AT Roberts was selected to play for the Army Under-21s.

Orienteering. The college team won the Royal Signals Junior Team Championship on 11 October and AT Sharpe won the junior title.

Cycling. At the Army roller cycling championships held at Chepstow on 22 November the college came first in the junior team championship and second in the senior event. AT McLellan was the junior individual champion.

Cross Country. In the combined NE, NW and Scotland District Championship held at Catterick last week, the college came first in the junior team championships.

Squash. The college won the individual, the team and the open plate competition of the Royal Signals championships held at the college in November.

Of course these are only the highlights of our sporting activity and there has been a very busy programme of league and friendly matches.

In athletics in 1986 the college were Army team champions in Zone B and winners of the triangular competition. ATs Thomkinson, Downer, Lothian and Bartcliffe represented the Combined Services. The PS were not to be outdone by being Minor Unit champions.

The junior cricketers retained the Army Cup in 1986 by beating Infantry Ouston (Coleman 61, Fardy 4 for 12), RA Bramcote (Cole 7 for 6), Junior Leaders RE (Lamb 5 for 12 including 4 wickets with 4 balls) and REME Arborfield in the final in which Lamb scored 54 and Cole took 4 for 52. In the triangular matches an unusual record was set in 1987 when the competition ended all square for the third year running. In the final year Major (Retired) Don Robinson finally hung up his white jacket after running the side for over twenty years.

The 1986–87 season brought a double-double for Penney Squadron when they again won the Army Apprentices' Challenge Cup and the Army Youth Cup. The final in the former was at Aldershot against the REME at Arborfield and was won by AT Harrison with a goal late in extra time. In the latter there were victories against King's Regiment Ouston, Scott Squadron, 88 Squadron RE and REME Arborfield in the final. The team was trained by Sergeant Andrews and the mainstays of the team included ATs Leyland, Stafford, McCarthy and Storey. Soccer tours to BAOR were very popular and in 1987 matches were arranged against 13, 16 and 21 Signal regiments. The college found playing against such teams was tough and although they lost them all they were only by the odd goal.

The finals of college boxing were attended by John Conteh on 18 February 1987 and he presented all the prizes. The Champion Squadron at senior level was Rawson Squadron with AT Duggan awarded the best boxer prize and AT Moffat the best loser. The junior champions were also Rawson and AT Dickson was best boxer and AT Hunt best loser. Captain Coffey then took nine boxers to the Army junior championships in March at Shorncliffe where AT Henderson, in his first year of boxing, became the first Army champion that the college had produced for many years.

The hockey season's highlights were made by the PS when they became NE District Minor Unit champions when they beat King's Division by 2-0. Of the ATs, AT Roberts excelled and represented the Army and Combined Services; he was also top scorer of the season with nine goals. The team went on to reach the final of the Army Junior Cup against REME. The tour to BAOR was popular during which the team played in the Rear Combat Zone and corps six-a-side competitions for a total of 11 exhausting matches.

This was a period of strength for college squash. In 1987 both the Under-19 and the junior team were Army champions. ATs Roberts, Piers and Wood were the senior team. ATs Rossiter, Barker, Hinton, Glove and JLs Stonstreet, Glover and Philips represented the juniors.

The arrival of Major Mike Fisher in Bradley Squadron brought about the formation of 'The Arrowgate Archers' on 18 June 1987. It started with membership of about 48 but soon became very popular indeed. In the same year the college entered a team in the Army (UK) indoor championships. AT Burke won the individual gold medal and the handicap award. The team of JLs Overal, Cruickshank, Ward and AT Evans also won the Gatgan Shield as junior champions. The senior team won the silver medal. Archery remained popular until the college closed.

In February 1987 WO2 (SSM) Townsley entered the UKLF Alpine skiing championships at Aviemore. He swept the board in his events and was Army champion, Army UKLF champion, Army veteran champion and the corps champion.

Judo remained a popular sport with a membership of about 40. The team won the Triangular Games with ease and this was the first time that the college had won the event since its inception in 1976. Winners included ATs Leatherbarrow, Whitrow, Holland, Whitehead, Porter and Hitchin. The team also won 11 medals in the Army judo championships which secured the runners-up award.

The 1986–1987 season was a bumper year for the canoeists with upwards of 25 paddlers attending the training sessions at Slenningford Mill, Bishop Monkton or the swimming pool. JL Downey, AT Lewis-Walker and AT Broders won the Army junior slalom championships and were selected to represent UKLF against BAOR in which they subsequently

destroyed all opposition at the dreaded Tryweryn Falls. The summer months brought about the 1st Royal Signals sprint and marathon championships followed by the Army championships in which the club captured an amazing 19 medals. Colours in 1987 went to JLs Downey, Howie, Harper and Vanandeland and AT Clifford. Canoeing was in the safe hands of Mr Archie Miles.

1987 also brought success to the college cyclists in the Army Cycling Festival staged at Dover. AT Paul McClellan won the 25-mile time trial and, supported by ATs Mark Leak and Peter Barber, won the team event. Sergeant Bob Young established a new twelve-hour roller cycle world record when he completed 312 miles at an average of 26 miles per hour. The Mayor of Harrogate's Fund benefited by £1000 from his efforts.

The college swimming team suffered because the pool was out of use for months on end. Major MJW Lord put this right by using the local pools at Harrogate Ladies' College and the Police Training College. As a result the college were runners-up in the Army junior championships and ATs Hobson, Ledger, Evans and JL Douglas were selected for the Army. Success came in the Triangular Games in July 1987 when ten months of hard training were rewarded with a win.

At the Army Youth Rugby Challenge Final of 16 December 1987 it appeared that the college were

Army Rugby Youth Cup winners 1987. Back row: *ATs Hayes, LCpl Ball, Cpl Clapham, JL Shaw, ATs Wilson, Clark, Leaser, JL Clark.* Middle row: *SSgt Thompson, ATs Williams, LCpl Tubbs, Parr, Coombs, JL Ridges, ATs LCpl White, LCpl Bembridge, Sergeant Stevenson, Lt JW Cooper (OIC).* Front row: *AT LCpl Waley, JL LCpl Whitworth, AT SSM Browning (captain), ATs Sgt Millar, Cpl Bradley, LCpl Noble.*

heading to be worthy losers. Chepstow led at half time but inspired play by AT Browning, AT Tubbs and JL Whitworth took the college to a narrow 14-13 win. Browning scored 10 of the points.

Some individual successes included AT Corporal Sharp who was the Army orienteering champion and AT Coleman was the Army junior tennis champion. AT Young was the Army football young player of the year. AT Foss won the college golf competition in 1988.

The WRVS Club continued to thrive under Mrs Sheila Cotter. There were many darts, snooker, games evenings and table-tennis competitions. In December 1986, at the last event organised by Sheila, AT Patterson was the snooker champion, Piercy won the darts, JL Cuthbertson the table tennis and AT Moffat the pool. She stated, 'I am very sorry to be leaving the club but I hope it will continue to be home from home for ATs and JLs for many years to come.'

A further unit moved into Hildebrand Barracks in 1987 in the form of D Company, 1st Battalion Yorkshire Volunteers. On 25 April 1993, they were retitled C Company, 4th/5th battalion, The Green Howards. They were disbanded on 21 March, 1999.

Colonel Garton completed his tour and was escorted from the camp in an appropriate manner, 'My time at the college was thoroughly enjoyable and my departure by Smiths' Ales grey horses was memorable and, perhaps, fitting!'

General knowledge test.
Q. *What is the Pentagon?*
A. *A group of countries playing each other at sport.*

18

ROYAL VISIT AND CHANGES DUE
TO THE CAREER REVIEW

Colonel KP Burke – January 1989 to September 1990

Colonel KP Burke (Keith) assumed the appointment of Commandant in January 1989. He was born in Pembrokeshire and his father had been a senior officer in Royal Signals. He was educated at Welbeck College and was commissioned into the corps in 1960. He went on to study for an electrical engineering degree at the Royal Military College of Science, Shrivenham. His military service had taken him to 4th Signal Regiment BAOR, Singapore, the Army Staff Course, Northern Army Group and Northern Ireland. He had held staff appointments in 1st British corps, RMCS, Operational Requirements in MOD and the Procurement Executive. He had commanded 7th Signal Regiment, the largest regiment in the corps.

Colonel Burke arrived at the college when there were significant changes taking place in the Royal Signals trade structure. The trade structure of the 1970s and 80s did not meet the demands of the 1990s and this had been identified in the 'Review of Career Employments'. In his opening remarks in *The Gate* he stated:

Some changes should and would occur as a direct result of the recent Review of Career Employment. We are now in the difficult process of setting ourselves up for the demands of the 1990s and the inevitable further advances in technology and their introduction into the Army and its equipment. There is much planning completed and I shall be looking to you all, apprentices, junior leaders and both civilian and military members of the permanent staff, to play your part in our joint future.

For Technicians' Wing the outcome was that the college then taught a common syllabus for technicians, whose final trade selection was not made until towards the end of their time at the college just before the equipment phase of training. This took place for three months at Catterick after graduation from Harrogate. The split in training was necessary because there was insufficient training equipment for Catterick, Blandford and Harrogate; especially 'Ptarmigan'. The choice of trade was telecommunications technician (radio) or telecommunications technician (radio relay). This change in trade

May 1989 – The Commandant presents the Imperial Service Medal to Mr Charles Allan who joined the college in June 1962 and served for twenty-eight years. Previously he had served with the Royal Marines for thirteen years.

Signalman Paul Meredith received a Commander Training Group's Commendation for saving a man's life after a traffic accident in Harrogate. His award caught up with him when Air Vice Marshal Crwys-Williams made the presentation in the Falkland Islands.

Her Royal Highness, the Princess Royal, inspects the apprentices at the Graduation Parade on 3 August 1990.

structure coincided with changes in the BTEC diploma requirements. The syllabuses needed to be rewritten and some of the modules had to be reconfigured. The gaining of a BTEC diploma was a considerable attraction in the recruiting of technicians, so meeting the requirements was essential.

Telegraphist Wing trained telecommunications operator (telegraph), telecommunications operator (systems), telecommunications operator (special) and telecommunications operator (linguist). The linguists and special operators continued with the equipment phase of their training at the Intelligence and Security Group, Loughborough, once they had graduated from Harrogate. The systems operators were also required to go on to pass the HGV driving test and so the telegraphists were the only tradesmen who departed from the college as fully trained soldiers. One of the main changes in the wing was the arrival of a new keyboard trainer, the typing skills trainer (TST) which replaced the T100 teleprinter. The TST could simulate both Cossor and Trend teleprinters. The Cossor was the operational teleprinter and the Trend was used in 'Commcens'. The TST was excellent equipment which could test tradesmen and produce the results. However, it was found later that some of the cleverer operators could

reconfigure the software to print out false results; higher of course!

In 1996 Colonel Burke reflected on some of the incidents during his time at the college:

When rehearsing for the visit of Princess Anne as Reviewing Officer to the summer 1990 pass-off parade, a bomb alert was telephoned in to the college. Major Mike Fisher who was the officer responsible for operations and security and was manning the Operations Room for just such an event; alerted us and the local civilian Police. We had reached the stage in the rehearsal when Princess Anne had concluded the parade and was in the process of meeting a number of personnel in groups of ten. We decided we would play the incident for real and therefore attempted to remove Princess Anne in a speedy manner via a simulated helicopter, at the same time dispersing the crowds. As you would imagine this caused quite a stir and we never really got to the bottom of the telephone call but we rather believed it was probably a hoax.

Mike Fisher again. Mike ran and organised the Great Northern duck race. This consisted of selling about 4000 yellow plastic ducks at £1 each which are then dropped centrally off a bridge into a river, they flow downstream and the winner is the duck which passes a nominated line first. It makes a lot of money for the winner and even more for charity. Knaresborough were having their annual fête and Mike had spent a lot of time selling these ducks. However, when we heaved them over the bridge with due ceremony, they fell into what can only be described as slack water. We had had a dry summer and there was hardly any water in the river and these ducks moved off at a very very sedate pace. As the winner was due to get £1000 we were somewhat concerned that they were never going to reach the spot by the end of the fete. Various methods were used such as throwing stones and sticks, and people in boats kicking them on, but the net result was that we had to shorten the course. A winner was selected and everyone was happy. However, the old hearts fluttered a bit.

I had been told that a graduation parade had never been rained off and taken place in the Drill Shed, that being the planned wet weather programme. I regret to say that this happened during my time; it bucketed down and as bad luck would have it, it was not just an ordinary Army General coming, it was Air Vice Marshal Brown who was Chief of CIS for the Air Force. However it went off very well even if it was considerably less impressive than the show we normally put on.

The Commandant's Walk takes place each term and there was an occasion when I was out on the course with Claire and the Chief Instructor, Lieutenant Colonel Chris Melhuish. We had been told about something called 'Petrified Moss' which was apparently famous and was to be found at a particular waterfall that we were passing. Everyone therefore wanted to stop and have a look. Led by the Commandant and the chief instructor a number leant forward towards the waterfall to inspect whatever Petrified Moss was present. There was certainly quite a lot of moss, so much so that the water on the round rock on which we were standing had made it slippery and the Commandant did a dive fully regaled in all his walking kit, spectacles, stick, etc. straight into the pool which was very deep and very cold. The chief instructor was heroic and helped to pull the Commandant out, nearly being pulled in for his trouble. All of this had a certain amount of amusement, but the assembled staff were not quite sure how the Commandant was going to view it after he got out of the water. There was a stunned silence awaiting me as I rose from the depths, pretty bedraggled, very cold and pretty relieved to have got out. I am happy to say that there were only two choices – cry or laugh – so I chose the latter which broke the tension. I then had to walk for the remainder of the day in saturated kit which did gradually dry out as we went round on one of these wonderful walks. Claire wrote an amusing little article which was in the college magazine, the 'Commandant's Splash' would be a better name in future.

During my time I introduced something which I thought made quite a bit of difference to the parades and this was to invite the Guardsmen present to wear Public Duties Dress. We got permission from the Guards Depot and from the Household Brigade for them to be issued with their bearskins and dress suits and it has made a very big difference, I believe, to the splendour of the graduation parade.

Another first, I think, was that I managed to persuade our corps Band to allow the College Band, particularly our Pipes and Drums, to perform with them at the Old Comrades' Weekend up in Catterick. In fact they helped them to Beat Retreat in front of Richmond Castle. This really was a first and took quite a lot of doing. Professionals it appears do not wish to be mixed in with amateurs. The outcome was excellent.

Colonel Burke mentioned the visit of The Colonel in Chief Royal Signals, Her Royal Highness the Princess Royal GCVO. This was for the graduation parade on 3 August 1990 when 66 junior leaders and 155 apprentices graduated with AT RSM I Davis in command of the parade. Her Royal Highness arrived in the camp by helicopter and inspected the troops escorted by the Master of Signals. This was a time when future cuts in the Armed Services were imminent and mention was made:

Whatever the future of our Armed Services, communications will remain crucial. The skills and values you have here at the college will remain crucial in a most worthwhile career as well as in the service of your country.

Her Royal Highness then presented 20 awards. Following luncheon in the officers' mess the royal party departed for the Royal Signals Adventurous Training Centre, Whernside, in the Lake District. The day had been an outstanding success and WO1 (RSM) R Ritchie, Scots Guards, was pleased with the way those on parade had performed.

Major General PD Alexander inspects the Quarter Guard with the Commandant. Chin-straps are down to protect against the fierce Penny Pot wind.

Another royal event for the college occurred in the Queen's Birthday Honours List of 1989 when Mr Keith Thomas of Operator Wing was awarded the British Empire Medal. Keith, born at Deri in South Wales, first trained as a radio officer in the Merchant Navy. He then served nine years with the RAF and afterwards became an instructional officer at 14 Signal Regiment, Gloucester where he also qualified as youth leader. In 1969 he transferred to Harrogate and voluntarily formed the Penny Pot Youth Club. Under his leadership this flourished. From 1976 to 1979 he worked with the Physically Handicapped and Able Bodied Youth Club (PHAB) in Harrogate where he ran discos, camps, dances, games nights and visits. He was also the mainstay in the College's Duke of Edinburgh Award Scheme. His efforts over a long period of time were appropriately recognised.

Operator Wing, with Major (Tfc) Dave Tunmore QGM and his 34 staff, were moving with the technological times and on 24 July 1989 took delivery of the 'Scicon' automatic message switch. This was the same operational equipment as was deployed in Hong Kong and Northern Ireland and enabled Mr Terry Buss to give the ATs realistic training during their course. *Exercise Homebase* was to become a well known part of the course.

Technician Wing were also forging ahead. A new transmission lab was installed by Mr Wilson, Mr Steel and Sergeant Tomkins. Mr Gorman designed a new soldering lab and the courses were redesigned with a much higher practical content to simulate field conditions.

Meanwhile, Military Training Wing was being kept busy with the level of new recruits. There were 84 in Intake 89A, 237 in 89B and 182 in 89C. The dreaded final hurdle, *Exercise Warrior's Quest* seemed to come around all too often. The culminating tests of home defence, range management, fitness, NBC, first aid and basic battle skills were always approached with a measure of caution. Other codes such as YW SLR, YW Defence, YW SAA and WQ 1 & 2 would also set the heart racing. Nothing seemed to stir the blood more than the prospect of a good military training exercise. The wing also had to prepare for the arrival of the new rifle, SA80, in 1991.

The period saw moderate success at hockey which was still played on shale at the college although astroturf was coming into vogue. The PS team were District Cup winners under Captain Dave Luckett in 1989. AT Cunnion played for the corps and he, Emsen and Hopkins represented Army U25.

The AT rugby team was narrowly defeated by Arborfield, 15-13, in the 1988/89 final despite the best two tries of the match being scored by AT Sergeant Jones. ATs Benbridge, Williams, Clarke, Hayes and Parr played for the Army Colts with the last two being selected for the Combined Services team.

The 1990 football team had seven players in the Army Youth squad: ATs McBean, Chester, McLachlan, Briggs, Todd and JL McNeill. The swimmers were Army junior champions and the Triangular Cup winners. Captain Wallace managed the team and his efforts included a trip to Berlin with them The cricketers beat Arborfield in 1989 to take the Army Cup. Corporal Wilson scored 85 and AT Siggs took 3 for 19 and scored 30. In tennis ATs Hope and Whitford were Army junior and district doubles champions. The ski team won the junior championship in 1989 and retained it in 1990. The junior leader team won the Army Nordic ski championships: JLs Mollon, Finch, Powell, Carter and Greenwell.

The Duke of Edinburgh Award Scheme continued to be very well supported with about 20 members. ATs Morgan, Campbell and Eaves were all presented with their gold awards at St James's Palace by His Royal Highness, The Duke of Edinburgh. Private Linda Eden WRAC received a Silver Award.

Adventurous training exercises continued to abound. ATs McHenry and Macgillivary went to Israel on a wilderness trail. *Exercise Viking Lope* took the skiers to Norway in January 1990. *Exercise Snowscapes* continued to provide the college with a stream of competent skiers. *Exercise Norscape* saw JLs Morrow, McCully, Johnson, Icke and Mitchell in Norway. The sub-aqua club mounted expeditions to Scotland, Plymouth and Cyprus during 1989–90 and qualified 21 novices, 15 spots divers and three diver leaders in so doing.

Colonel Burke saw out the 1980s and departed in September 1990 just as the outcome of the Government's drive to make financial savings was gaining momentum.

Apprentice to Instructor.
"But surely, if you put the D11 transmitter on full power it must improve the reception".

19

THE FINAL COUNTDOWN
GREATCOATS ON... GREATCOATS OFF...

Colonel WH Backhouse – October 1990 to December 1991
Colonel CJ Walters – January 1992 to July 1995
Lieutenant Colonel P Richards Royal Signals – July 1995 to August 1996

The title of this chapter draws attention to both the demise of the college and the 'stop-start fashion' in which it was managed by the Ministry of Defence. To create the clearest picture from some very blurred situations that were created, the final drawdown is best portrayed in a single chapter. It does not make for easy or comfortable reading and says little for Ministry of Defence clear thinking and planning. It was certainly the most turbulent time in the history of the college.

Colonel WH Backhouse took command of the college in October 1990. Previously he had been Chief Instructor at the School of Signals and this, combined with his background as a former captain of corps rugby, made him an ideal selection. Although his tour only lasted fifteen months before he was promoted to command 11 Signal Brigade, it was a very important era in the history of apprentice training which was brought about by significant changes in the defence policies of western governments. He was succeeded by Colonel CJ Walters in January 1992 who was the third Old Welbexian in succession. The short gap in the appointment was unavoidable as Colonel Walters was serving in Northern Iraq on *Operation Haven* at the time. He had previously commanded 28th Signal Regiment and 259 Signal Squadron. He had served in Hong Kong, Cyprus, the Ministry of Defence, Germany and the UK. He was a keen sportsman and had played hockey, cricket, rugby, squash, tennis, golf and soccer at representative level. The college would not be short of encouragement on the sporting field. In turn, he was succeeded by Lieutenant Colonel P Richards R Signals, who had previously been the Chief Instructor since summer 1994, and whose experiences would serve him well during the final year of the college.

The worldwide decline of communism, which was symbolised by the fall of the Berlin Wall in November 1989, had brought about a 'Peace Dividend'. There was no longer an easily identified

Lieutenant Colonel Peter Richards, Royal Signals, the last Commandant of the Army Apprentices' College, Harrogate.

The Earl of Arran inspects the Quarter Guard with the Commandant – October 1991.

Soviet threat across the inner German border and western governments took the opportunity to make significant cuts in their defence spending; in view of the deep recession this was welcome news in the UK. It was initially decided, for instance, that the British Army should be reduced to a trained strength of 104,000 soldiers. This was later increased to 106,500 when the troubles in the former Yugoslavia underlined our inability to meet defence commitments. 'Options for Change' brought about significant, and well publicised changes, to the NATO, and hence British, defence posture. As a part of the restructuring programme there was also a complete 'Review of the Training Base (RTB)' which was carried out by the Inspector General of doctrine and training and it looked at all aspects of military training. It was this latter review, the aim of which was to save money and manpower, that had such a profound effect on the future of the college and on Royal Signals training as a whole.

The first results of the RTB were announced on 4 February 1991 and stated that there were to be only eight establishments that would deal with initial (Phase 1) training in the Army. There were to be five Army Training regiments (ATRs) for new recruits, a single Army technical college for apprentices and two Army Junior Leader regiments (AJLRs), one of which was to be at Harrogate. Much of this reorganisation was to be undertaken quickly in order to make the necessary savings.

The setting up of the ATRs heralded the demise of 11th Signal Regiment and the final parade was held on 11 December 1992 at Helles Barracks, Catterick. Commencing on 1 January 1993 all Royal Signals recruit training was carried out at ATR Bassingbourn. The first pass-out parade to be taken by a senior Royal Signals officer at the new establishment was on 8 April 1993 by Colonel CJ Walters, Commandant of the Army Apprentices' College, Harrogate.

The plan for a single Army technical college (ATC) for apprentices became a complex issue. Eventually, Arborfield was selected as the ATC for RE, R Signals and REME Apprentices, with a 'wing' at Aldershot for the ACC. Training was to commence on 6 September 1993 and this would enable the colleges at Harrogate and Chepstow to be closed by December 1993 and June 1994 respectively. The aim was to produce a one-year foundation course at the ATC which would be followed by a further one year 'Special-to-Arm course' at the appropriate trade (Phase 2) training centre (8th Signal Regiment in the case of Royal Signals). Plans were made to set up the ATC to the extent that the course content was devised and the moving of equipment from the closing colleges was arranged. The pilot foundation course commenced at Harrogate with apprentice Intake 92B in September 1992. On completion of the first year of the course it was intended that the apprentices would

Major General Boyle with the staff of the newly formed C Company displaying their many cap badges.

continue training in 8th Signal Regiment, Catterick. However, on 16 December 1992, in a further Ministerial announcement, there were two 'bombshells'. Firstly, plans for the single ATS were aborted and the various corps were instructed to retain the apprenticeship within their own Phase 2 training organisation.

The initial overall plan had required that Harrogate should phase out apprentice training by December 1993. Meanwhile, it should hurriedly convert to an AJLR for which Intake 92C, comprising 75 All Arms junior leaders, arrived on 26 October 1992. The aim was to take a maximum of 1000 junior leaders each year, in four intakes, from RE, R Signals, Infantry and the new Royal Logistic Corps (RLC). Training would be in 'cap badged' companies and as the initial intake was predominantly infantry, C Company was set up first under command of Major N Parker PWO. The six-month long course of instruction for the junior leaders had been piloted by the Junior Leader Regiment, Bramcote, which was to be the other AJLR. This had enabled the staff to iron out many of the problems that had occurred on the course which was known as the Common Military Syllabus (Junior Entry) (CMS{JE}) and comprised twenty-one weeks of intensive training. At this time there were 29 different cap badges in the college which was reminiscent of the days of the original school.

Whilst the AJLR was being established at Harrogate there were still Royal Signals junior leaders from Intake 92A, who were completing their one-year course, which ended with the parade on 17 December 1992. The Reviewing Officer for the parade was Brigadier JD Stokoe CBE who himself had been an apprentice at the college in Intake 64. This also brought about the demise of Bradley Squadron which went into suspended animation after over twenty years. It was a sad but moving farewell in the sergeants' mess on 28 November 1992 when the last intake of 32 junior leaders on the one-year course dined out in the presence of Major General PEM Bradley CB CBE DSO and his wife. In his speech he, reflected on the importance of junior leaders to the corps in the past and the numbers that had gone on to long and distinguished careers.

From this it is evident that during the second half of 1992 there were four different courses being held simultaneously at the college: the two-year apprenticeship course; the one-year apprenticeship foundation pilot course; the Royal Signals one-year junior leader course and the new CMS(JE).

The second 'bombshell' contained in the ministerial announcement was that there was no longer to be a junior leader entry in the Army. This would enable the AJLRs at Harrogate and Bramcote to be closed with corresponding finanancial savings. In future the Army would adopt a single-entry system commencing in September 1993; the only exception being an annual intake of about 1000 apprentices of which 267 would be Royal Signals trained as described previously. By this time, the second report of the RTB had been published and was not to the liking of the majority of the Royal Corps of Signals. The report decreed that all Royal Signals training should be carried out in a single 'Centre of

Excellence' located at Blandford. This would necessitate the whole of the training group functions, including 8th Signal Regiment, Catterick and the Army Apprentices' College, being transferred to Dorset by mid-1995.

The arrangements for the future of the college had taken yet another complete about turn. This meant that Intake 93A of All Arms junior leaders were the second and final course of its type. So it was, on 18 June 1993, that Brigadier JM Macfarlane MA, Director of Educational and Training Support for the Army (DETS[A]), was the final Reviewing Officer for junior leaders in the British Army. Fittingly, the weather was kind as the 39 junior leaders of C Company paraded with a total of 17 different cap badges representing Royal Signals, The King's Division, the Queen's Division and Staff. This second pass-out parade was the last, after which C Company was disbanded. But they had made their indelible mark on the college and at the prize-giving Brigadier Macfarlane presented the Champion Squadron Trophy to JL Sergeant Napper. Deservedly, C Company had won it only four days earlier. It had been twenty-seven years since a company had been victorious and was prior to the formation of the college from the school in 1966.

The officers' mess in 1995. Third row (l to r): *Capt D Kerridge, Lt KM Levins, Capt PA Moorehouse, Capt ADM Angus, Lt BA Northover, Lt CFS Waudby, Capt AM Churchill.* Second row (l to r): *Maj BW Maltby, Maj M Davis, Maj GL Hegarty, Maj (Retd) BM Hudson, Maj MD Bailes, Capt A Middleton MBE, Capt G M Rutherford, Maj DJ Lumb, Padre CW Gibbs.* Front row (l to r): *Maj DS Smith, Maj PM Castle, Lt Col P Richards, Col CJ Walters, Maj D Bornstein, Maj D Shawyer, Maj GJ McNeill.*

The Apprentices' Pipes and Drums in 1994.

The departure of C Company reduced the college population to 342 apprentices who were reorganised into Scott and Rawson squadrons. The staff overall was reduced to cater for the intended annual intake of up to 267 apprentices, the course for whom had by now reverted to the original two-year apprenticeship.

The college went through an extended period of uncertainty and turmoil. The civilian staff were unsettled because of this but they remained completely loyal throughout. The local employment situation had been made worse by parallel news from the RAF restructuring programme. The MOD offices at St George's Road were to move from Harrogate to Cambridgeshire in 1995 with a loss of over 1300 jobs. There had also been losses of jobs at a number of the major civilian firms in the town due to the recession. Harrogate was not going to be an easy place to get employment for the foreseeable future and as at June 1993 no further use had been found for Uniacke and Hildebrand Barracks.

The military staff were also unsettled by the three rounds of redundancy that occurred in successive years from 1991. This had combined with the setting up and dismantling of the AJLR, all within eight months, bringing a good deal of uncertainty and scepticism. The restructuring of the Army brought about the formation of the Adjutant General's corps on 5 April 1992, and the Royal Logistic corps on 5 April 1993. There were appropriate occasions in each case to make the necessary changes in cap badges and other accoutrements but, noticeably, none of the PS volunteered for a formal parade. The college also suddenly found its Royal Signals Chief Clerk, WO2 (ORQMS) BD Durlik, wearing a very smart green beret which supported the AGC(SPS) cap badge; he was also retitled RAOWO.

Amongst all these changes training on the ground went on much as normal. One of the major historical events was in September 1991 when 31 female apprentices (Apprentice Tradeswoman – ATW) arrived for the first time with Intake 91B. The intake was also to provide the first ATW SSM when ATW SSM JA Willis was promoted on 1 March 1993. Intake 91C was to go one stage further when ATW K Moore became the best recruit in her squadron before becoming ATW SSM in June 1993 and the first female AT RSM on 6 September 1993. In 1999, after passing her Regular Commissions Board, she went on to attend the Commissioning Course at the Royal Military Academy, Sandhurst and to be commissioned into Royal Signals. There was to be further surprise on 10 July 1993 when the Scott Squadron

The first apprentice tradeswomen on parade.

ATW Karen Moore was the first female apprentice RSM and she commanded the graduation parade on 22 October 1993.

was decided to run a number of basic recruit training and trade courses (Phase 2) at the college for adult soldiers or single-entry (SE) as it became known. The maximum number of students was to be 200 and the courses covered were telegraph operators and telegraph technicians; stores accountant was added later. To meet this heavy commitment personnel of 2 Squadron, 8th Signal Regiment, under command of Major Brian Smith, moved into the college and commenced training 41 SE recruits from Bassingbourne on 5 September 1994. Shortly afterwards they were retitled Bradley Squadron.

One of the final 'hat-tricks' that the Ministry of Defence performed was to abolish the plan to hold apprenticeship courses at Blandford. The final decision was to centralise a forty-two-week course at Arborfield. Unfortunately, it did not include trade training and so was to be more akin to the junior leaders course of old. The trade aspect would follow on at Blandford together with the SE recruits. Those apprentices of Intakes 95B and 95C who were at Harrogate when it closed but had only completed one year of their course moved to Blandford as Rawson Troop under command of Lieutenant G Oliver. The 71 ATs of Intake 95B completed their course and graduated on 9 August 1997 when the Reviewing Officer was Major General JD Stokoe CBE. It was appropriate that an ex-apprentice should review on such a memorable occasion. AT SSM SR Pritchard was the senior apprentice who won four

female team won the junior drill competition and ATW Corporal N Sweeney was judged to be the best Squad Commander.

The arrival of female apprentices did not change the training programme in any way; this was a major policy decision. They carried out exactly the same programme as the males including PT, military exercises and external leadership. Females were accepted into all six trades. It has to be said that the discos in the NAAFI took on a new meaning and there was no longer the need to import local girls from town. There were also strict rules about access to accommodation of the opposite sex which, as some found to their cost, was an expensive rule to disobey!

In the spring of 1994 the plans were still in place to move the apprenticeship to Blandford by July 1995 but there were more surprises still to be drawn out of the hat by the Ministry of Defence. It was decided to close down 8th Signal Regiment in Catterick by October 1994 although Blandford would not be ready to take on the training commitment. To ensure that recruiting into the corps did not completely dry up it

On 10 February 1996 Colonel G Dickson-Gribble, Commander of Menwith Hill Station, was the Reviewing Officer at the passing-off parade of Intake 95C.

Education Wing staff with the Director of the Education Training Services (Army) 18 June 1993. Back row: *BS Allen, M Steele, 2Lt HC Campbell, DM O'Donnell, T Page, JM James, 2Lt SJ Hulm, A Gallacher, AAR Ferguson.* Middle row: *SSgt PD Ashworth, Mrs W McLeod, DT James, R Trenam, D Wolstencroft, A Miles, C Gray, R Walden, D Kearns, DW Robinson, Lt LE Hambly.* Front row: *Capt A Bishop, A Harwood, Maj NJ Wilson, Col CJ Walters, Brig JM Macfarlane, Lt Col DWM Magee, Maj WB Kerslake, A Green, R Cooper, LT SV Roberts.*

major prizes including the Worshipful Company of Information Technologists' Prize. AT SSM RW Dunlop commanded the troops on parade at the graduation parade of Intake 95C when the last of the Harrogate ATs finally passed into men's service from Blandford.

One could be forgiven for thinking that all of the orders and counter-orders that occurred during this drawdown phase might have brought on a time of 'doom and gloom' in the college, but reality was far from this. Lieutenant Colonel Richard Hewitt, the Chief Instructor, saw that each of the departments was ensuring that the apprentices and single-entry recruits were getting full value from their courses.

Education Wing was moving with the times initially under Lieutenant Colonel John Taylor and later Lieutenant Colonel David Magee. There was considerable course design to meet the needs of the various courses and in 1994 the RSA computer literacy and information technology (CLAIT) course was introduced for everyone. Thirty new 386X computers were procured for the Science Department. The 'Educators' played their full part in college life especially in supporting sport and adventurous training. Lieutenant Lorna Hambly played hockey and tennis for the Army. Skiing, sub aqua and canoeing relied on the staff of the

wing. In 1991 Mr John Primrose left the Maths Department after nearly thirty years' service with the college. A shock came to the Young ETS officers when the Commandant decided that they should all command AT Troops in addition to their educational duties.

Operator Wing had redesigned its courses to meet the needs of the Royal Signals trade review and *Exercise Mercury 1* to 5 were introduced. This was a progressive series of exercises ending with deployments to Stirling, Weston-super-Mare and Dartmoor on *Mercury 4* and over 20 tests on *Mercury 5* before final graduation. WO2 Ashworth established *Exercise Monitor 3* and *Big Ears* for the specialist operators and linguists respectively. Major Chas Birchall also reported, 'A number of our recently departed ATs have written to us reporting on their success in the Gulf War.'

Technician Wing came under command of Majors Cliff Webb, Bryan Maltby and Peter Shawyer. Keeping up with the changes was no easy matter. Visits to industry remained an important part of the learning process which included GEC Plessey Telecomms to witness the manufacture of ISDX printed circuit boards. They said farewell to Mr Mike Wilson who retired after thirty-six years' service to the college; a stalwart to say the least.

THE FINAL COUNT DOWN – GREAT COATS ON... GREAT COATS OFF...

General Training Wing, which included military and external leadership training, redesigned their courses of instruction to meet the new challenges. Military training under Major Bob McDonald introduced a series of progressively tough exercises encompassing *Exercise Tenderfoot, Military Training 1 to 3* and *Exercise Young Warrior Defence*. The latter was known as *'DIG'* as it included forty hours of trench digging in the Catterick training area. Captain Dee Kerridge APTC expanded the external leadership courses to include EL Basic, EL Snow and Ice (winter), EL Caving, EL Canoe (summer), EL Expedition, EL Rock (Spring) and *Exercise Highland Endeavour*.

Adventurous training went from strength to strength with many ambitious and successful expeditions. This resulted from a combination of dedicated staff who were prepared to make considerable personal effort and a range of ATs who were keen to take advantage of every opportunity that came their way. The most newsworthy was *Exercise Uniacke Express* to Nepal in April 1992. The leader was Major David Craig RAEC. He took a party of 18 white-water rafting on the Sun Koshi river and the event was reported on the TV programme 'Blue Peter'. Exactly one year later Lieutenant Tim Smith lead Exercise Chaklagdo Jindagi of 11 personnel to the Helambu region of central Nepal where they trekked to a height of 14,000 feet. In February 1994 Captain Stu Moffat and WO2 (RQMS) Eccles took a party of 12 skiers to Scotland and on to Norway. On 28 July 1995, Lieutenant Kerry Levins and a party of 12, set out on *Exercise Alps Wander* to explore the mountains of Italy. Captain Andy Churchill and Mr Archie Miles ventured to Costa Rica on *Exercise Big Wednesday* in September 1995. Canoeing the giant Pacuare river and sea kayaking the Pacific coast is something that ATs Turnock, Belton, Hadley and Vernon will not forget. Mr Mike McHale was exceptional in leading four expeditions each year; one skiing to Austria and three sub-aqua diving. The

latter went to Gibraltar, Scapa Flow, Kyle of Lochalsh, Benbecula or the Ascension Islands. The 1993 trip to Ascension assisted the Royal Navy by carrying out an underwater inspection of a survey ship and thereby avoided the need for a specialist team to be flown out from the UK. Mr Rod Trenam was equally dedicated with his efforts for downhill skiing to ensure that *Exercise Snowscapes* took place each year in such places as Austria and Bulgaria.

During this time there was a stalwart of a man being rewarded for devoting over forty-eight years to the corps; of these, forty years of loyalty had been given to the college. Mr Peter Sharp had joined Royal Signals at Catterick as a boy soldier and was one of those to transfer to Harrogate in September 1948. Having trained as a telecommunications mechanic and returned to Harrogate as a staff sergeant he then retired from the Army and stayed on as a civilian instructor. He served 12 commandants as senior instructional officer and pioneered many aspects of training qualifications. On 24 November 1994, at the London International Press Centre, he received the Royal Signals Institution Silver Medal from Major General AC Birtwistle CB CBE DL, the Master of Signals. This is regarded as a rare award that marks the attainment of an outstanding professional achievement in the corps. It could not have been better earned.

The college also had its share of sporting success some of which was encouraged by the adventurous training exercises. For a number of years the college team excelled at the various forms of skiing. In 1991 nine first places were won at the Nordic skiing championships. The PS team comprised Major Heritage, Captain Ashton, WO2 Rafferty and Lance Corporal Clinton. The junior leaders' team comprised JL Daeth, Lello, Picken, Stenning and Wall. There is no doubt that the seeds of skiing success in the college were sown by Major David Pugh who departed in 1991 after six years as OC HQ Squadron. Successive teams went on to perform just as successfully with Staff Sergeant Steve Major as the leading instructor. At the UKLF downhill championships in March 1993 the college teams, led by Captain Andy Frost and AT Doughty, took ten major trophies including Regular Army Inter-Unit champions and Junior Unit champions.

The cover of the June 1993 edition of the *Wire* showed the fencing team with prizes gained at the Army fencing championships. As a result, ATs Dawes, Evans and Trundley were selected for the Army squad. There was also considerable success in the Army individual swimming championships in 1993 resulting in AT Lance Corporal Barr, AT Carnegie and AT Horner being selected for Army honours. Sportswomen also made their mark with ATW Sergeant Tippett representing the Army at basketball and Sergeant Carthy was in the ladies Combined Services volleyball team.

On 28 July 1995, Colonel Cliff and Mrs Walters departed in style as Major General AH Boyle and WO1 (RSM) Humphreys look on.

145

The cricket team of 1992. Back row: JL Thornton, ATs Donaldson, Lance Corporal Carter, JL Lance Corporal Mayhead, AT Weirmouth. Front row: ATs Staff Sergeant Porter, Lance Corporal Topping, Sergeant Clayton (captain), Major R Grieve RA, Lance Corporal Chapman, Groundsell, Kelly.

A memorable event took place at the college inter-squadron boxing competition on 26 November 1993. The spectators included a number of members of the Wakefield Branch of the RE Association, three of whom were ex-apprentices, AT CSM John Dickson (48B), AT Les Emmery (48B) and AT Sergeant Ben Lewis (48A). Les had boxed at the school some forty-five years earlier. During the prize-giving he presented a trophy for the best loser which on this occasion was awarded to AT Divine. Rawson Squadron won the event by 10-8 and the best boxing award went to AT Sergeant Robinson.

The major sports continued to flourish and in 1991 the PS rugby team nearly pulled off a major success when they were narrowly beaten in the final of the Army Cup at Aldershot. Sergeant Tredwell scored the only try in a narrow 17-6 defeat by 5 Airborne Brigade Logistic Battalion.

The ATs were Army junior cricket champions in 1991 when they comfortably beat Arborfield by seven wickets. AT Corporal Clayton was captain and he had good support from ATs Lance Corporal Chapman, Sergeant Todd and Junior Leader Thubron.

The football team registered a number of worthy seasons, not least of which was in 1994–95 when, under Major David Bornstein and Sergeant D Hukin, they beat Arborfield to become Army Youth Cup winners and they were also Quadrangular Games winners. AT Lance Corporal Borrill was Army Youth player of the year. The team undertook an annual tour of Germany with the hockey team where they faced the opposition of 13, 16 and 28 Signal Regiments. These were always good experience and tough matches especially 28 Regiment who were among the top teams in Germany.

The strength of the college team often depends upon the availability of good coaching. It was thus that, under Captain Sue Roberts and with support from the chief instructor, the swimming team became very strong. In the Army junior championships ATs Carnegie, Barrs, Palmer, Fielding, Pincott, Horner and Teesdale swept all before them with consummate ease. This included a very strong water polo team. Full advantage was taken of having the swimming pool 'on tap' and training was often to be heard early in the morning.

Tennis became the coaching responsibility of Mr Rod Trenam who also encouraged social tennis for the permanent staff. Lieutenant Lorna Hambly represented the Army and with Colonel Cliff Walters won the district doubles. The ATs won the Triangular competition of 1991 with ATs Conley, Clark, Cleghorn, Unsworth and JLs Brind and Higgins.

Orienteering and cross-country running were well supported. On 12 November 1991 the college team won both the Minor Unit and Junior Team events at the corps orienteering competition. WO2 Case and AT Lance Corporal McClelland won their classes. In the district cross-country championships of 1995/96 held at Catterick on 11 December 1995 the college had a clean sweep. ATWs Wood was the first female and ATs Caddywould, Lucus and Jones were the first three males. Caddywould went on to RMA Sandhurst and followed his father into the corps.

Life for ATs and SE recruits remained as lively and varied as it ever had. Fund-raising for the good of those who were less fortunate continued apace. *Exercise Mables* was established in this respect. This became an annual event in which civilian companies such as Flexpack, Courtaulds, Coopers & Lybrand, and Simpson Curtis subscribed to send their employees on team building weekends. Archie Miles and Mike McHale, ably assisted by ATs, put the teams through their paces on the North Yorkshire moors. Many thousands of pounds were donated to BLESMA and the participants could not get enough of it. To support Comic Relief in March 1991, ATs Goodbody, Hendricks, Gray and Parnham completed a 40km cycle ride and 10km run and presented £180 to their chosen cause. In April 1991, Penney Squadron had a sponsored car wash at Morrisons, Safeways and Great Mills. Although this was financially successful by generating £1000 for National Children Homes, it is known that one individual drove to all three car parks, paying at each one, before he had a car 'that didn't look like a zebra!'

It is often said that soldiers are at their best when supporting their own. This was true in 1993 when a fund-raising campaign was initiated by Rawson Squadron to support AT Sergeant Dylan Arnold who had had a tragic accident. Whilst climbing with friends on the south coast he had fallen down a cliff and received very serious injuries. He was in a coma for some time and remained in hospital for a lengthy period. He was left with severe disabilities. With the £2000 that was raised the Commandant was able to visit him at his home in Hereford on 12 February 1993 and present him with a modern computer suite.

In the early 1990s it was planned that the 'final Freedom parade' should be held in Harrogate on 5 June 1992. This was undertaken with the usual military precision which was overseen by the Mayor's secretary Lynne Mee. In the end it was not the final parade because the life of the college was extended until 1996. Nevertheless, junior leaders and apprentice tradesmen paraded outside the Municipal Offices under command of the Commandant, Colonel CJ Walters. The inspection and salute were taken jointly by the Representative Colonel Commandant of the Royal Corps of Signals, Major General CN Last CB OBE, and the Deputy Mayor, Councillor R O'Neill; the Mayor was unavailable as she had recently taken up office and was otherwise committed. The march ended at the Royal Bath Assembly Rooms where college and townsfolk gathered for a celebratory 'pie and pint'. Major General Last also presented the Deputy Mayor with a framed copy of the Royal Corps of Signals print, 'The Cable

Wagon'. This was a lasting tribute to the happy relationship that generations of soldiers had made with the town.

The final Freedom parade was eventually held on 5 July 1996 when the college presented a sun-dial to the Borough Council as a lasting memorial to their presence in Harrogate.

In the early 1990s, when it became evident that there was neither a future for the Army Apprentices' College, Harrogate, nor for the Royal Signals Training Brigade, Catterick, Brigadier JH Almonds, the Training Brigade Commander, set up a small committee with his subordinate commanders. The aim of this group was to determine the memorial that should be left to represent the Royal Signals training units that had been established in Catterick, Harrogate and Ouston. Consideration was given to a wide range of options to which the commanding officers agreed to subscribe. Finally, it was decided that a stone plinth supporting a suitably inscribed pyramid should be erected in Blandford. This was finally unveiled by the Master of Signals, Major General AC Birtwistle CB CBE DL and Brigadier Almonds in the area of the soldiers' restaurant. The three sides of the pyramid were inscribed:

Councillor Bob O'Neil, the Mayor of Harrogate, takes the salute at the final Freedom parade on 5 July 1996.

*The Army Apprentices' College
1947–1996
Royal Signals Soldier Training
1924–1994
Training Brigade Royal Signals, Catterick
1924–1993*

Its location was later deemed to be inappropriate and it was moved to the main Hawke Square in line with the corps Memorial and the Canadian Cairn. The college was indelibly marked in corps history for all to see.

Planning had also been undertaken by Colonel Walters for three major events. The first was for a major reunion to take place before the college closed so that all the 'Old Boys' could revisit their roots. The second was to leave a lasting memorial of the college in Harrogate. After much planning the latter reached fruition on 5 July 1996 when a stone sundial of considerable magnitude was unveiled in the centre of the town near the War Memorial. The third event was to commission an acrylic painting by a local artist, Mr Maude. This was completed in 1993 and hung in College Headquarters until its closure. It was then moved to Arborfield and a copy was displayed in Blandford. The subject of the painting was 'The Three Churches' of Uniacke Barracks which had played so great a part in the lives of ATs over the previous thirty years or so. It was a fitting subject to utilise for a permanent record of the college and the barracks.

Major General AC Birtwistle, the Master of Signals, with Brigadier John Almonds, unveils the inscribed pyramid at Blandford Camp to commemorate the withdrawal of the Royal Signals training organisation from the North of England.

THE FINAL GRADUATION PARADE

The final graduation parade was set for Friday 2 August 1996; over forty-seven years since the first one. Beforehand, on 1 August 1996, there was to be the final graduation service with Oath of Allegiance in the church and 'The Last Supper' in the officers' mess. The speaker at the service was the Chaplain General, Reverend Dr V Dobbin MBE QHC DD, who reflected on what the college had achieved over the years. Many ATs had reaffirmed their Oath in the past and many had listened to the Apprentices' Prayer. It was a sad occasion to know that it was the final time that these words would echo around the college church. The Dinner Night was attended by the Master of Signals, the Signal Officer-in-Chief (Army) and 7 'Gammies'; Colonel Piddington being the earliest.

On the following day, 75 ATs of Intake 94C had the privilege of taking Penney Squadron and the Army Apprentices' College, Harrogate into the history books. The intakes of 95B and 95C moved on to Blandford where they became the only ATs ever to qualify in this way. The Reviewing Officer was Brigadier NF Wood ADC, Signal Officer in Chief (Army). There were 12 commandants and 8 RSMs of the college present to witness the historic event. AT RSM PS Gray had the honour of being the last AT RSM to grace the square as leader of a graduation parade. Like CSM Gittins, nearly fifty years earlier, he stood erect, confident and proud. The weather was better than the average for parade days and a combination of the corps Band and the college corps of Drums put a spring in the heal of those on parade and a tap in the foot of those spectating.

It was important for the college to leave a lasting monument of their time in Uniacke Barracks even though the future of the barracks was uncertain. It was decided to leave a suitably inscribed stone and this was unveiled by Colonel JR Piddington OBE MC, who was the earliest serving of the eleven former commandants present at the final parade. The inscription on the stone read:

*Army Apprentices' College, Harrogate
1947–1996*

1947	Army Apprentices' School
1956	Adoption
1961	Royal Signals Trades only
1965	School rebuilt within Uniacke Barracks
1966	Retitled Army Apprentices' College and badged Royal Signals
1972	Granted Freedom of the Borough of Harrogate
1996	Disbanded

Brigadier NF Wood ADC, Signal Officer in Chief (Army), takes the salute at the final parade.
The stick orderlies are dressed in battledress and WO1 (RSM) Humphreys looks on.

Twelve commandants meet at the final parade on 2 August 1996. Back row: *Major General SR Carr-Smith, Brigadier*
CT Garton, Brigadier KP Burke, Brigadier WH Backhouse, Colonel CJ Walters, Lieutenant Colonel P Richards. Front
row: *Colonel JR Piddington OBE MC, Colonel JW Eagle MBE ERD, Brigadier NA Butler, Colonel F Ramsbottom,*
Colonel MU Ryan, Colonel GC Verdon OBE.

All of those present filed past the monument to review the above words. The final curtain had fallen on the Army Apprentices' College, Harrogate. At Arborfield items of Harrogate significance where installed in the Royal Signals Squadron titled Harrogate Squadron. At Blandford, 3 (Harrogate) Squadron was established within 11th Signal Regiment. The Squadron Headquarters is the home of Harrogate memorabilia. One of the new buildings in Blandford camp was designed as the Education Wing for the apprenticeship. When plans were changed it became the Headquarters of the Royal School of Signals but by then had been named Harrogate Building. The Catterick Building in the camp also displayed a number of important items from Harrogate:

> *Photographs of all the commandants*
> *The Borough of Harrogate sword*
> *A Board of all apprentice RSMs*
> *The Harrogate coat of arms from the*
> *college gate*
> *The Adoption Scroll*
> *The Freedom of Harrogate Scroll*
> *The 'Three Churches' Painting*

So, although the apprenticeship does not live on at Harrogate its memory lives on in places that are prominent to the soldiers and officers of the modern Royal Corps of Signals.

The inscribed stone unveiled by Colonel Jack Piddington at Uniacke Barracks on 2 August 1996 to commemorate the closure of the college.

Irate educator to two Apprentices
scuffling in the corridor
"Come on you two, you didn't join the Army to fight".

APPENDIX I

1 Feb 49	Maj Gen CB Callandar CB MC	DG of Military Training
25 Jul 49		
3 Feb 50		
21 Jul 50	Lt Gen Sir Richard N Gale KBE CB DSO MC	DG of Military Training
30 Jan 51	General Sir John T Crocker GCB KBE DSO MC ADC	Adjt General
19 Jul 51	Fd Marshal Sir William J Slim GCB GBE DSO MC	CIGS
5 Feb 52	Lt Gen Sir Philip M Balfour KBE CB MC	GOCinC Northern Comd
23 Jul 52	Her Royal Highness The Princess Royal Colonel-in-Chief	
6 Feb 53	Gen Sir Ouvry L Roberts KCB KBE DSO ADC	QMG
22 Jul 53	Fd Marshal Sir John Harding GCB CBE DSO MC ADC	CIGS
29 Jan 54	Lt Gen Sir Geoffrey Evans KBE CB DSO	GOCinC Northern Com
21 Jul 54	Brig RJ Springhall CB OBE	Comd E & W Ridings Area
1 Feb 55	Maj Gen JC Walkey CB CBE	E-in-C
20 Jul 55	Maj Gen MS Wheatley CB CBE	Director of Signals
31 Jan 56	Brig DA Kendrew CBE DSO	Brig AQ Northern Comd
18 Jul 56	Maj Gen AH Hornby CB CBE MC	Rep Col Comdt RA
30 Jan 57	Lt Gen Sir Geoffrey Evans KBE CB DSO	GOCinC Northern Comd
17 Jul 57	Lt Gen RW Goodbody KBE CB DSO	GOCinC Northern Comd
23 Jul 58	Maj Gen GA Thomas CBE ADC	COS Northern Comd
5 Feb 58	Brig AJD Turner DSO MC	Dir of Boy's Training
17 Dec 58	Maj Gen RJ Moberly CB OBE	SOinC
29 Jul 59	Gen Sir Hugh C Stockwell KCB KBE DSO ADC	Adjutant General
17 Dec 59	Maj Gen HHC Sugden CB CBE DSO	EinC
27 Jul 60	Lt Gen J D'Arcy Anderson CB CBE DSO	DG of Military Training
14 Dec 60	Maj Gen AMW Whistler CBE	SOinC
26 Jul 61	Lt Gen Sir William Pike KCB CBE DSO	VCIGS
11 Apr 62	Brig WD Tarr	Insp of Boys Training
Aug 62	Lt Gen Sir Charles L Richardson KCB CBE DSO	DG of Mil Training
12 Dec 62	Brig JB Ashworth CBE DSO ADC	Insp of Boys Training
Easter 63	Maj Gen GF Upjohn CBE	GOC Yorkshire District
31 Jul 63	Maj Gen Sir William A Scott KCMG CB CBE	Master of Signals
Dec 63	Rt Hon J Ramsden MP	Sec of State for War
15 Apr 64	The Mayor, Councillor Hitchen	
12 Aug 64	Air Chief Marshal Sir Alfred Earle KBE CB RAF	
Dec 64	Maj Gen GF Upjohn CBE	GOC Yorkshire District
13 Apr 65	Maj Gen GG Rawson CB OBE	
Aug 65	Lt Gen Sir Geoffrey Musson KCB CBE DSO	GOCinC Northern Comd
Dec 65	Maj Gen AMW Whistler CB CBE	Rep Col Comdt R SIGNALS
13 Apr 66	Maj Gen RH Whitworth CBE BA	GOC Yorkshire District
Aug 66	AVM MD Lyne AFC RAF	AOC 23 Group RAF
Dec 66	Maj Gen PM Bradley CBE DSO	SOinC(A)
Apr 67	Maj Gen AJ Deane-Drummond DSO MC	GOC 3 Div
9 Aug 67	Maj Gen DGT Horsford CBE DSO	GOC Yorkshire District
13 Dec 67	Maj Gen AF Stanton OBE	COS Northern Comd
10 Apr 68	Maj Gen EF Foxton OBE	Director Army Education
7 Aug 68	Lt Gen Sir Walter Walker KCB CBE DSO	GOCinC Northern Comd
11 Dec 68	AVM H Burton CBE DSO RAF	AOC 23 Group RAF
9 Apr 69	Maj Gen MD Price OBE	VQMG
7 Aug 69	Maj Gen The Earl Cathcart DSO MC	GOC Yorkshire District
10 Dec 69	Lt Gen Sir Cecil Blacker KCB OBE MC	GOCinC Northern Comd

8 Apr 70	Maj Gen JE Anderson CBE	ACDS(Sys)
5 Aug 70	Maj Gen PF Pentreath MBE	SOinC(A)
9 Dec 70	Air Marshal JH Hunter-Tod CB OBE MA RAF	Instr Tech Dept
14 Apr 71	Lt Gen Sir William Jackson KCB OBE MC	GOCinC Northern Comd
11 Aug 71	Maj Gen PEM Bradley CB CBE DSO	Master of Signals
15 Dec 71	Maj Gen JM Sawers MBE	SOinC(A)
13 Apr 72	Her Royal Highness The Duchess of Kent	
11 Aug 72	Maj Gen JMW Badcock MBE	Dir Manning (Army)
15 Dec 72	Lt Gen Sir William Jackson KCB OBE MC	GOCinC Northern Comd
13 Apr 73	Maj Gen AJ Woodrow MBE	GOC Wales
10 Aug 73	Lt Gen Sir Allan Taylor KBE MC	DCinC UKLF
14 Dec 73	Maj Gen JM Strawson OBE	COS UKLF
11 Apr 74	Her Royal Highness Princess Margaret, The Countess of Snowdon	
9 Aug 74	Maj Gen JM Sawers CB MBE	SOinC(A)
13 Dec 74	Maj Gen A Farrar-Hockley DSO MBE MC	DCD
10 Mar 75	The Marquis of Normanby CBE DCL KStJ	HM Lieutenant of N Yorks
31 Jul 75	Maj Gen G de E Collin	GOC NE District
18 Dec 75	Mr Robert Brown MP	PUS of S
8 Apr 76	Maj Gen PAM Tighe MBE	SOinC(A)
12 Aug 76	Lt Gen Sir Hugh Beach KCB OBE MC MA	DCinC UKLF
16 Dec 76	Maj Gen WT Macfarlane	COS UKLF
14 Apr 77	Maj Gen H Woods MBE MC MA	GOC NE District
11 Aug 77	Maj Gen P Baldwin	CSO BAOR
15 Dec 77	Maj Gen L Howell	Director Army Education
13 Apr 78	Maj Gen AAG Anderson	SOinC(A)
10 Aug 78	Maj Gen HAJ Sturge CB	ACDS(Sys)
14 Dec 78	Maj Gen JA Ward-Booth OBE	Director AAC
11 Apr 79	Maj Gen PEM Bradley CB CBE DSO	Master of Signals
9 Aug 79	Maj Gen MJH Walsh DSO	DAT
12 Dec 79	Maj Gen J Akehurst CBE	GOC 4 Armd Div
10 Apr 80	Maj Gen EJ Hellier CBE	MG Admin UKLF
7 Aug 80	Maj Gen IH Baker CBE	GOC NE District
11 Dec 80	Maj Gen AC Birtwistle CBE	SOinC(A)
9 Apr 81	Mr K Henshaw QPM	Chief Constable N Yorks
13 Aug 81	Maj Gen AJ Jackson	
17 Dec 81	Maj Gen DM Woodford CBE	ACGS (Trg & CD)
15 Apr 82	Gen Sir John Stanier KCB MBE ADC	CinC UKLF
14 Aug 82	Maj Gen AJ Trythall MA	GOC NE District
30 Mar 83	Maj Gen BW Davis CBE	COS LE(A)
5 Aug 83	Maj Gen JMW Badcock CBE MBE DL	Master of Signals
21 Dec 83	Maj Gen R Benbow	SOinC(A)
30 Mar 83	Maj Gen BW Davis CBE	COS LE(A)
14 Apr 84	Field Marshal Sir Edwin Bramall GCB OBE MC	Chief of the Defence Staff
3 Aug 84	Mr C Sampson QPM	Chief Constable W Yorks
21 Dec 84	Maj Gen PA Inge	GOC NE District
4 Apr 85	Lt Gen Sir Charles Huxtable KCB CBE	Comd Trg Estbs
2 Aug 85	Lt Gen Sir Geoffrey Howlett KBE MC	GOC SE District
20 Dec 85	Maj Gen GR Oehlers	ACDS(CIS)
13 Jun 86	Brig RF Maynard MBE	Comd Trg Gp R SIGNALS
2 Aug 86	Maj Gen PD Alexander MBE	SOinC(A)
19 Dec 86	Maj Gen R Benbow	SOinC(A)
15 Jun 87	Maj Gen GR Oehlers	ACDS(CIS)
31 Jul 87	Maj Gen IOJ Sprackling OBE	DMSI
18 Dec 87	Maj Gen CN Last OBE	VMGO
3 Jun 88	Maj Gen WT Macfarlane CB	Colonel Commandant
29 Jul 88	Maj Gen PD Alexander MBE	SOinC(A)
21 Dec 88	Maj Gen DM Naylor MBE	GOC NE District
4 Aug 89	Maj Gen RFL Cook	SOinC(A)

21 Dec 89	Maj Gen IOJ Sprackling OBE	Colonel Commandant
7 Jun 90	AVM JPR Browne CBE RAF	Chief RAF CIS
26 Oct 90	Maj Gen GR Oehlers CB	Colonel Commandant
3 Aug 90	Her Royal Highness The Princess Royal GCVO	
21 Dec 90	Maj Gen HM Rose CBE QGM	GOC NE District
2 Aug 91	Gen Sir David Ramsbottom KCB CBE ADC Gen	Adjutant General
20 Dec 91	Maj Gen PD Alexander CB MBE	Colonel Commandant
31 Jul 92	Maj Gen AC Birtwistle CB CBE DL	Master of Signals
23 Oct 92	Brig AH Boyle	SOinC(A) Des
17 Dec 92	Brig JD Stokoe CBE	Comd Comms BAOR
13 Aug 93	Maj Gen PR Davies CB	Colonel Commandant
18 Jun 93	Brig JM Macfarlane	DETS(A)
22 Oct 93	Maj Gen PAJ Cordingley DSO	GOC 2 Division
17 Dec 93	Maj Gen WJ Robins OBE	ACDS (CIS)
5 Aug 94	Maj Gen PD Alexander CB MBE	Colonel Commandant
16 Dec 94	Maj Gen JF Deverell OBE	DG Army Manning & Recruiting
28 July 95	Maj Gen AH Boyle	SOinC(A)
2 Aug 96	Brig NF Wood ADC	SOinC(A)

APPENDIX II

THE CHAMPION COMPANIES AND SQUADRONS

Year	Unit	Year	Unit	Year	Unit	Year	Unit
1951	B COY	1964	D COY	1974	PENNEY	1985	BRADLEY
	A COY		D COY		PHILLIPS		BRADLEY
1952	A COY		D COY		RAWSON		RAWSON
	B COY	1965	D COY	1975	RAWSON	1986	PENNEY
1953	C COY		C COY		PENNEY		PENNEY
	A COY		D COY		BRADLEY		PENNEY
1954	A COY	1966	B COY	1976	BRADLEY	1987	BRADLEY
	A COY		C COY		BRADLEY		BRADLEY
1955	A COY	1966	PENNEY		RAWSON		PENNEY
	A COY	1967	PHILLIPS	1977	PENNEY	1988	PENNEY
1956	D COY		SCOTT		PHILLIPS		BRADLEY
	B COY		SCOTT		PENNEY		SCOTT
1957	D COY	1968	RAWSON	1978	SCOTT	1989	BRADLEY
	B COY		RAWSON		PENNEY		RAWSON
1958	C COY		RAWSON		PENNEY		SCOTT
	D COY	1969	RAWSON	1979	RAWSON	1990	SCOTT
TIE	C COY		PENNEY	1980	PENNEY		RAWSON
	D COY		SCOTT		SCOTT		SCOTT
1959	B COY	1970	PENNEY		RAWSON	1991	SCOTT
	D COY		PENNEY	1981	PENNEY		SCOTT
1960	C COY		PENNEY		RAWSON		BRADLEY
	D COY	1971	RAWSON		SCOTT	1992	BRADLEY
1961	B COY		PHILLIPS	1982	PENNEY		SCOTT
	B COY		PENNEY		PENNEY	1993	C COY
1962	D COY	1972	BRADLEY	1983	SCOTT		
	B COY		PHILLIPS		BRADLEY		
	B COY		PHILLIPS		BRADLEY		
1963	D COY	1973	PHILLIPS	1984	BRADLEY		
	D COY		PENNEY		PENNEY		
	D COY		PHILLIPS		RAWSON		

APPENDIX III

COMMANDANTS

COLONEL WH LANGRAN MC	APR 47–APR 48
COLONEL DA KENDREW CBE DSO	AUG 48–OCT 50
COLONEL RN THICKNESSE	SEP 50–MAR 54
COLONEL JP CARNE VC DSO	APR 54–APR 57
COLONEL NAC CROFT DSO MA	MAR 57–MAY 60
COLONEL JP NORTH CBE	MAY 60–JAN 64
COLONEL JR PIDDINGTON OBE MC	JAN 64–SEP 66
COLONEL JW EAGLE MBE ERD	SEP 66–AUG 69
COLONEL JC CLINCH	FEB 70–DEC 71
COLONEL NA BUTLER	DEC 71–MAR 74
COLONEL WG NEILSON	APR 74–OCT 75
COLONEL F RAMSBOTTOM	OCT 75–JUN 78
COLONEL MU RYAN	JUN 78–APR 81
COLONEL GC VERDON OBE	APR 81–APR 84
COLONEL SR CARR-SMITH	SEP 84–OCT 86
COLONEL CT GARTON	OCT 86–JAN 89
COLONEL KP BURKE	JAN 89–OCT 90
COLONEL WH BACKHOUSE	OCT 90–JAN 92
COLONEL CJ WALTERS	JAN 92–JUL 95
LIEUTENANT COLONEL P RICHARDS	JUL 95–AUG 96

REGIMENTAL SERGEANT MAJORS

WO1 (RSM)	T	REES	WELSH GUARDS	SEP 47–MAR 48
WO1 (RSM)	S	LONSBOROUGH	COLDM GUARDS	MAR 48–SEP 55
WO1 (RSM)	D	KING	WELSH GUARDS	SEP 55–OCT 58
WO1 (RSM)	T	ROCKLEY	COLDM GUARDS	OCT 58–DEC 63
WO1 (RSM)	DT	EVANS	WELSH GUARDS	DEC 63–MAY 67
WO1 (RSM)	DR	BOAK	WELSH GUARDS	JUN 67–MAY 70
WO1 (RSM)	AW	CUNNINGHAM	IRISH GUARDS	MAY 70–JAN 73
WO1 (RSM)	L	MEADE	SCOTS GUARDS	JAN 73–MAR 75
WO1 (RSM)	H	FORREST	SCOTS GUARDS	MAR 75–JAN 77
WO1 (RSM)	PF	RICHARDSON	GREN GUARDS	JAN 77–AUG 78
WO1 (RSM)	T	CONNOR	IRISH GUARDS	AUG 78–APR 81
WO1 (RSM)	L	BAILEY	COLDM GUARDS	APR 81–DEC 83
WO1 (RSM)	RE	LYNE	COLDM GUARDS	DEC 83–SEP 85
WO1 (RSM)	JF	FALOONE	IRISH GUARDS	OCT 85–JUN 88
WO1 (RSM)	R	RITCHIE	SCOTS GUARDS	JUN 88–JAN 91
WO1 (RSM)	DR	MACRAE	SCOTS GUARDS	JAN 91–APR 92
WO1 (RSM)	K	ROBERTS	WELSH GUARDS	APR 92–DEC 93
WO1 (RSM)	K	HUMPHREY	COLDM GUARDS	DEC 93–AUG 96

ROLE OF APPRENTICE REGIMENTAL SERGEANT MAJORS

MD GITTINS (CSM)	FEB 49	RMR GRAHAM	SUM 67	GD WILSON	WIN 81
R STANIFORD (CSM)	JUL 49	AS COPELAND	WIN 67	RA MULHOLLAND	SPR 82
RA HOWSON	FEB 50	WJ HITCHENS	SPR 68	DM RICHARDS	SUM 82
R HYLANDS J	UL 50	JG CALLAWAY	SUM 68	NP LONGLEY	WIN 82
E McDONAGH	FEB 51	J KERR	WIN 68	L GRIFFIN	SPR 83
JE WINTER	JUL 51	WR KIRKWOOD	SPR 69	SP NORRIS	SUM 83
J INNES	FEB 52	A DAVIE	SUM 69	AK PHILLIPS	WIN 83
DR PHILPIN	JUL 52	JS BAILES	WIN 69	D ROOK	SPR 84
D MURRAY	FEB 53	WT PATERSON	SPR 70	MAC REED	SUM 84
N KENNARD	JUL 53	WT PATERSON	SUM 70	IL BUDD	WIN 84
M CHERRY	JAN 54	D BOYD	WIN 70	JR ROBERTS	SPR 85
MW HOWLAND	JUL 54	T HARDINHAM	SPR 71	JE SUTTON	SUM 85
G ANDREWS	FEB 55	T HARDINHAM	SUM 71	CJ BUDDING	WIN 85
P TOMLINSON	JUL 55	K THOMSON	WIN 71	A IRONSIDE	SPR 86
J FINDLAY	JAN 56	RJ DIXON	SPR 72	A IRONSIDE	SUM 86
F COLEMON	JUL 56	T TURNBULL	SUM 72	EM O'HALLORAN	WIN 86
BR LAY	JAN 57	DA RUDD	WIN 72	ED MUNDY	SPR 87
BJ ATTKINS	JUL 57	MJ FLAHERTY	SPR 73	P STOREY	SUM 87
DM RANCE	FEB 58	MJ FLAHERTY	SUM 73	JR TRIMMER	WIN 87
PJ BAILY	JUL 58	PL CRISP	WIN 73	LJ LEYLAND	SPR 88
DM BLAKE	DEC 58	JE WAKENSHAW	SPR 74	J PORTER	SUM 88
IC ROTHWELL	JUL 59	S HALL	SUM 74	JP WALSH	WIN 88
J TURNER	DEC 59	K LIVERMORE	SPR 74	SP BEMBRIDGE	SPR 89
D JOHNSTON	JUL 60	S BALDWIN	SUM 75	RD JONES	SUM 89
PA REE	DEC 60	RL HILL	WIN 75	JL BURKE	WIN 89
BS DYER	JUL 60	EF CLARK	SPR 76	MA BROWN	SPR 90
D HAMILTON	DEC 61	I LUMSDEN-GORDON	SUM 76	I DAVIS	SUM 90
A HARWOOD	APR 62	J JEFFERSON	WIN 76	RM PARR	WIN 90
R HARRIS	JUL 62	SC JOHNS	SPR 77	GJ SEEDS	SPR 91
GS SPEARPOINT	SEP 62	GT GREIG	SUM 77	PM PLATT	WIN 91
CE WILLIAMS	APR 63	S DAVIES	WIN 77	C GUNN	SUM 92
DEW GARDENER	JUL 63	CW SKELTON	SPR 78	LJ LAWSON	WIN 92
PL SMURTHWAITE	DEC 63	HB BARCLAY	SUM 78	DM PERRY	SPR 93
R DRANSFIELD	APR 64	PM CAHILL	WIN 78	K MOORE	SUM 93
JA CORNFORTH	AUG 64	AD LOBB	SPR 79	DA CHAMBERLAIN	WIN 93
JM KIRKMAN	DEC 64	AD MARJORIBANKS	SUM 79	D ROBINSON	SUM 94
CA ARUNDEL	APR 65	DC LAYCOCK	WIN 79	S OWEN	WIN 94
P LEECH	AUG 65	DC LAYCOCK	SPR 80	DJ MEMS	WIN 95
D HIRST	DEC 65	BM BINGHAM	SUM 80	PS GRAY	SUM 96
PA MACKAY	APR 66	CN MACKAY	WIN 80	PRITCHARD PS (SSM)	SUM 97
PB CHILDS	WIN 66	CN MACKAY	SPR 81	DUNLOP RW (SSM)	WIN 97
AC ARMSTRONG	SPR 67	MA RIDLEY	SUM 81		

APPENDIX IV

THE ASSOCIATION OF HARROGATE APPRENTICES

One of Colonel Thicknesse's major innovations was in June 1952 when he announced that it had been decided to form the Harrogate Apprentices' Association. This was primarily for the benefit of past and present apprentices but civilian and military staff could join as associate members. He advised that there would be a distinguishing tie and coat badge. The royal blue tie would be made of silk with a series of small AAS Badges worked in red, gold and silver. The badge would be of gilt with colours in red and blue enamel.

Within a few months the Association of Harrogate Apprentices had been formally established. During the July 1952 parade, Her Royal Highness the Princess Royal agreed to be Patron. The President was Field Marshal Sir John Harding GCB CBE DSO MC, Chief of the Imperial General Staff. Brigadier Langran and Colonel Kendrew, who were both past commandants of the school, accepted invitations to be Vice-Presidents. The Commandant was the Chairman of the Executive Committee. The inaugural General Meeting of the Association was held on 1 February 1953.

Life Membership was 10 shillings (50p) which included a gilt and enamel coat badge! Each new member received a small red membership book which gave his Association number, and a tie could be purchased for 10s.6d. The first annual general meeting was held in September 1953. By 1956 it was possible to purchase an embroidered blazer badge for 36s.6d (£1.82p) and a silk square for 26s (£1.30p). The badge was the school badge set in the shape of a shield with 'AOHA' on the cross, 'HARROGATE' on a scroll above it and 'OLD – HARROGATE - BOYS' on a scroll below it. In 1957 life membership was raised to 15s (75p) and by 1958 it was possible to purchase a copy of the Nominal Roll of all members from 47A to 56B for only 1s (5p).

An enormous effort was put into encouraging membership to AOHA. In 1957, AT KCA Stewart was presented with an Association Blazer Badge for being the 1000th member. This had doubled by 31 July 1963 when AT RA Pearce was presented with a tie for being the 2000th member. In 1966 there were 3000. Regular contributions were made to the school and college journal and there were annual reunions and annual general meetings in the usual way. It was recorded that, 'The Association Dance in October 1966 was held in the NAAFI because of the lack of heating in the Hildebrand gymnasium!!' In 1963, the Association purchased an embroidered 'AOHA Pipe Banner' and it was presented to the Pipes and Drums by WO2 (FofS) D Willis (49A).

The Association appeared to thrive until the late 1960s. The last recording in the *Gate* for some time was in summer 1968. It shows a photograph of Messrs DP Tyrie, LWT Strange, E Sladdin, EC Dodd, WJE Bevan and CF Oakley. The Secretary of the Association had always been the chief instructor but, on this occasion, during the hand-over of chief instructors and commandants, the Association seems to have been lost. Lieutenant Desmond Barry stated in the 1990s that, 'As far as I remember neither Colonel Joe Eagle nor Lieutenant Colonel Malcolm Scott made mention of the AOHA during the hand-over period.' Thus it was that the Association disappeared completely until it made a very brief reappearance in 1973 when, 'On 4 August some 64 ex-boys of various vintage met in the NAAFI while the drill competition was on... Having established the desire within the corps for an active Old Boys' Association we shall now go ahead to achieve this. Captain R Staniford will be the Secretary.' There are no records of any subsequent activity although it is believed that occasional meetings were held from time to time.

The next concerted effort to re-establish the Association came at the final reunion in 1994. This was proposed by a number of 'old boys' and was put in writing to the Commandant by Douglas Dickason (54A). It has to be said that the Commandant was sceptical and thought that, 'The nostalgic heart was ruling the pragmatic head.' However, having been pressurised again at the final parade and at Royal Signals Association weekends, Colonel Walters agreed to support the proposal to resurrect the AOHA. Tireless work was done by Douglas Dickason who had agreed to act as Secretary and had obtained members for other posts. On 9 October 1999 an AGM and Annual Reunion was held at Uniacke Barracks with considerable assistance from Major Mick Davis who had remained at Uniacke Barracks as 'Caretaker Quartermaster' after disbandment and, Bryan Maltby who lived locally in Harrogate. The AGM Minutes recorded that:

Colonel Cliff Walters	Honorary Chairman
Douglas Dickason	Honorary Secretary
Chris Longmore	Honorary Treasurer
Terry Cawthorne	Reunion Organiser
Alan Lafferty	Newsletter Editor

And One Hundred and Eighty members and Wives were present.

The Secretary reported that in January 1999 there were 95 members and in October 1999 there were 301 members. The Association Of Harrogate Apprentices was once again up and running with every intention of having annual meetings at Harrogate and spreading the good word through the AOHA Newsletter.

APPENDIX V

RELATIONSHIP WITH THE LOCAL COMMUNITY

This information is based on a series of articles written in the late 1960s by Mr G Kenyon-Muir BA, a lecturer at the College.

The relationship between any military unit and the local community is always very important. Most of the military staff remain in the unit for only a comparatively short period of time and they rely upon the local facilities for their well-being and leisure. On the other hand they bring a large source of income to the community and it is important that they play a full part in assisting the locals rather than causing any harassment. It is evident that during the formative years of the cchool great emphasis was placed, by the staff, on fostering good relationships with a wide range of the local community. In return the township went out of their way to make all members of the school feel at home. This two-way flow of effort and respect continued to the day the college closed.

One of the earliest customs to be established was representation at Remembrance Sunday. On 7 November 1948 a small contingent of one officer, one sergeant and thirty boys paraded in Harrogate behind the Town Band along with the other representatives. This started a tradition that continued without break, but true to form the weather was ghastly and this was a feature that affected many of the parades from that day onwards.

The earliest assistance given to local charities probably came from the Church. The carol service of 1948 resulted in two guineas being sent to the Harrogate General Hospital and a year later £8 13s 0d went to Dr Barnado's in Hampsthwaite. A donation was also made to St George's Crypt for unemployed men in Leeds.

IN LOCO PARENTIS

In May 1956, by a special resolution, the Council formally adopted the school and agreed by such adoption to stand 'in loco parentis' to the personnel of the school. The Certificate of Adoption adorned the Commandant's office thereafter and when the college closed it was moved to Blandford and displayed in Catterick Building. It bore the Corporation Seal and the signatures of the Mayor and Town Clerk of the day, Councillor RJ Riley and Mr J Neville-Knox respectively. The certificate was engrossed by Miss M Raisbeck of Harrogate; a member of the Society of Scribes. It presented her with several technical problems. The main one was the colouring of the school badge. The yellow was comparatively simple because real gold leaf was used. White presented difficulties because silver would tarnish and platinum was too expensive. In the end she used aluminium which presented its own problems when 'or' and 'argent' were adjacent. The script was in clear medieval hand using Chinese ink made from pure carbon to prevent fading. The outcome was a finely decorated white calf-skin vellum. The resolution passed by the Council formed the main inscription of the certificate and it read:

Whereas the Council of the Borough of Harrogate at a special meeting at the Royal Hall, Harrogate, on 3rd May 1956, by resolution formally adopted the Army Apprentices' School at Harrogate, agreed by such adoption to stand in loco parentis to the personnel thereof.

The certificate was accepted by the Commandant, Colonel Carne from the Mayor, Alderman Riley. This resolution was often referred to by visiting mayors at speeches on graduation days and usually with a humorous touch; the Mayor suddenly realising that the size of his, or her, family had increased considerably on taking up office! The term 'in loco parentis' has legal connotations which date back to Roman times. To the school, and indeed to the 'parents', it had much wider implications.

Just over six weeks after the adoption by the Council, the new Mayor, Councillor Edwin Pickard presented the school with two ornamental plaques. These were to be fixed to the gates which at this time graced the main entrance. One plaque was the coat of arms of the Borough, and the other was the original school cap badge. The aim was, 'To set a seal, in a public place, on the adoption that had taken place'. The gates had been built by apprentices at Chepstow, and the entrance had been constructed by the sapper apprentices of the school. The coat of arms was moved to Blandford when the college closed and was displayed in Catterick Building. A year after the adoption, on 6 May 1957, the occasion was celebrated with an anniversary ceremony in the Royal Hall. Present were Brigadier JDB Houchin DSO MC, Commander East and West Riding Area, Colonel Croft, the Commandant in his first official civic function, the Mayor, Councillor Edwin Pickard, and most of the school. The Mayor stated that the adoption would be celebrated every three years and this became an important event in the school calendar. After the ceremony, the Commandant led the parade of 750 officers and apprentices past the Victoria Memorial, where the salute was taken by the Mayor.

Subsequent mayors always had an affinity for their role as 'in loco parentis'. Councillor Leonard

Roberts, the Mayor in 1960–61 remarked during a graduation speech:

I have always been impressed by the bearing of the boys in town, and at one Harvest Festival which I attended, I was full of admiration for the beautiful display which the apprentices had done in the Camp Church.

Councillor Roberts was a military man himself having served for five years in each of the two wars; including two at Penny Pot Camp. In his speech he remarked that the Reviewing Officer had spoken for twenty-three minutes, the Commandant for seventeen minutes and so, knowing what the audience was now thinking, he would be brief! On another occasion he suggested to the Commandant, Colonel North, that selected apprentices should attend the conference dances as guests of the Council. What a good 'parent' he was.

Councillor Roberts was also much to the fore on 22 June 1960 when the links were further strengthened. The Borough Council at a special meeting in the Royal Hall, renewed the adoption of the school by the town. As well as members of the school, General Sir Michael West KCB DSO, GOC-in-C Northern Command, was also present. The speeches noted the importance of the apprenticeship in providing more than eighty-five percent of skilled technicians for Royal Signals. More important was the first public announcement that over £1.75 million was to be spent on completely reconstructing the barracks. After the ceremony five companies of apprentices marched through the town, past the Victoria Memorial, where the salute was taken by the Mayor, Councillor Roberts.

Another most popular Mayor of the day was Councillor Gwen Stepney who was in office from 1967–68. She showed great interest and a deep understanding of the problems of her 'young family' and stated:

The apprentices are very popular in town and I have always been particularly impressed by the atmosphere that is apparent between apprentices and staff. I find the candidness and freedom of speech of the boys during conversation most refreshing. I like the boys and I like their sense of humour too.

The subsequent Mayor, Councillor Alan Mais also had words of praise when he stated:

We (The Council) consider that the apprentices, by their bearing and behaviour, show a most creditable standard and are an example to the youth of this town. Their training and discipline make them stand out wherever they are. In consequence of this we want to make the college feel that it is a part of the family of Harrogate and that is why we are proud to stand in loco parentis. Whenever events take part in the town we like the apprentices to take part also.

A further example of the give and take between town and college occurred whilst Colonel North was in command. The band needed leopard skins for the drummers, both as protection and to improve appearances. These, at £65 each, were more than the band funds could manage and the Council were asked for help. Councillor Smethurst stated that, 'They often play in the town without charging, though it would cost £15 each time. We ought to be more generous and purchase three skins; one for each drummer.' Three were duly purchased and presented to the band.

The college has provided ceremonial guards on many occasions mainly in support of official events. Typical of this was on 17 May 1988 when the Lord Mayor and Lady Mayoress of London visited the Town. It was on the occasion of the seventy-fifth anniversary of the opening of the Pump Rooms Annexe; a ceremony originally carried out by the Lord Mayor in 1913, Sir David Burnett. The Honour Guard was inspected by Sir Greville Spratt in the presence of the Harrogate Mayor, Councillor John Marshall.

THE BOROUGH PRIZE

On 6 May 1957, at the anniversary ceremony of the adoption which was mentioned earlier, the Mayor announced that £10 prizes would be awarded twice a year (the school had two terms each year in those days), and would be given to the apprentice who wrote the best papers on local government. The prize was to be known as The Council of The Borough of Harrogate's Prize (but it became affectionately known as The Mayor's Prize). When the Mayor read the resolution about the prize, the main idea behind this gesture was not just to foster interest in civic affairs of Harrogate, but was also to give the apprentices a breadth of outlook which would be of value to them in understanding local government wherever they settled in later life.

To support this initiative, officials from various departments gave hour-long lectures at the school on a Wednesday morning. These included the Town Clerk, the Borough Engineer, the Medical Officer for Health and the Entertainment and Publicity Manager. A series of about six lectures was given in the final term and culminated in the apprentices writing four essays. The school staff selected the best ten essays and sent them to the Town Clerk for final adjudication. Three years later, the prizes were changed to three times each year, in line with the new school policy of having a three-term year. To equalise chances the prizes were also shared equally between technician and operator apprentices.

This system continued for twenty-five years until 1982, when due to increased pressure on the two-year course, there was insufficient time to continue with the local government project. The prize was changed and was awarded to the person who was considered to have given the greatest service to the community. This normally went to a junior soldier but exceptionally on 31 July 1992 it was awarded to Mr Keith Thomas BEM; an instructor at the college. He had spent many years assisting with The Duke Of Edinburgh Award Scheme and helping people in the community who were handicapped in some way.

There was also another exception later in the year when on 23 October 1993 the Mayor, Councillor Barbara Hillier, presented her prize to AT Sergeant Arnold who was in a wheelchair. During the Easter leave he had been the victim of a very serious climbing accident. He had returned to the college for the first time since his accident, to receive his award.

THE DISPLAY ROOM IN THE MUNICIPAL OFFICES

The next major event that cemented the relationship between town and school occurred in 1959. This coincided with the seventy-fifth anniversary of the Borough of Harrogate's Incorporation on 18 February 1884. At the time of the celebrations, the Commandant, Colonel NAC Croft, suggested that the school's contribution to mark such an occasion should be the construction of a suitable display room in the Municipal Offices. The room was to house the various gifts which private citizens, firms and organisations in town had presented to the Corporation. It was built in what had become a broom cupboard made out of an old lift shaft. The design was undertaken by Mr CT Schofield; a supervising instructor in the Joiners' and Carpenters' Department. Together with the fine work of the apprentices he constructed a magnificent room and an inscribed plate was placed over the door which read:

This room was constructed for
THE BOROUGH OF HARROGATE
on the occasion of the 75th Anniversary of its
Incorporation on the
1st February 1884 by The ARMY APPRENTICES'
SCHOOL, HARROGATE

Subsequently the room housed about 80 items which ranged from the mace and the Mayor's chain of office, to a loving cup presented by Her Royal Highness, The Princess Royal who at the time was the Colonel-in-Chief of the Royal Corps of Signals. The Royal Navy and the Royal Air Force were also well represented, as was local industry. Unfortunately, during the late 1980s there was increasing pressure to rebuild a lift for disabled people, in the Municipal Offices, and the display room had to be reconstructed to its former use. There is no longer any trace of the work of Mr Schofield and his apprentices.

FREEDOM OF THE TOWN AND THE LASTING MEMORIAL

At precisely 1630 hours on 5 June 1972, 12 Jet Provosts from RAF Leeming flew over Harrogate in an 'H' formation. As they did so, 850 apprentices and staff of the college marched up Station Parade towards the Queen Victoria memorial. This was the march past that celebrated the college's acknowledgment of being honoured with the Freedom of Harrogate: an honour which was in effect a further strengthening of the ties beyond the adoption. The College Band was playing, the officers had swords drawn and the senior term marched with bayonets fixed. The salute was taken jointly by the Mayor, Councillor FA Rotherham, and the Colonel Commandant of the Royal Corps of Signals, Major General Sir John Anderson KBE.

Earlier, in the Royal Hall a full meeting of the Borough Council agreed to a motion proposed by Alderman Harold Hitchen and, seconded by Alderman Rodney Kent, granting the college the Freedom of Harrogate in its silver jubilee year. The ceremony was graced with over 1400 guests and included two former commandants in Colonel (now retired) North and Brigadier Clinch. Other military guests included Brigadier PAM Tighe MBE, Commander Training Group R Signals. To commemorate the occasion the Mayor presented the college with a wooden stand surmounted by a glass cage which was to house a display, in the college church, of a Roll of Honour of the names of signallers killed in the 1939 to 1945 war. In return the Colonel Commandant presented the Borough with a solid silver statuette of 'Jimmy'.

The scroll was of the design described for the adoption. It was inscribed on white vellum and was received by the Commandant, Colonel NA Butler. The inscription included the following:

Whereas, we, the Mayor, Aldermen & Burgesses of the Borough of Harrogat in the West Riding of the County of York, have formally adopted your College and agreed to stand in loco parentis to the personnel thereof by resolution of the Council, dated 19 March 1956, and being sensible of your close proximity to our Borough for some twenty-five years and being further desirous of recognising, cementing and fostering the intimate association which now and in the past has been enjoyed between our Borough and your college.

Do, by these presents, confer upon you the title, privilege, honour and distinction of marching through the streets of the Borough of Harrogate on all ceremonial occasions with bayonets fixed, colours flying and bands playing.

The scroll subsequently adorned the Commandant's office and was displayed alongside the Scroll of Adoption. When the college closed they were both taken to Blandford where they were displayed in Catterick Building. The words were a most poignant reminder of the relationship between college and town, '...further desirous of recognising, cementing and fostering the intimate association which now and in the past has been enjoyed...'

After that, freedom parades were held on 6 August 1978, 30 July 1982, 3 May 1986 and 5 June 1992. The final parade to exercise the Freedom of the Town was held on 5 July 1996. The Mayor, Councillor Philip Broadbank was the Reviewing Officer. During the parade the Commandant made a presentation to the Borough of a sun-dial. There was considerable consideration and consultation to determine what permanent reminder there should be of the near fifty-year association of the College with Harrogate. It was finally decided that a stone sun-dial should be placed on the western lawn of the War Memorial site in the town centre. The sun-dial was of granite and created by Michael Dan Archer and a team of masons at a quarry in Cornwall. It weighed 10 tons and had a diameter of 12ft. So heavy was it that it was moved into position on blocks of ice which then melted allowing the dial to be lowered into position. The project was co-ordinated with Andrew Stewart, Harrogate's Assistant Museum Curator. The sun-dial was accepted by the Mayor and Mayoress of Harrogate, Councillor Philip Broadbank from Lieutenant Colonel Peter Richards who stated, 'Harrogate has meant a lot to everyone who was fortunate enough to be trained or work at the college and we did not feel we could depart without leaving behind a lasting testament to our presence.' The inscription read

PRESENTED BY THE ARMY APPRENTICES COLLEGE, TO THE BOROUGH OF HARROGATE, TO COMMEMORATE THE CLOSE ASSOCIATION BETWEEN THE COLLEGE AND THE BOROUGH. 1947–1996.

Harrogate would not (alas could not) forget the college!

SUPPORT FOR CHARITIES AND THE LOCAL COMMUNITY

All military units take pride in their efforts to support charities and the local community; the college has been no exception to this. In the case of a junior training organisation, as well as being a form of necessary support to the community, it is also a reminder that there are people who are much less fortunate than ourselves. In an account of this size it is not feasible to even scratch the surface of the support that has been given. For instance, in 1992 alone, over £15,000 was donated in largesse. Nevertheless, it is possible to give a flavour of the efforts that have been put in.

From early days there was a close relationship with the Ian Tetley Memorial School, near Killinghall. This is a Barnado's school for physically handicapped children. The choir archives show that at Christmas 1963 they spent a most enjoyable evening singing carols with the children. On 22 July 1971 the children of the Memorial School were special guests

at a college parade when Colonel JC Clinch presented a custom-built Ford Transit bus to Mr Robert Richardson, the Headmaster, and Mr VL Cornish, the Director of Child Care. The apprentices had raised £1363 by means of sponsored walks arranged by Major Jon Roberts, Royal Signals, OC Bradley Squadron.

Of a different nature was the assistance given by the apprentices to the villagers of Hampsthwaite and Killinghall on 2 July 1968. During the day the most violent storm in living memory sprang up and was described in the *Gate*:

…the sky grew darker and darker, the wind stronger and stronger, the rain heavier and heavier. The wind increased to a furious gale … rain in solid sheets …water driven horizontally. When the storm seemed to have become as bad as it possibly could, it proceeded to become ten times as ferocious … everyone left the classrooms and headed for ground level feeling certain that our new college could not withstand such an onslaught. Yet no one left the buildings, as it was clear they would be swept away or drowned, or knocked out by the enormous hailstones which were an inch or more in diameter and were now mixed with sheets of rain … it was black as night and the power failed.

…the staff set out for home to survey their damaged homes, patch up broken windows, attend to chimney pots, greenhouses, garages and caravans. … no one was hurt.

The local community were not so lucky and teams of helpers were despatched to the villages. There were many letters of thanks and typical was the appreciation recorded by Mr Alfred Hawkridge:

…we live in the hamlet of Knox, near Killinghall. Whereas the stream is normally at the bottom of the garden, on that day the garden was at the bottom of the stream! … and having viewed the situation the Council sent an SOS to the Army Apprentices' College. Within a short space of time an Army lorry arrived and five bright lads, armed with whiter than white mops and squeeges, were allotted to each of the five houses, and, overlooked by a captain and sergeant, they got stuck into the job of cleaning up the water and mud. … Later the mobile canteen arrived … with tea that tasted better than any NAAFI stuff I drank in the last war.

Typical of the endeavour to raise funds were the efforts in February 1993 when ten members of the gymnasium staff, led by Cpl Scott, accepted a sponsored challenge; 7500 parallel dips; 2500 baskets at alternate ends of the basketball court; 2,000 lengths swimming; 1000 rope climbs. This all added up to 13,000 exercises which were completed in twelve hours in aid of Multiple Sclerosis.